AF371603

Lux et Veritas Pushing a white wall

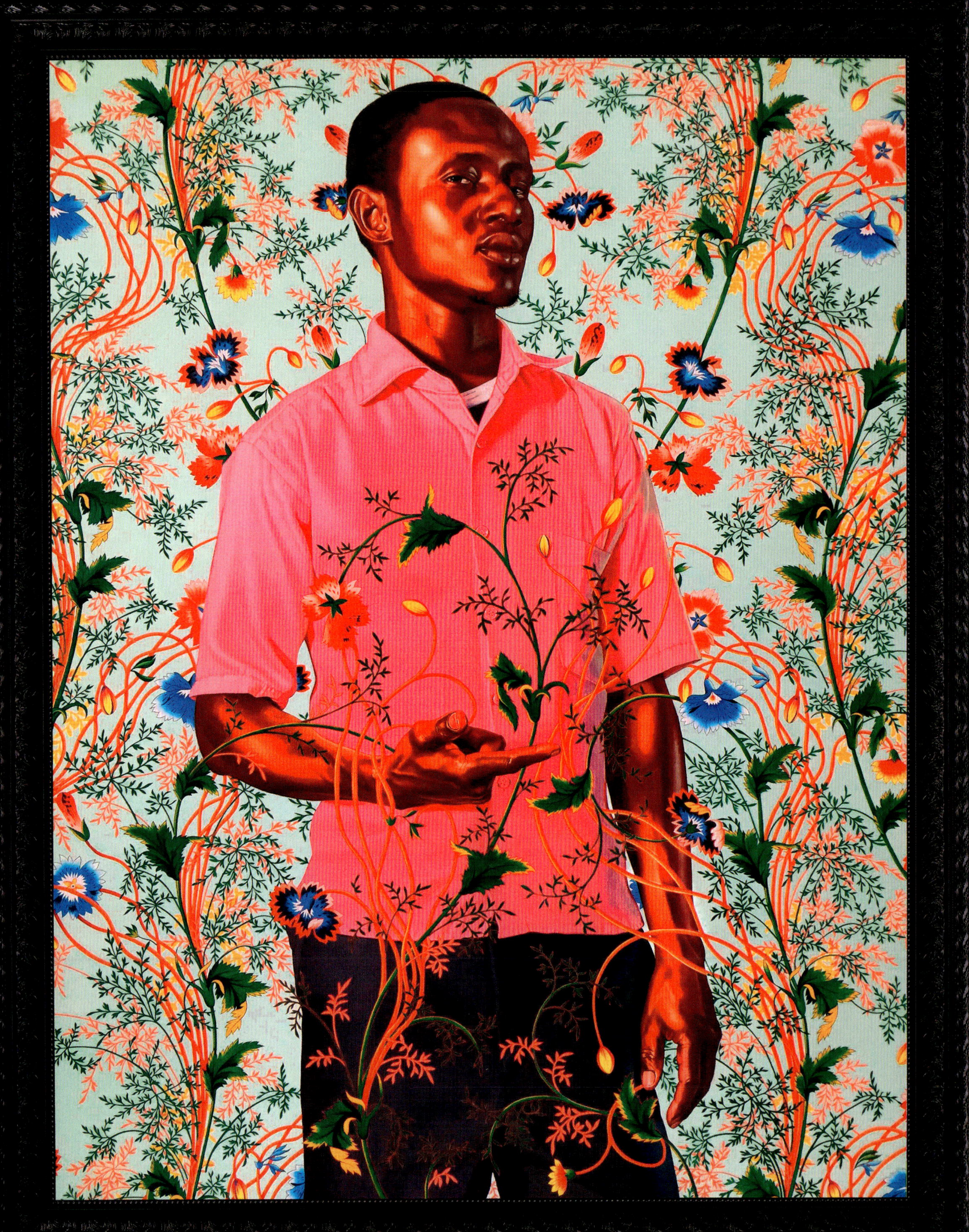

Lux et Veritas
Pushing a white wall

edited with text by
Bonnie Clearwater

with text by
william cordova

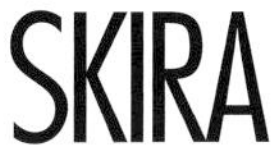

Published in association with
NSU Art Museum Fort Lauderdale
One East Las Olas Blvd.
Fort Lauderdale, FL 33301

Lux et Veritas
NSU Art Museum Fort Lauderdale
April 2, 2022-January 8, 2023

Cover
Photograph by
Adrian Martinez Chavez

Page 2
Karl Spindler
2017
Oil on linen
72 × 60 in
Courtesy of S. Donald Sussman.
© Kehinde Wiley

Design
Luigi Fiore

Editorial Coordination
Vincenza Russo

Copy Editing
Anna Albano

Layout
Barbara Galotta

First published in Italy in 2022
by Skira editore
Palazzo Casati Stampa
via Torino 61
20123 Milano
Italy
www.skira.net

Printed and bound in Italy.
First edition

ISBN: 978-88-572-4855-4

Distributed in USA, Canada,
Central & South America by
ARTBOOK | D.A.P.
75, Broad Street Suite 630,
New York, NY 10004, USA.
Distributed elsewhere in the world
by Thames and Hudson Ltd.,
181A High Holborn, London
WC1V 7QX, United Kingdom.

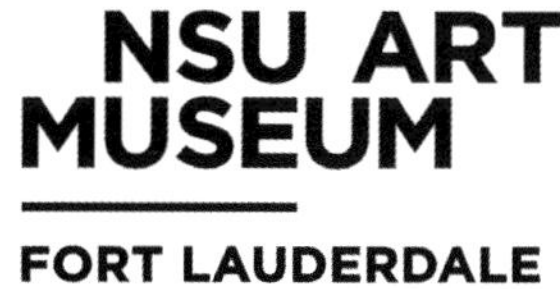

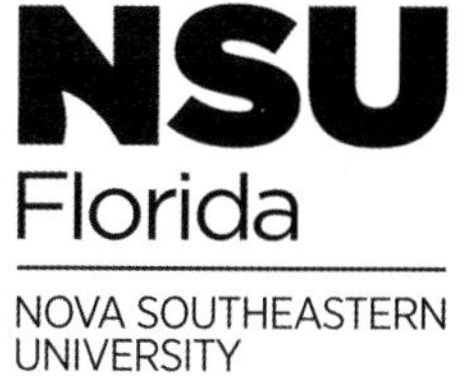

Video of *Lux et Veritas*
Roundtable Discussion
April 2, 2022

Video of Artists Talks
April 2, 2022

Penumbras
Lux et Veritas

Major support for NSU Art Museum Fort Lauderdale is provided by the David and Francie Horvitz Family Foundation, the City of Fort Lauderdale, Community Foundation of Broward, the Broward County Cultural Division, the Cultural Council, and the Broward County Board of County Commissioners, and the State of Florida, Department of State, Division of Arts and Culture, the Florida Council on Arts and Culture, and the National Endowment for the Arts.

Support has been provided by the following Funds at the Community Foundation of Broward: Barbara and Michael G. Landry Fund for Broward, Peck Family Fund, Julia C. Baldwin Fund, and Frederick W. Jaqua Fund.

Lux et Veritas is made possible by
the generosity of Presenting Sponsor
S. Donald Sussman.
Additional support provided by Funding Arts Broward, Inc.

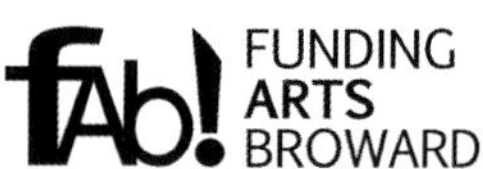

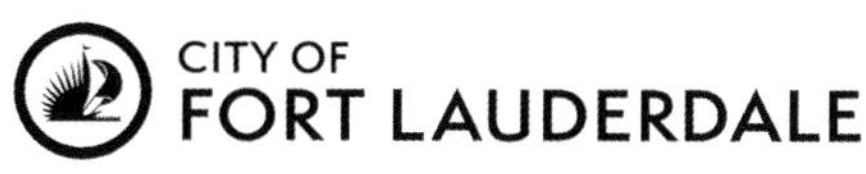

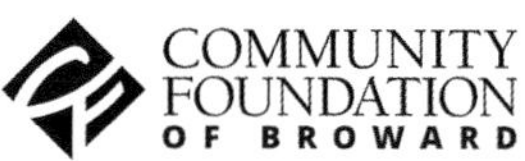

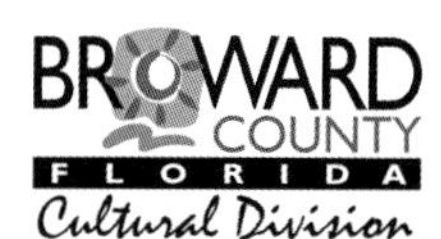

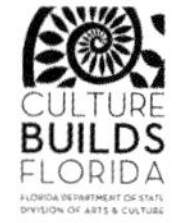

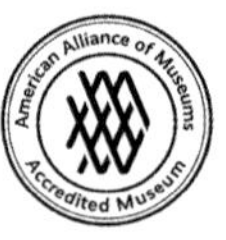

Bonnie Clearwater

Introduction

The exhibition *Lux et Veritas* explores a transformative period in contemporary art by focusing on an exceptional generation of artists of color who attended the Yale School of Art for graduate studies between 2000 and 2010. The exhibition's title alludes to Yale University's motto, "Lux et Veritas," which translates from Latin to "Light and Truth." In the context of this exhibition and publication, the title references how these artists thought critically about their work and their movement through institutional structures. The subtitle of the book, *Pushing a white wall*, references the performance *Pushing White Walls/360 (a resistance study)*, 1998, by Keith Obadike (MFA Yale Sound Design 2004). A private action, the work was documented in photographs and on a DVD. (ill. pp. 140–141)[1] The work and augmented title of this book point with conceptual heft, addressing the Sisyphean task of challenging a predominately white institution to expand. Both the exhibition and book were guided by the aim to "present these artists' distinct works, highlighting philosophical and idiosyncratic approaches that both challenged and reimagined modern and contemporary art convention," and "how in the process they pushed and created space for an expansion of criteria based on multivalent parameters."[2]

As with similar programs, the Yale School of Art, in New Haven, Connecticut, had not been historically diverse, which spurred these art students to form affiliations across the departments of painting, graphic design, sculpture, photography, and art history. They filled gaps in the school's curriculum and counteracted the lack of diversity among the faculty by inviting artists, curators, and writers of color as advisors and guest speakers, developing an interdisciplinary forum, publishing art journals, organizing exhibitions, and documenting their experiences in video and photography. The relationships they formed at school evolved into communities that networked and provided essential support and feedback for one another, often passing on these efforts beyond graduate study. Their reevaluation of the Western art canon, and commitment to the method and practice of teaching has contributed to a greater recognition of artists of color, challenged stereotypes and enriched the overall shared spaces of learning and thinking about art and the art praxis.[3]

The exhibition *Lux et Veritas* provided a public forum in which to address the directions these artists followed based on the explorations that took place in graduate school and were instilled thereafter in their practice. I became interested in this generation of Yale artists in the early 2000s when william cordova (MFA Painting 2004), John Espinosa (MFA Sculpture 2001), and Luis Gispert (MFA Sculpture 2001) attended the school for their graduate studies. All three were active in the Miami scene when I was Director and Chief Curator of the Museum of Contemporary Art North Miami and were included in exhibitions there. Concurrently, cordova organized seminal exhibitions that included several of his peers at art galleries located across the street from MOCA North Miami and at Rush Arts Gallery in New York.[4] cordova's practice was motivated by the artist collectives who came before, such as AfriCOBRA, Miami Black Arts Workshop, the Hairy Who, ASCO, Dark Room Collective, and L.A. Rebellion, among others. As with these prior collectives there was a bond among the Yale graduates that was moving art and art discourse in a new direction and that together they were bringing previous generations of artists of color who sacrificed so much to the fore as well as mentoring and championing younger artists.

My interest in this generation as a whole crystallized while working with Eric N. Mack (MFA Painting 2012) on a solo exhibition in 2020 for NSU Art Museum as his work and curatorial activities seemed consistent with that of earlier Yale graduates. I consulted cordova for his perspective on Yale, and discovered that he, in fact, cared deeply to archive and collect materials on the trajectory of his peers who attended the School of Art. He generously shared a concept for the exhibition outlining key issues, concerns, and perspectives that he started observing in 2009 and formulated in email correspondence with artist, curator, and writer Coco Fusco in 2010 about race and accountability in major art institutions throughout the USA.[5] Our initial exchange was a revelation, for cordova detailed how these artists operated as a collective with a stated purpose. Their collective actions brought about positive changes in art and society that were as significant as their individual achievements as artists. It was imperative to record the history of this collective to provide context for these artists' work and their contribution to an important period in art history. We embarked on this project with cordova convening an advisory committee of his peers and me as curator. In addition to cordova, the committee consisted of Mike Cloud (Yale MFA Painting 2003), Leslie Hewitt (Yale MFA Sculpture 2004), and Irene V. Small, Associate Professor, Contemporary Art & Criticism, Princeton University (Yale Ph.D. 2008). The advisory committee proposed parameters of the exhibition and invited artists who were aligned with this cohort.[6] The committee was also instrumental in bringing context to the exhibition including discussion in terms of shared language, timeline narrative, the design concept for the cover of this book and the archival images in the Appendix.

This exhibition is not a survey of all artists of color who attended the Yale School of Art during this period. Nor is it a history of the school. Two recent publications marking the occasion of the 150th anniversary of women at the Yale School of Art provide an in-depth study of the history of the school from the perspective of women students and faculty: *On the Basis of Art*, the catalogue of an exhibition of the same title held at Yale Art Gallery, and *History of an Art School*, by Marta Kuzma, the School of Art's first woman Dean.[7] *Lux et Veritas* instead focuses on the artists who actively formed affiliations with each other during their time at Yale and beyond. Coco Fusco wrote about her first-hand observation of the institutional challenges these artists faced at Yale and their extensive efforts to expand the school beyond the status quo in her 2014 article, "One Step Forward, Two Steps Back? Thoughts about the Donelle Woolford Debate."[8] The 2004 film *Still Black at Yale*, produced by two Black Yale University students, Monique Walton and Andia N. R. Winslow, chronicled the influence of Black culture on campus through a series of interviews with Black students and professors university-wide with the aim to "serve as a visual meditation of notions of identity and belonging within the historical hegemony of the institution that is Yale University." The challenges documented in the film were consistent with those also faced by the artists of color at the Yale School of Art at the time. As the narrator of the film reports, "It became apparent with our time at Yale, that despite the significant strides that were made by the many Black students who came before us, Black students still did not fit the face of what Yale has come to represent."[9]

The *Lux et Veritas* book features extensive installation photographs of the exhibition and provides an in-depth overview of this generation of artists by documenting their experiences, relationships, and work through oral histories and transcriptions of public discussions. Readers can access videos of the public programs and the documentary film *Penumbras: Lux et Veritas*, 2022, produced by cordova by using the QR codes on page 5.

[1] Although Keith Obadike was an MFA student in the Yale School of Drama, he played a vital role in the early collective period under consideration here. The DVD of *Pushing White Walls/360 (a resistance study)* was included in the exhibition *Skillz* curated by william cordova at Ingalls and Associates, North Miami, April 7 – May 7, 2004.

[2] Statement by Artist Advisory Committee, January 20, 2021.

[3] Yale University announced in 2021 that 51 percent of the incoming class identified as students of color. See Stephanie Saul, "Top Colleges Cling to Favoring Alumni's Children," *New York Times*, July 14, 2022, p. 1A. For the academic year 2021 to 2022, 62 percent of enrolled MFA students at the Yale School of Art identified as students of color (correspondence with Taryn Wolf, Assistant Dean of Academic Affairs, July 19, 2022).

[4] cordova had previously shared information of this collective of Yale artists of color with Coco Fusco, who included it in her article, "One Step Forward, Two Steps Back? Thoughts about the Donelle Woolford Debate," *The Brooklyn Rail* (May 2014). The first group exhibitions cordova curated that included his Yale peers are: *Why don't we do it in the road*, Ambrosino Gallery, North Miami (2002), which included Mickalene Thomas et al; and at Ingalls & Associates, North Miami, *Skillz* (2004), which featured cordova, Rashawn Griffin, Leslie Hewitt, Loren Holland, Wardell Milan, Keith Obadike, et al.; and *Being There* (2006) which included cordova, Hewitt and Milan; at Rush Arts Gallery, New York: *Passin' it On* (2006), with Torkwase Dyson, Monique Walton, Hewitt, Griffin, et al.

[5] Email from cordova to Bonnie Clearwater, September 20, 2020.

[6] Doreen Adengo (MA Architecture 2005), Lourdes Correa-Carlo (MFA Sculpture 2009), SunTek Chung (MFA Sculpture 2001), Micah Ganske (MFA Painting 2005), Doreen Adengo (M.Arch 2005 Keith Obadike (MFA Sound Design 2004), Jennifer Packer (MFA Painting 2012), Carol Pereira-Olson (MFA Painting 2003), Tavares Strachan (MFA Sculpture 2006), Monique Walton (BFA 2004), Andia Winslow (BFA 2004), Forrest Young (MFA Graphic Design 2006), are among the artists who were associated with the artists whose work was included in the *Lux et Veritas* exhibition. In addition, Derrick Adams (MFA Columbia University 2003), although not a Yale artist, created access to the Yale artists of color through the alternative space Rush Arts in New York.

[7] *On the Basis of Art: 150 Years of Women at Yale*, intro. Elisabeth Hodermarsky, essays by Helen A. Cooper, Linda Kinheim Kramer, and Marta Kuzma (New Haven: Yale University Press, 2021); Marta Kuzma with Angela Y. Davis and Linda Nochlin, *History of an Art School*, ed. Angie Keefer (New Haven: Yale School of Art, 2021). For an overview of theories regarding teaching art in the new millennium see *Art School (Propositions for the 21st Century)*, ed. with an introduction by Steven Henry Madoff (Cambridge, MA: The MIT Press, 2009). Madoff was a Visiting Critic at the Yale School of Art. Abigail DeVille (MFA Sculpture 2012), recalls him assigning the book.

[8] See Fusco, "One Step Forward, Two Steps Back?," cit. The impetus for Fusco's article was to provide context for the decision by the Black artists group Yams Collective to withdraw from the 2014 Whitney Biennial in protest of the show's inclusion of artist Joe Scanlan's art performance in which he, "a white middle-aged male art professor, outsources a black female character of his own invention to a series of younger, lesser-known black women artists." As Fusco notes, this incident "forced a long-standing private conversation among artists of color into public view." Fusco centered her article on the origins of this work by Scanlan to his time as a faculty member in Yale's Sculpture department, in which he initially featured one of his Black female students—Namik Minter, who subsequently removed herself from the project. As a Visiting Associate Professor at the school from 2004 to 2005 who maintained a relationship with many of the former students, Fusco observed how Scanlan's performance and the ensuing debate was emblematic of the "banishment" of critical and open debate about institutional racism, politics and gender identity at the Yale School of Art.

[9] *Still Black at Yale* ©, a film by Andia N. R. Winslow and Monique Walton, Walton Winslow Productions, 2004.

Acknowledgments

I extend my very deep appreciation to the essential contribution of william cordova, for providing important guidance every step of the way, identifying key issues, producing the documentary film, *Penumbras: Lux et Veritas* for the exhibition, sharing archival documents and photographs for the exhibition and book, writing an introductory essay and connecting me with the artists. I thank the advisory committee members Mike Cloud, Leslie Hewitt, and Irene V. Small for generously dedicating their time to this exhibition and publication, and for their valuable insights. It was a great pleasure to get to know and work with the participating artists and an honor to include their work in the exhibition. I extend my appreciation to Peter Halley (Director of Graduate Studies for Painting and Printmaking 2002–2011), Dr. Kymberly Pinder, Dean School of Art (2021–present), Shinique Smith (Visiting Artist 2010), Robert Storr (Dean 2006–2016), and Sue Szary, former Department of Painting and Printmaking Secretary, for sharing information regarding their experiences with the Yale School of Art.

Special thanks for assistance with this exhibition go to Galeria Livia Benavides 80M2, Lima, Peru, Valentina Branchini, Emily Cooper, Melissa Diaz, Ian Dickman, Ed Diven, Imari Elefteriu, Jonathan Fraser, Nicole Crawford Freeman, Emily Gachot, Susan Grogan, Jeffrey Grove, Marissa Mackey, Meg Malloy, Astrid Meek, Paul S. Murawski, Truth Murray-Cole, Brittany Nelson, David Nolan, Mendi + Keith Obadike, Julie and Bennet Roberts, Sol Saks, Deepka Sani, Chana Sheldon, Trevor Schoonmaker, Sikkema Jenkins & Co., New York, Franklin Sirmans, Cree Solomon, Sam Suddaby, Glenn Scott Wright, Emily Vera, Susanne Vielmetter, and Sam Yehros. For the fabrication of Torkwase Dyson's installation, our appreciation goes to Fernanda Carlovich, Hansi Liao, Pace Gallery, New York, and Dave Yepez and Axios, New York. Thanks to Steven Brooke for installation photographs, Adrian Martinez Chavez for the cover photograph, and Aaron Glickman and Alex Kreisberg for videography of the artists' talks and the roundtable discussion.

I am thankful to NSU Art Museum's curatorial staff for providing exceptional support for the research assistance, coordination, and realization of the exhibition and book: Cathie Conn, Oliver Loaiza, Caroline McNabb, Jordyn Newsome, Chuck Ross, Arasay Vazquez, Ariella Wolens, and the installation team. Many thanks to Lisa Quinn and the education staff for the coordination of the public programs. I thank the entire museum staff for their efforts for bringing this exhibition and publication to fruition. Appreciation is also extended to Skira for editing, designing and publishing this book. A special note of gratitude goes to my husband James Clearwater.

Thanks go to the many private collectors and institutions who so generously loaned works to the exhibition. Special thanks go to the Board of Governors of NSU Art Museum for their generous support and to Collection Committee Chair Dr. Barry Silverman for his insight regarding this exhibition.

We extend our deep appreciation to Presenting Sponsor S. Donald Sussman whose early and enthusiastic support made it possible to realize this exhibition and publication. We also acknowledge Funding Arts Broward for their additional support. The public programs for the exhibition were made possible by the generous support of the Community Foundation of Broward: Support provided by Barbara and Michael G. Landry Fund for Broward, Peck Family Fund, Julia C. Baldwin Fund, and Frederick W. Jaqua Fund.

Bonnie Clearwater
Director and Chief Curator
NSU Art Museum Fort Lauderdale

Participating Artists listed by date of completion of MFA

The exhibition and publication focus specifically on the artists of color who formed a community of support and feedback during their graduate studies at the Yale School of Art (it is not intended as a comprehensive survey of all artists of color who attended the school during the decade.)

2000

Wangechi Mutu, Sculpture

2001

John Espinosa, Sculpture

Luis Gispert, Sculpture

Kehinde Wiley, Painting

2002

Mickalene Thomas, Painting

Anna Tsouhlarakis, Sculpture

2003

Mike Cloud, Painting

Torkwase Dyson, Painting

Shoshanna Weinberger, Painting

2004

william cordova, Painting

Leslie Hewitt, Sculpture

Wardell Milan, Photography

Mamiko Otsubo, Sculpture

2005

Rashawn Griffin, Sculpture

Jamerry Kim, Graphic Design

2006

Loren Holland, Painting

Titus Kaphar, Painting

2011

Njideka Akunyili Crosby, Painting

Abigail DeVille, Painting

2012

Eric N. Mack, Painting

Ronny Quevedo, Painting

Contents

Outlaw Culture: Or Southern Alchemy

Making art at Yale University between the years 2000–2010 was unique in many ways for MFA students of color. 2000 marked the transition to the new millennium but it also pointed out the last generation of students who had first-hand examples and were directly influenced by artists from the 1960s, '70s, and '80s, most of whom had not had major national and international success until the late 1990s.

It was these earlier generations of artists who provoked many students of color to create, develop, and achieve an alternative space and higher ground—a spiritual space that reflected and acknowledged those elders who came before and made their sacrifices so that the proceeding generations could have access and benefit from their struggles. This younger generation sought out to bridge and build, not always at the same time, through mentors like the late sculptor, Terry Adkins (Visiting Artist 2004), whose cautionary words and wisdom kept many from straying into generic assembly line art; Coco Fusco (Visiting Artist/Scholar 2004, Visiting Associate Professor 2004–2005), who connected students with broad historical insights as a way to contextualize their work; art historian Dr. Kellie Jones (Yale Ph.D. 1999) who enlightened countless students with her knowledge of ASCO, the Chicano artist collective made up of students/activists from East Los Angeles, and Latin American photography and cinema; and artist/curator, Deborah Willis, whose critical eye kept students focused on a rigorous trajectory of self-reflection and analysis. The multi-tasking of Howardena Pindell (Yale MFA 1967), the first Black female artist to be hired as a curator at the Museum of Modern Art (1968–1978), inspired younger generations to curate, author, and mentor as part of their studio practice.

2000–2010 at Yale produced artists and Ph.D. art history students who tended to think outside of the box, and whose influences often came from sources other than those that were part of the School of Art's curriculum. These graduate students pushed to broaden the conversation. Many Yale School of Art students of color related to one another by building support groups, collectives, and developing personal and professional relationships even after graduating from their programs. After completing their MFA degree, several went on to participate in the Studio Museum in Harlem Artist-in-Residence program with the guidance of Executive Director Lowery Stokes Sims, Director and Chief Curator Thelma Golden, and Curator Christine Y. Kim. This residency program helped transform the contemporary art landscape with artists of color whose work occupied and responded to a completely different set of principles and logic.

Artist Sol Sax (Yale MFA 1995) stated, "Hip-Hop was our urban university prior to the 2000s. Scholarship around Hip-Hop was not embraced by institutions of higher learning until after the 2000s… we were in the trenches before that." Certainly much credit is due to curator Franklin Sirmans, whose *Boom bap* approach to curating introduced the world to a generation of hip-hop influenced art with the exhibitions *One Planet Under A Groove* (2001), *Americas Remixed* (2002), and *New Wave*

(2002).[1] Isolde Brielmaier's *Maximum Flavor*
(2005) exhibition also focused on the roots,
aesthetics, and ideology of *Dirty South*.[2] Finally,
curator Trevor Schoonmaker's exhibition *Street
Level* (2007) was the next ~~Trojan horse~~ TRINERE
with a global lens on post-hip-hop.[3]

From 1998–2009, artist/curator Derrick
Adams, and subsequently Nico Wheadon had a
vision, through Rush Arts Gallery and Resource
Center, New York, to create an experimental
exhibition space that cultivated a unique
support environment for visual practitioners,
writers, and students of color while bypassing
many art world trappings. The sign of the times
was swinging a pendulum in a manner that
had not occurred prior to the 2000s.

"Create dangerously"—Edwidge Danticat,
Create Dangerously: *the Immigrant Artist
at Work*, 2010

© william cordova

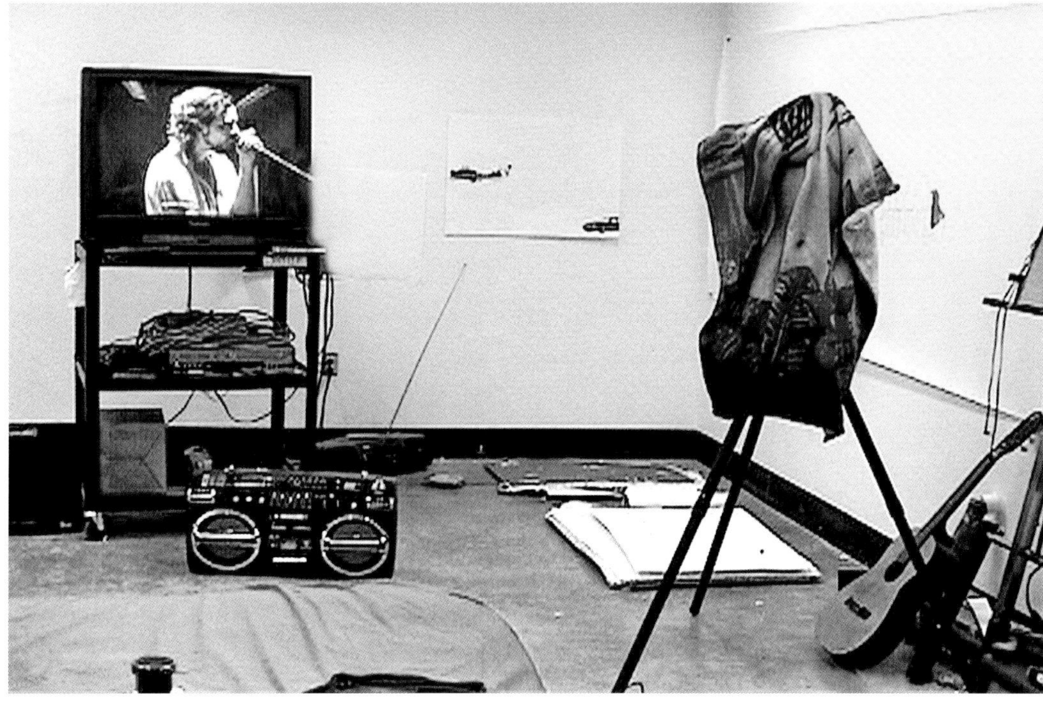

william cordova, Yale basement studio,
October 2002. Photo courtesy of w. cordova

[1] *One Planet Under a Groove: Hip-Hop and Contemporary Art*,
Bronx Museum of the Arts, October 26, 2001 – March 3, 2002
(traveled to the Walker Art Center, Minneapolis, Minnesota,
July 14 – October 13, 2002; and Spellman College Museum
of Fine Art, Atlanta, Georgia, Spring 2003); *Americas
Remixed*, Milan, Italy, 2002; *New Wave*, Kravets/Wehby
Gallery, New York, 2002.
[2] *Maximum Flavor*, Atlanta College of Art Gallery, Atlanta,
Georgia, May 26 – August 7, 2005.
[3] *Street Level: Mark Bradford, William Cordova & Robin Rhode*,
Nasher Museum of Art, Duke University, Durham, North Carolina,
March 29 – July 29, 2007.

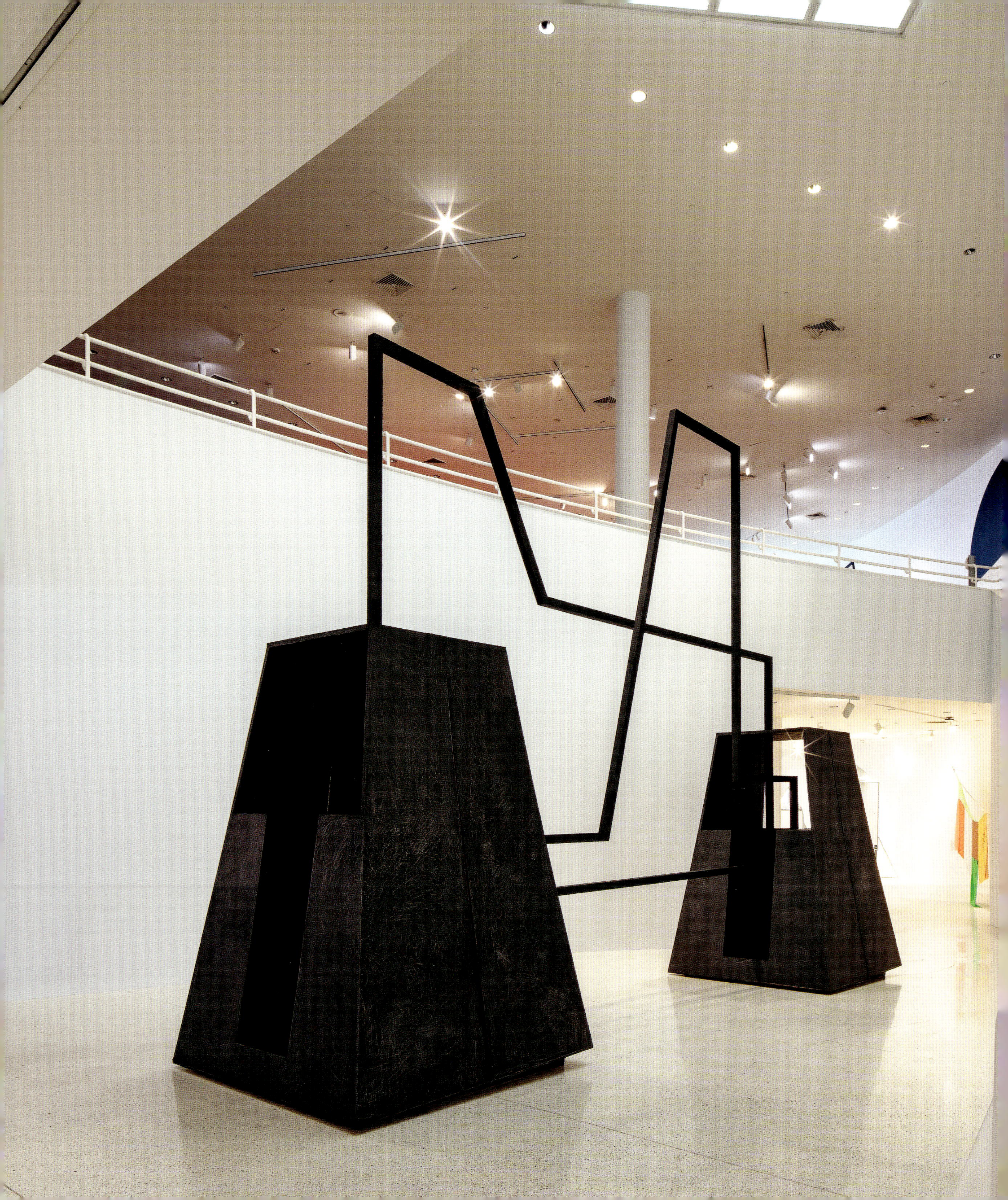

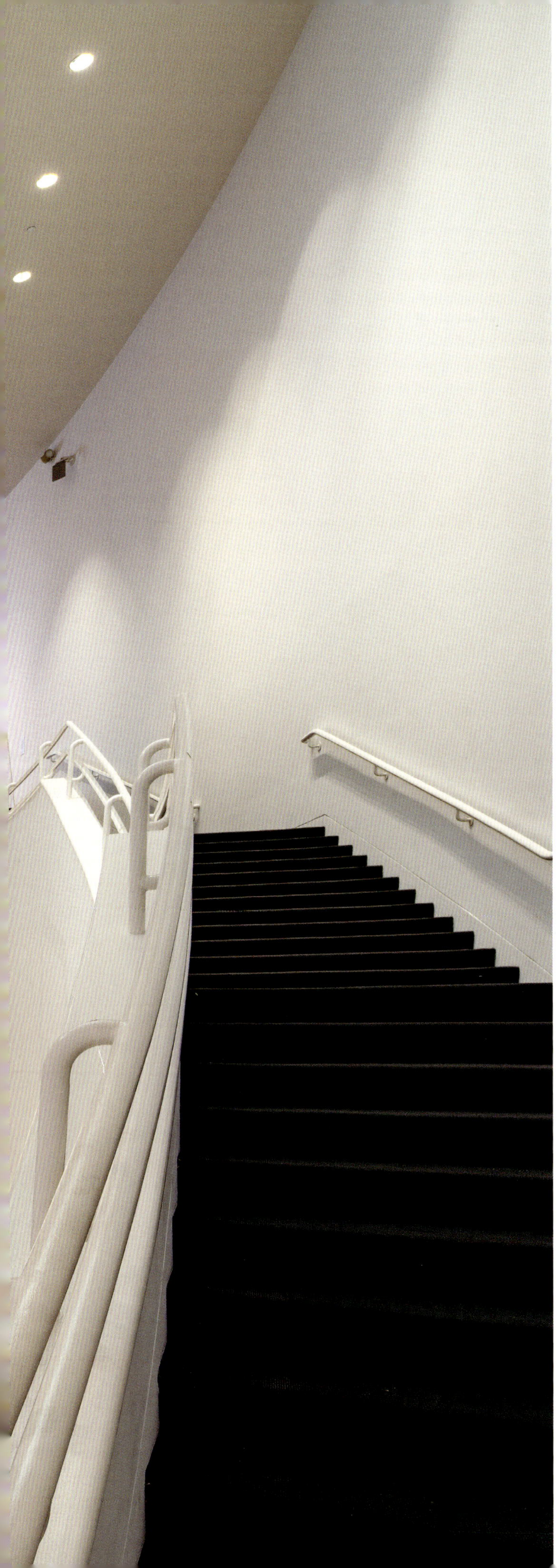

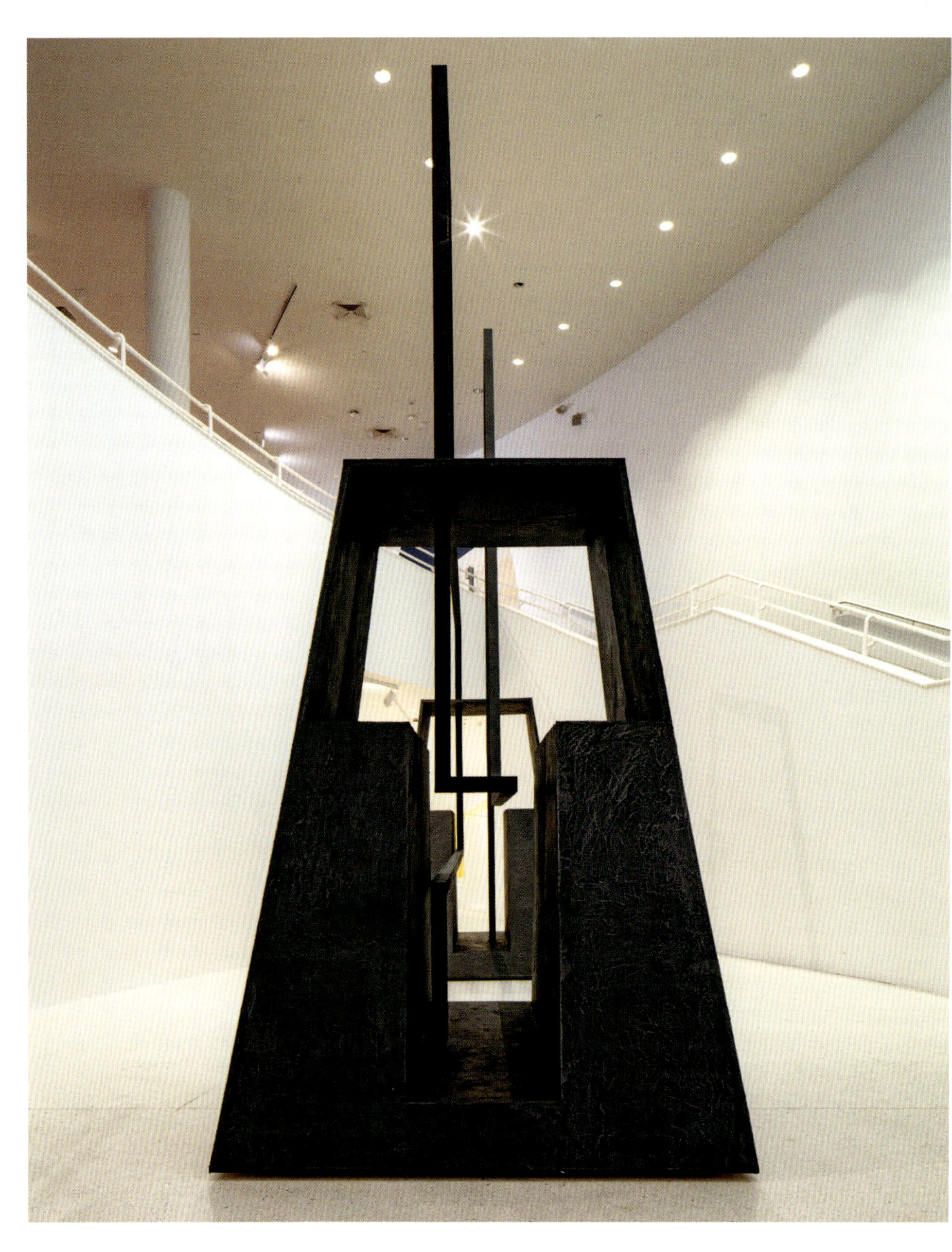

Torkwase Dyson
I BELONG TO THE DISTANCE (#2), 2022

Bonnie Clearwater

Lux et Veritas

Paradigm Shift

The artists included in the exhibition *Lux et Veritas* are among the first generation of art school graduates of the new millennium. The exhibition focuses on the artists of color who attended the Yale School of Art Master of Fine Arts program from 2000 to 2010 as they shared experiences and specific artistic and critical influences. It encompasses artists who thought more closely as a collective during this defining period and who came together out of mutual respect for each other's work. They identified their collective efforts under the group names of the coffee cup collective (CCC) and the BASE collective.

Cumulatively, their work contributed to a paradigm shift that occurred in the art created during the first two decades of the twenty-first century by which cultural context gained expression through formal experimentation. In 2014, artist, curator, and author Coco Fusco (Visiting Artist 2004, Visiting Associate Professor 2004–2005) recognized that these artists' significant successes were achieved through their mutual support in the face of institutional and art world biases.[1] *Lux et Veritas* reflects on the shared interests, values, philosophies, and theories of these artists as well as the catalytic role individual artists played in forming a cohort that sustained them through graduate school—and beyond.

These artists' formative years coincided with a period of reassessment of art history and cultural studies. The majority attended art schools as undergraduates where art theory and cultural studies were part of the curriculum. James Clifford's *The Predicament of Culture* (1988), Stuart Hall's "The Spectacle of the 'Other'" (1997), art historian Kellie Jones' multiple publications, Edward W. Said's *Orientalism* (1978), and Robert Farris Thompson's *Flash of the Spirit: African & Afro-American Art & Philosophy* (1983) were among the publications that were widely circulated in academia and art schools in the 1990s. Other influential texts were published in Kymberly Pinder's *Race-ing Art History: Critical Readings in Race and Art History* (2001), the first anthology of art history from the perspective of racial representation.

These new perspectives on art history and culture were disseminated to a wider public during the 1990s and early 2000s through several landmark museum exhibitions. Among these is the series of museum interventions by Fred Wilson that mined museum archives and collections for his installations.[2] Without any manipulation of objects other than their juxtaposition and placement, Wilson's installations drew attention to how models of categorization, collecting, and display embodied institutional biases. Hans Haacke, an early practitioner of Institutional Critique in the early 1970s, not only continued to be a strong presence in art exhibitions and public art in the 1990s, but was an influential professor at The Cooper Union for the Advancement of Science and Art in New York from 1967 to 2002 during the time Wangechi Mutu (MFA Sculpture 2000) and Leslie Hewitt (MFA Sculpture 2004) were enrolled there.

The 1993 Whitney Biennial, curated by Thelma Golden, John G. Hanhardt, Lisa Phillips, and Elisabeth Sussman, tapped into the marked shift in art-making by centering on cultural identity, politics, gender, and race. The Whitney Museum followed this sweeping overview with the groundbreaking 1994 exhibition *Black Male: Representation of Masculinity in Contemporary American Art*, curated by Whitney curator Thelma Golden. The exhibition included artists across race, culture, ethnicity, and generation, united through their interrogations of Black masculinity. As Golden notes, she "didn't expect that 'Black Male' would be part of a larger conversation that moved out of the art world and into the wider world—which it did, almost immediately."[3] Golden joined the Studio Museum in Harlem in 2000 as Deputy Director for Exhibitions (she became Director and Chief Curator in 2005) where she continued to organize exhibitions that not only shaped the public discourse but also had a direct influence on the work of a new generation of artists. *Freestyle* (The Studio Museum in Harlem, 2001), curated by Golden with the support of curatorial assistant Christine Y. Kim, proposed the concept of "post-Black" to identify a generation of Black artists who felt free to abandon or confront the label "Black artist," preferring to be understood as individuals with complex investigations of Blackness in their work. As Hewitt notes, the *Freestyle* exhibition "challenged everything,

creating a much-needed rupture that radically changed the discourse."[4]

The crash of the art market around 1990 (following the stock market crash in 1987 and the ensuing recession) had a monumental effect on the art world economically, philosophically, and artistically. Government support for the arts was jeopardized in the United States greatly due to political conflicts that flared in the late 1980s, while many commercial galleries that were hit hard financially by the recession, closed. There followed a general rethinking of the circulation of art that fostered the decentralization of the art world in search of new markets, collectors, and patrons, as well as new critical and curatorial voices. In contrast to the contemporary art market, which remained depressed for much of the decade, the Latin American art market was robust. Moreover, the occasion of the quincentennial of the "so-called discovery of America" (1992–1993) ignited widespread critical thinking about the colonial past and its impact on art.[5] The late 1990s also saw a significant move toward a global approach to art from non-Western perspectives, such as the eleventh edition of the monumental exhibition *documenta 11*, in Kassel, Germany (2002), organized by Okwui Enwezor, the first non-European to hold the title of Artistic Director.

The first decade of the new millennium was bracketed by the terrorist attacks in the United States on September 11, 2001, and the war in Iraq and Afghanistan at the beginning of the decade, and the Great Recession and the

election of Barack Obama as the first Black president of the United States towards the end of the decade. This was the moment in history that the artists represented in *Lux et Veritas* pursued their graduate studies.

Although these artists have remained in contact with each other and several have collaborated on projects and exhibitions, *Lux et Veritas* is the first major exhibition and publication to consider them as a collective. While each artist's work is distinct from the others in approach and concept, their commonalities came into sharper focus when viewed together. Among these is the creation of highly nuanced work that commands the viewer's prolonged attention and thought. Their work is a form of hidden communication represented through a formulation of personal and hermetic symbols, pictographs, codes, and formal pictorial language. These symbols are a gateway to their thinking and intensions. For some of the artists these personal symbols connected their work to cultural heritage: including textile encoding in Andean and other cultures for cordova, Buddhist symbols for Otsubo, and African symbols for Wiley. The incorporation of these symbols slows down the looking process, often leading viewers beyond the physical object to metadata in which meaning may reside in card catalogues, museum collections, books, or on the internet. Symbolic language also served as a strategy for giving voice to art students who felt stifled by their academic situation and society in general to address issues of race, gender, and identity.

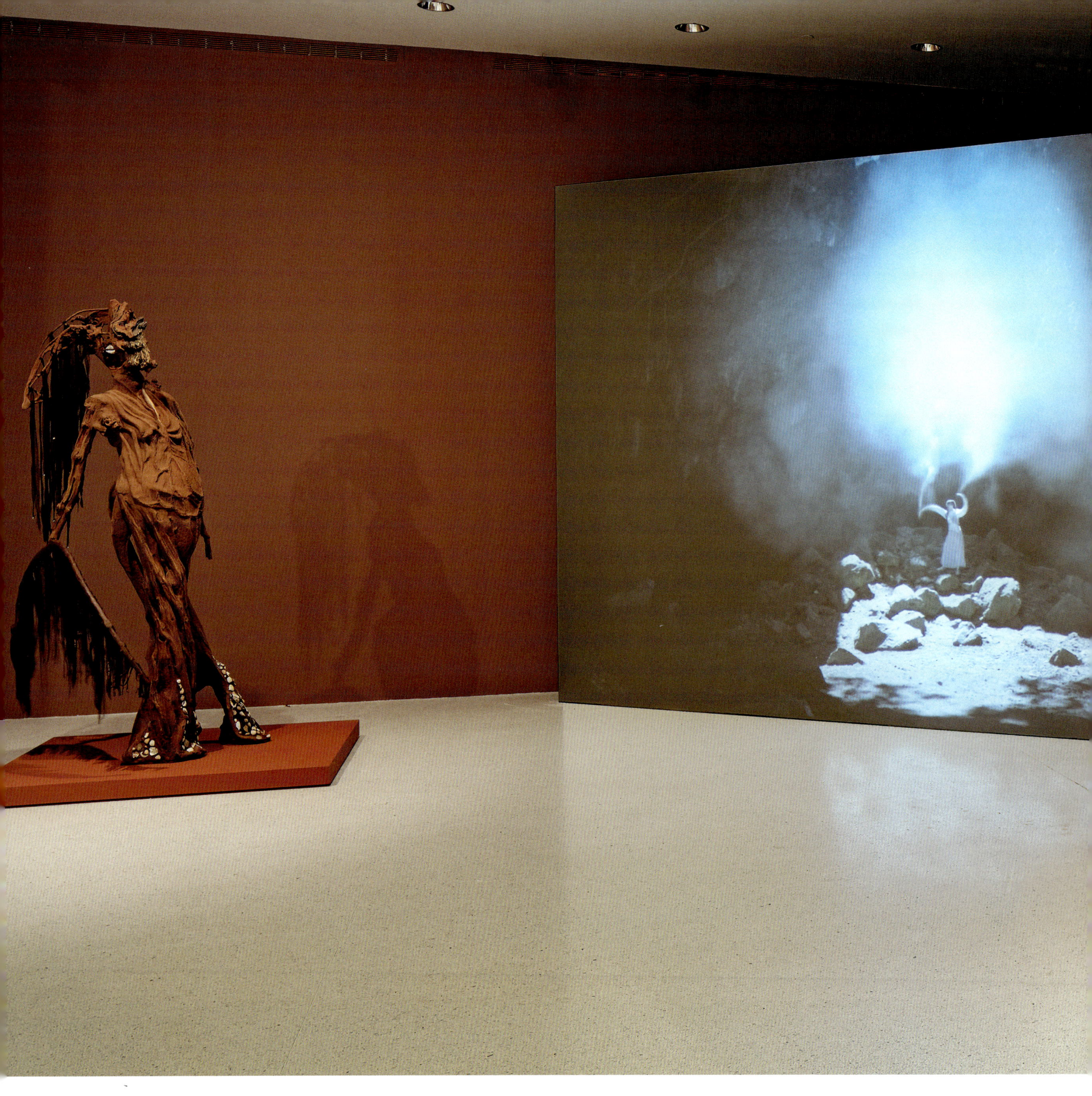

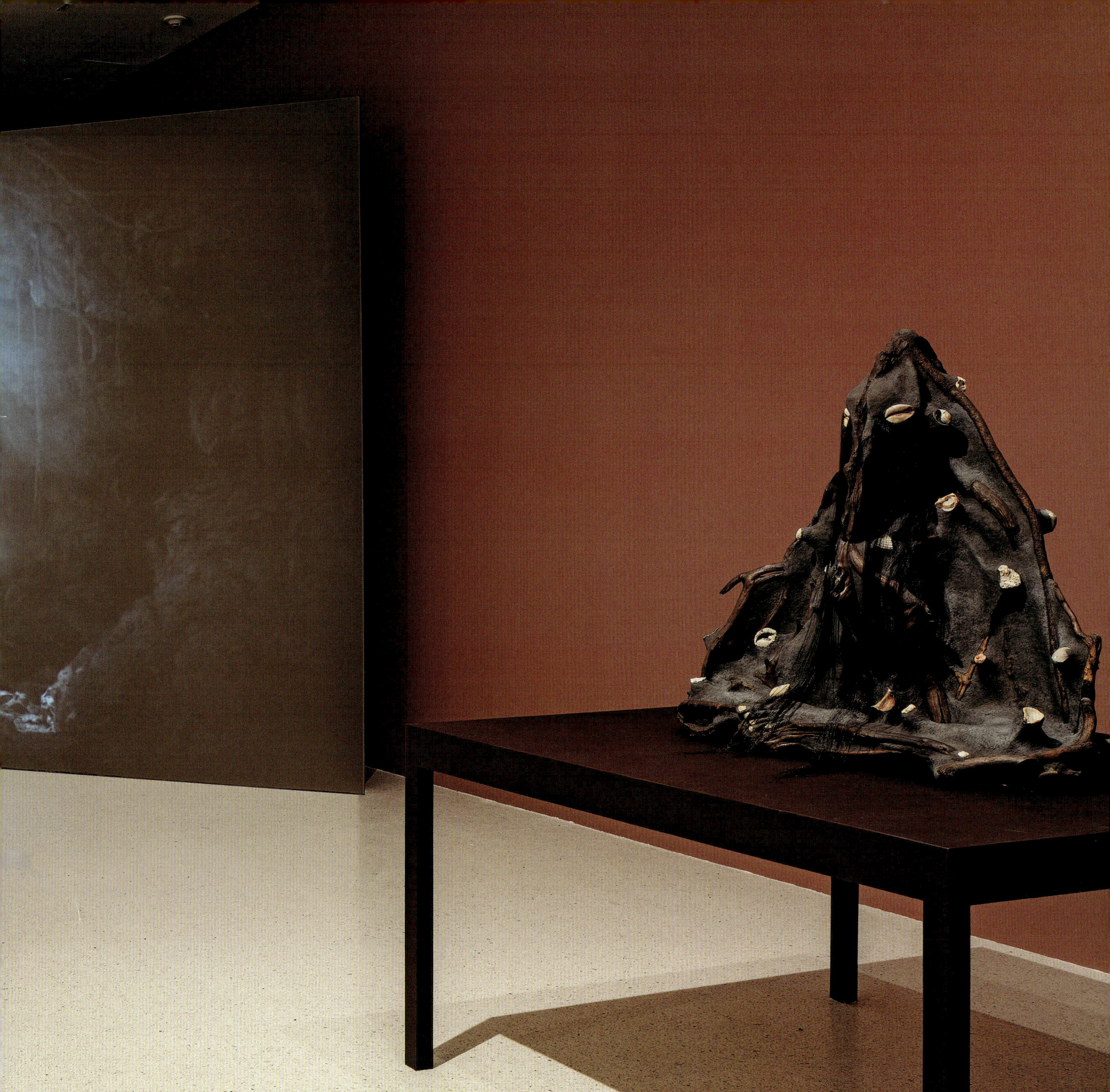

Wangechi Mutu

Sentinel VI, 2022

My Cave Call, 2021

Seeing Cowries, 2020

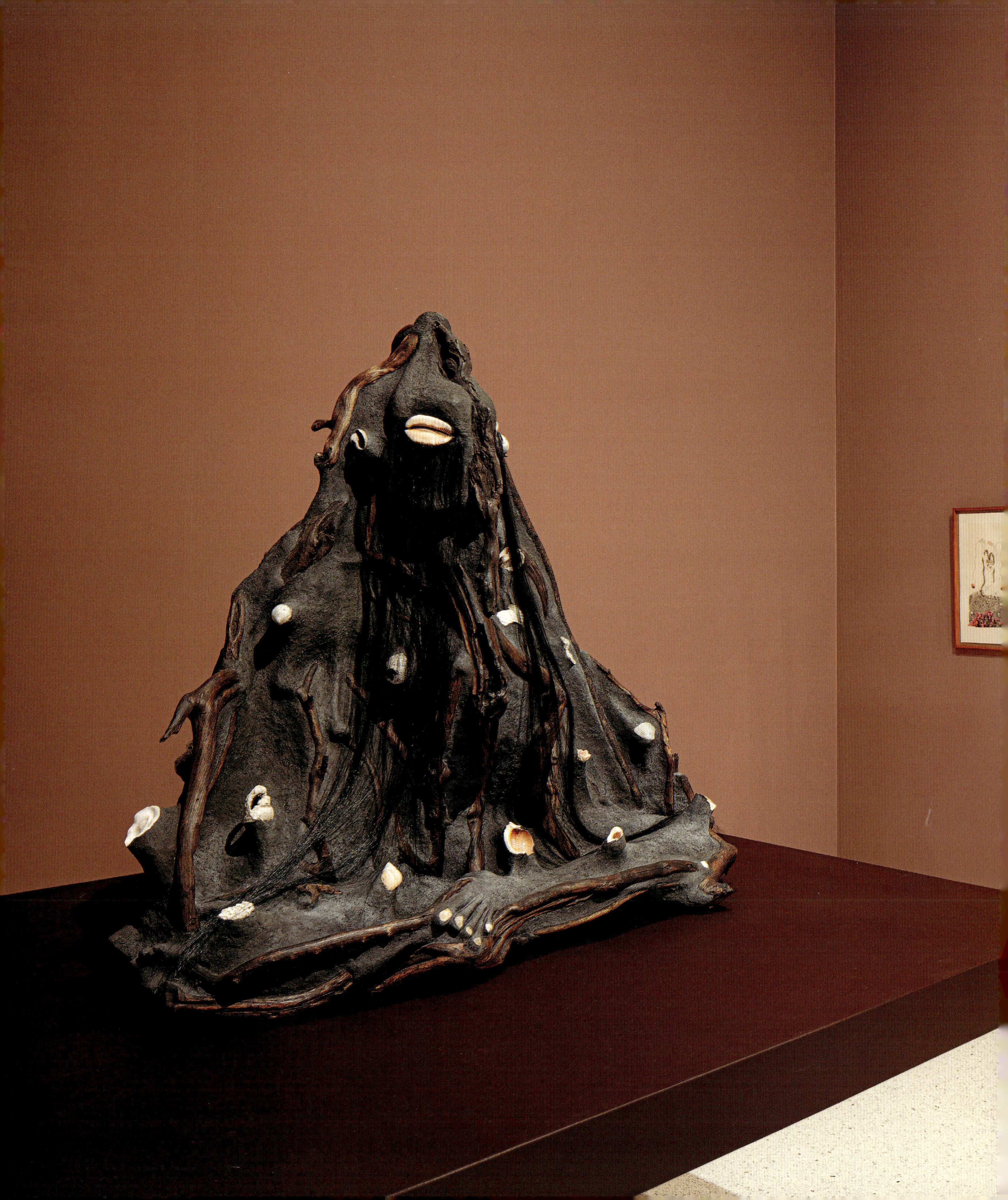

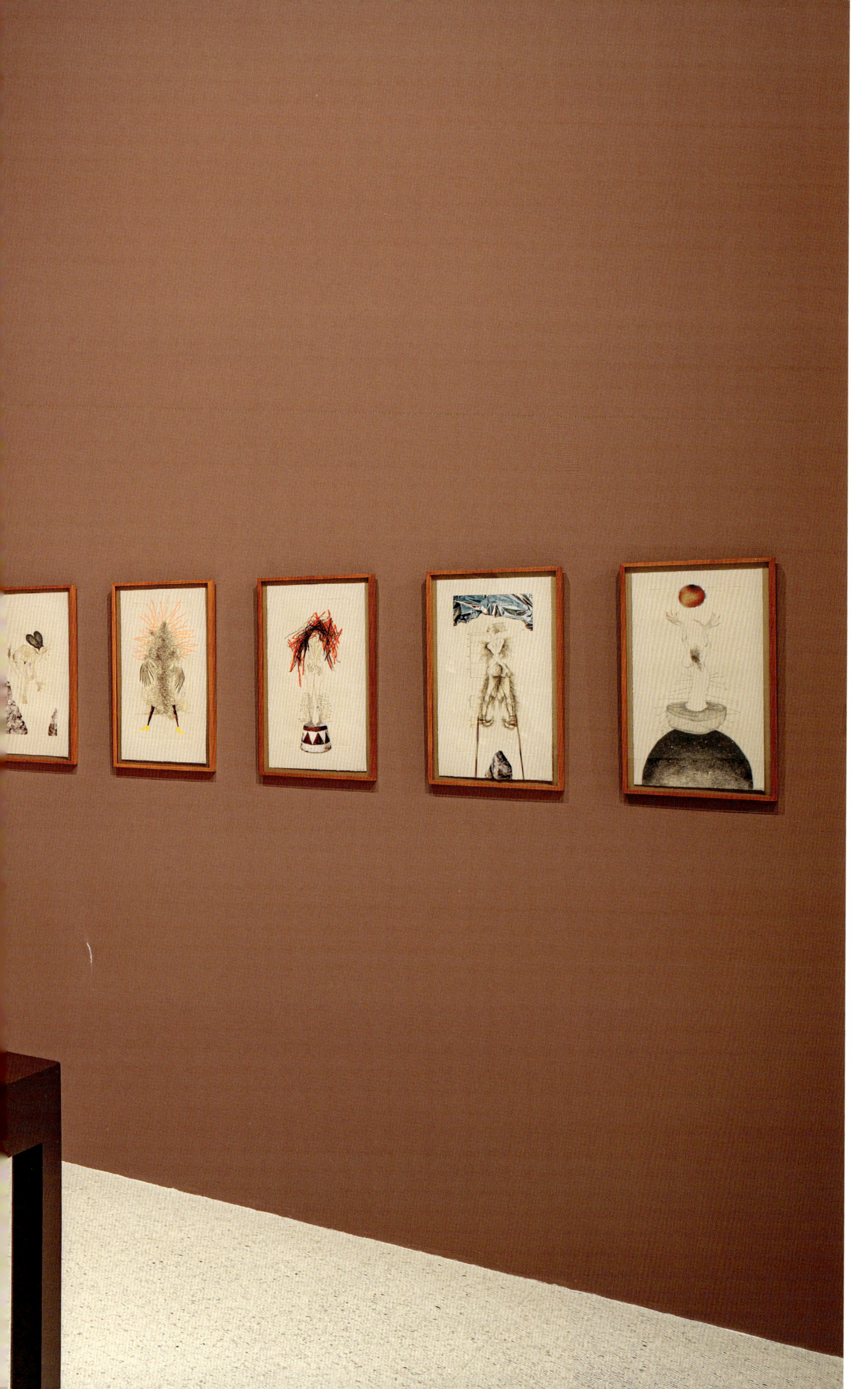

From left to right:
Wangechi Mutu
Seeing Cowries, 2020
The Original Nine Daughters, 2012

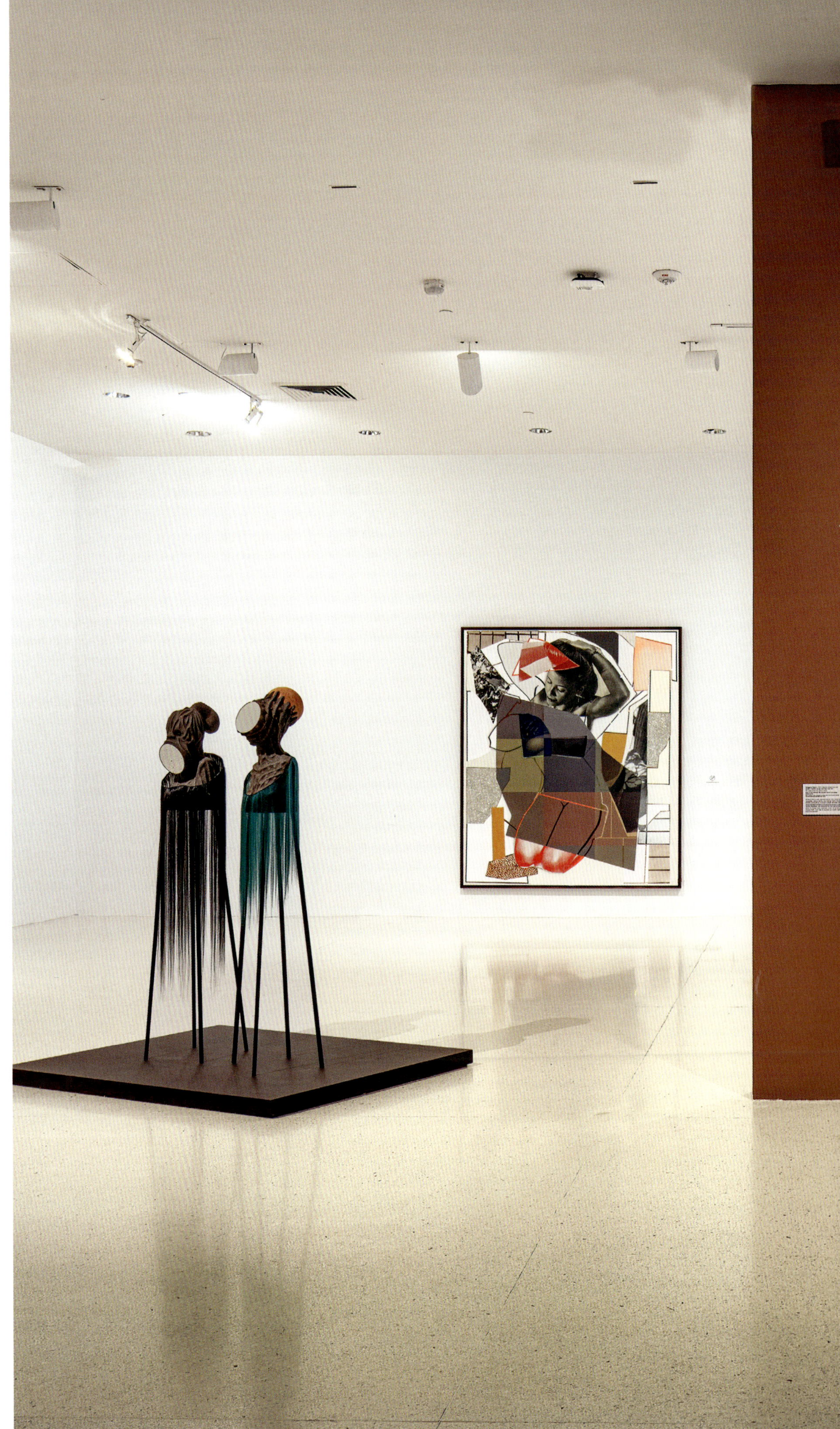

Left to right:

Wangechi Mutu

Mirror Faced II, 2020

Mirror Faced I, 2020

Mickalene Thomas

October 1950, 2021

Wangechi Mutu

The Original Nine Daughters, 2012

Sentinel VI, 2022

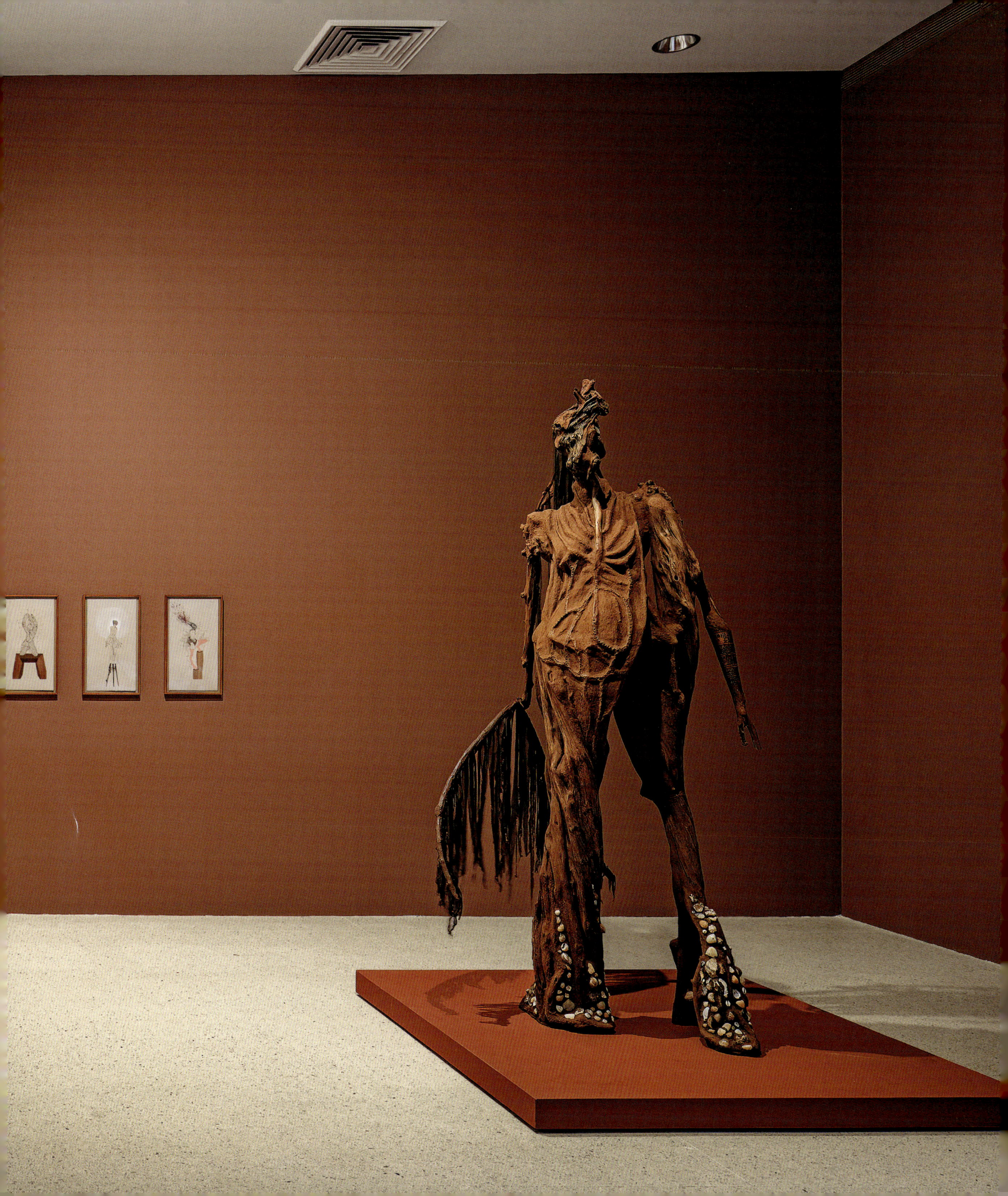

United in their critical reassessment of art history and the formal properties of each medium, these artists have pursued the establishment of new aesthetic paradigms that encompass a broader cultural worldview. Their interests in cultural and critical studies set a new course of artistic and cultural investigation that encompasses non-Western art, literature, film, and vernacular culture—including folk tales, spirit writing, outsider art, mass media, and hip-hop. Wangechi Mutu, Mickalene Thomas, Kehinde Wiley, Shoshanna Weinberger, Wardell Milan, Titus Kaphar, and Loren Holland reinvigorated figurative art with new relevance and urgency at the beginning of the decade, while Torkwase Dyson, Mike Cloud, Leslie Hewitt, Rashawn Griffin, Ronny Quevedo, and Eric N. Mack brought a fresh perspective to abstract art. Although there appears to be a divide between artists who work figuratively and those who create abstract work, they share an interest in the phenomenological relation of the body to space and architecture or to the work's narrative of bodily harm or exploitation. The body is implied even in its absence; and in several works, the absence of the body *is* the meaning of the work.

The twentieth-century medium of collage, with its breaks in time and juxtapositions, is effectively employed by most of these artists. For Thomas collage is Cubism filtered through artists Romare Bearden and Faith Ringgold, while Mike Cloud's appropriation of internet headline news can be traced to the newspapers Picasso and Braque collaged or painted into their Cubist compositions. Collage and three-dimensional assemblage also are associated with vernacular culture—of making art out of scraps and found materials—such as quilting. For cordova it is rooted in the hip-hop aesthetic of appropriation and sampling, as well as the sacred. Hip-hop, states cordova, was "about self-determination, aggrandizement, alternative methods of being, constructing different dimensions of existence… we were making Arte Povera without being aware of its European reference. Poor art is what we were making in some ways."[6] Most of the artists select their medium and materials for their nuanced properties that contribute to the symbolic meaning of the work and to the viewer's experience. Gold, mirrors, textiles, wood, and books are among the materials that appear most frequently, while other elements are incorporated to appeal to the sense of hearing, smell, and touch. The introduction of personal items such as the tenderly folded embroidered handkerchief in Hewitt's photographic still-life, *Typlologies (folded memory object)*, 2017 (ill. p. 110) attest to the presence of the artist, a way to acknowledge their own existence. To a certain extent the material culture that defines this generation overlaps with the work of the previous generation of artists, including Félix Gonzalez-Torres, Nari Ward, Jessica Stockholder (Director and Professor of Graduate Studies in Sculpture 1999–2011), Visiting Artists William Pope.L (2003)[7] and Shinique Smith (2010–2011) who uses textiles and other forms of personal adornment.

The exploration of abstract painting by this generation of artists coincided with scholarship and exhibitions that focused attention anew on abstract painting by Black artists in the 1960s, '70s, and '80s. Among these influential revisionist studies was Kellie Jones' exhibition *Energy/Experimentation*: *Black Artists and Abstraction 1964–1980* at The Studio Museum in Harlem (2006).[8] During the 1960s abstract painting was a controversial mode for Black artists who were marginalized by the mainstream art world and by the Black Arts Movement that favored figurative art to promote social and political engagement. These new studies focused on how the formal experiments by many of these abstract artists reflected or addressed social and political subjects. Concurrently, a new generation of Black abstract painters achieved prominence in the early 2000s, including Mark Bradford, Ellen Gallagher, Rashid Johnson, Julie Mehretu, Odili Donald Odita, and Shinique Smith, among others, who use form, color, materials, and personal archetypes to address social structures and interactions, history, and aesthetics.

Some of the shared subjects and praxis were not evident to the artists until they participated in the opening events for the *Lux et Veritas* exhibition. Chief among these was how many works had interior spaces that viewers could enter while others forbid entry. This tendency to reveal and conceal was evident in such works as Weinberger's paintings of headless

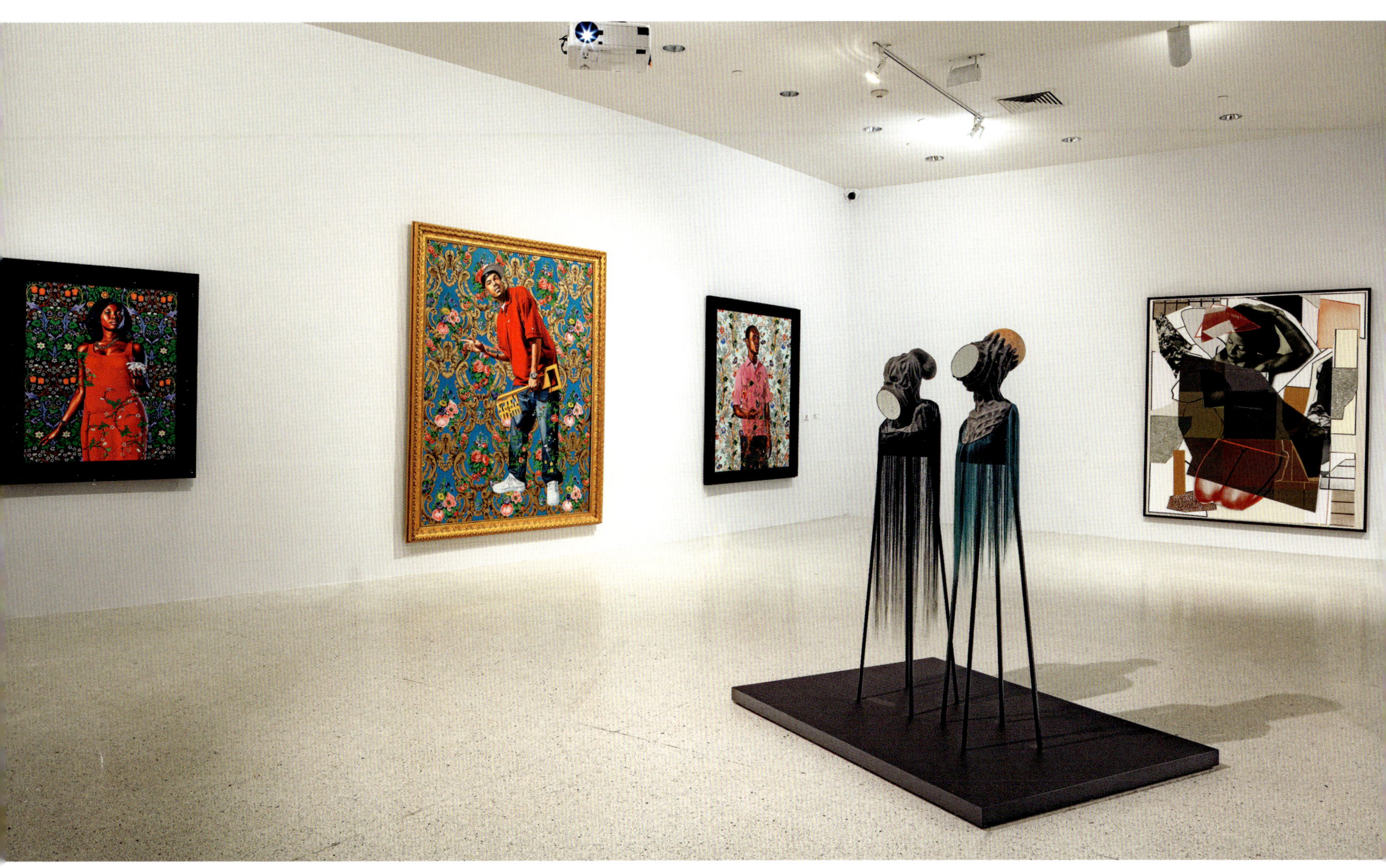

Left to right:

Kehinde Wiley
Sir Richard Owen 1804–1892, 2013
The Apostle Peter, 2006
Karl Spindler, 2017

Wangechi Mutu
Mirror Faced II, 2020
Mirror Faced I, 2020

Mickalene Thomas
October 1950, 2021

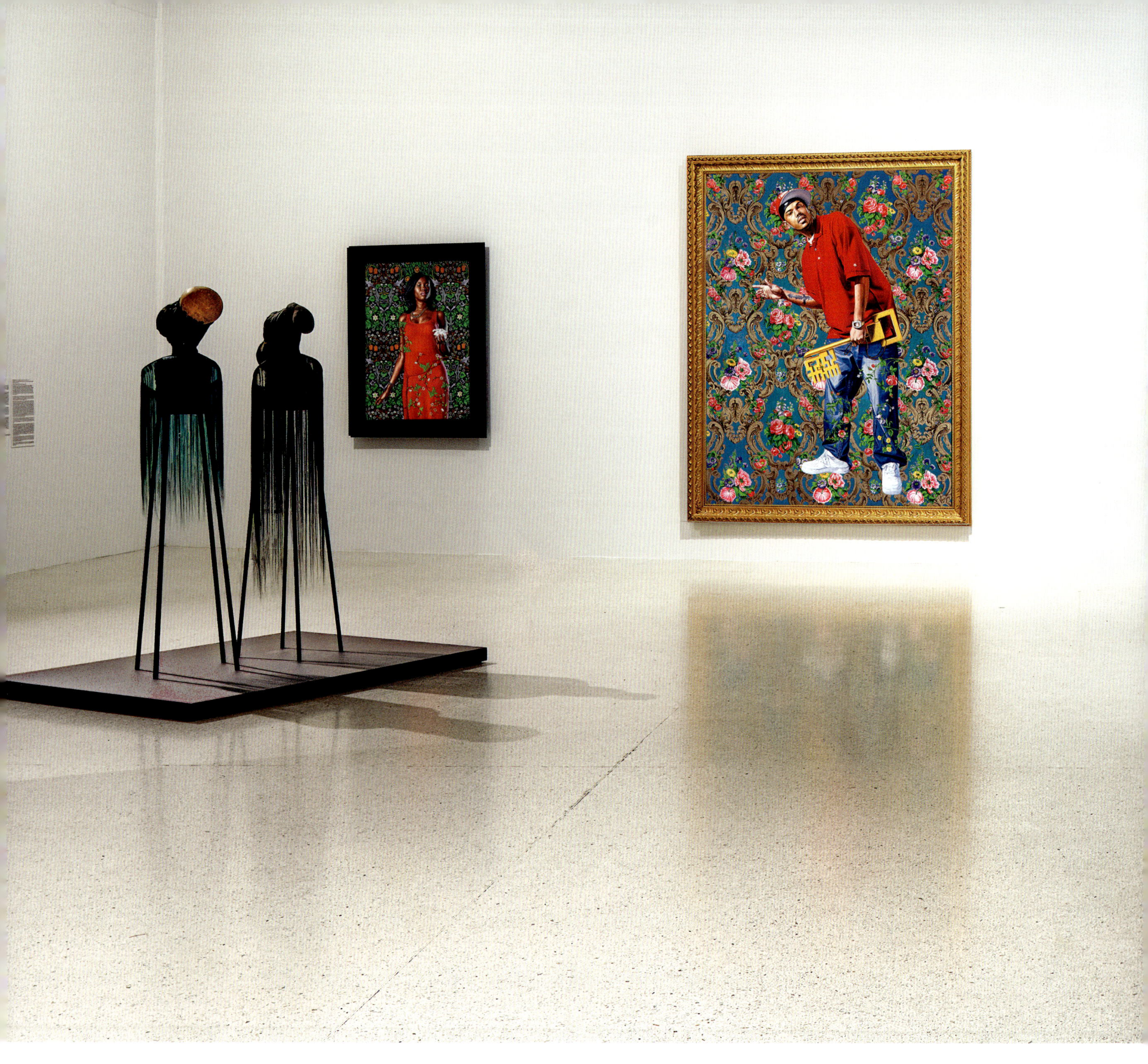

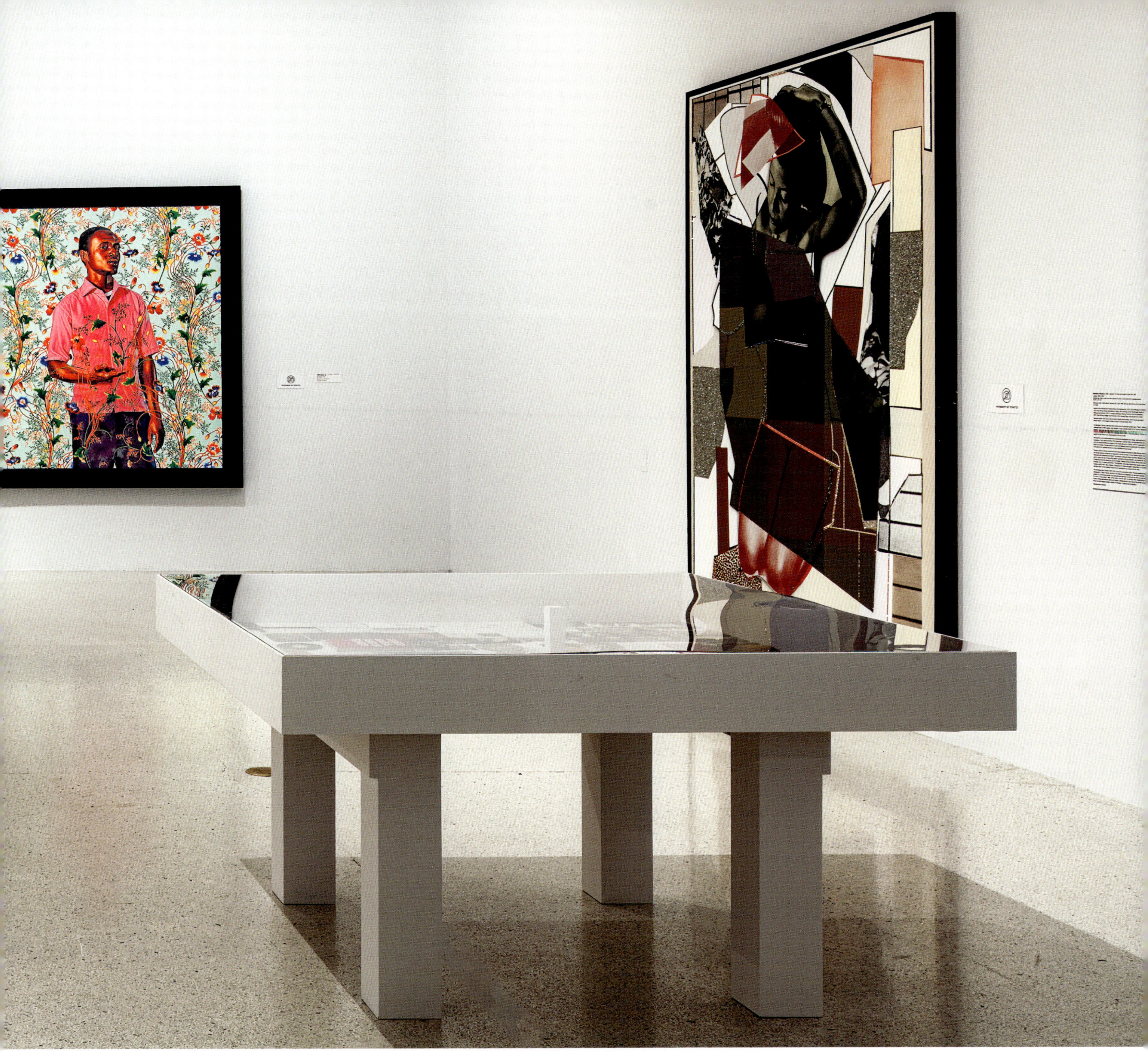

Left to right:
Wangechi Mutu
Mirror Faced II, 2020
Mirror Faced I, 2020

Kehinde Wiley
Sir Richard Owen 1804–1892, 2013
The Apostle Peter, 2006
Karl Spindler, 2017

Mickalene Thomas
October 1950, 2021

Left to right:

Titus Kaphar

Another Fight for Remembrance, Study, 2014

Top to bottom:

Titus Kaphar

Untitled 8, 2009

Untitled (Self-Portrait), 2007

Wardell Milan

Battle Royale, 2007

Left to right:

Titus Kaphar

Another Fight for Remembrance, Study, 2014

Top to bottom:

Titus Kaphar

Untitled 8, 2009

Untitled (Self-Portrait), 2007

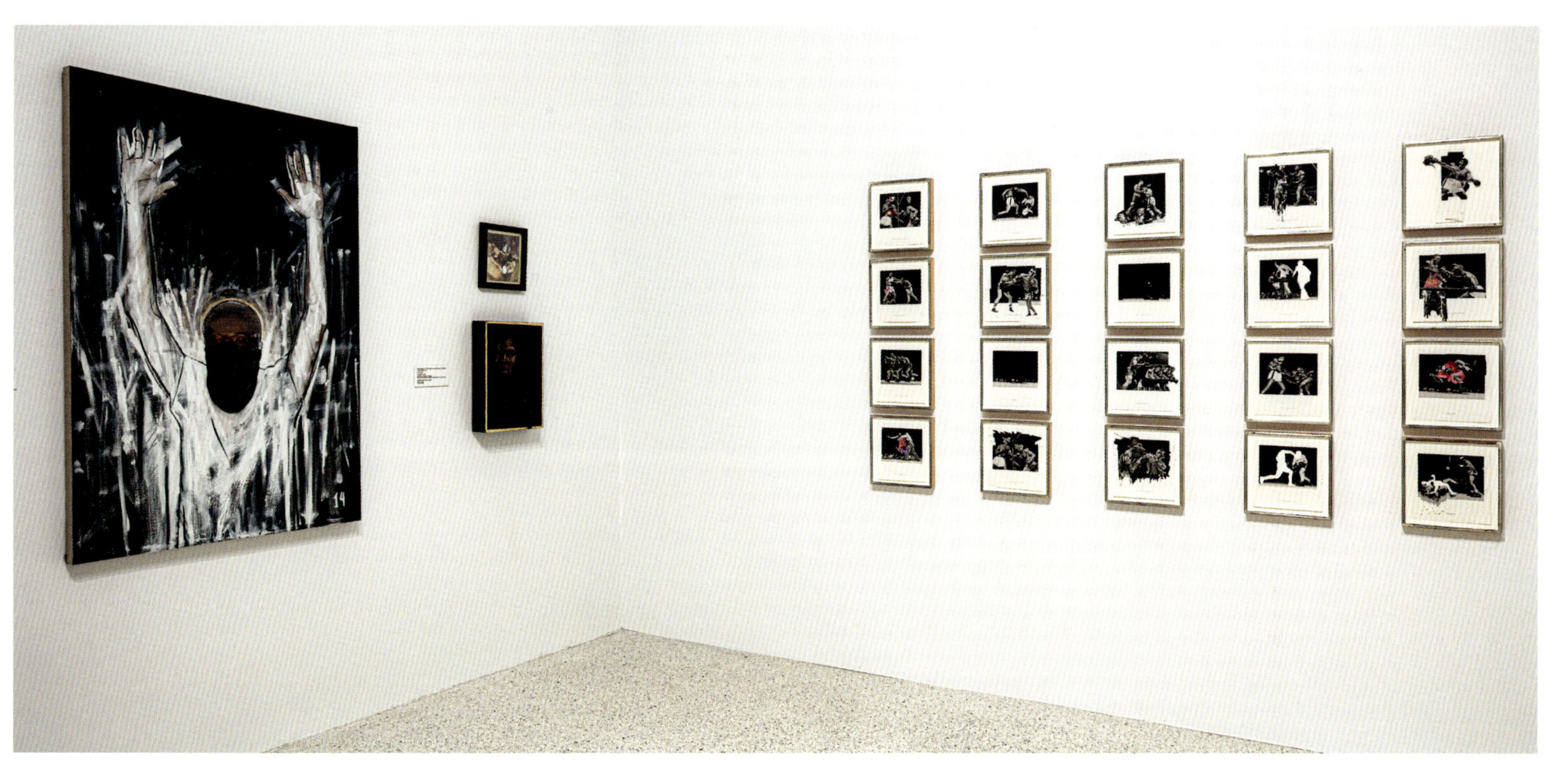

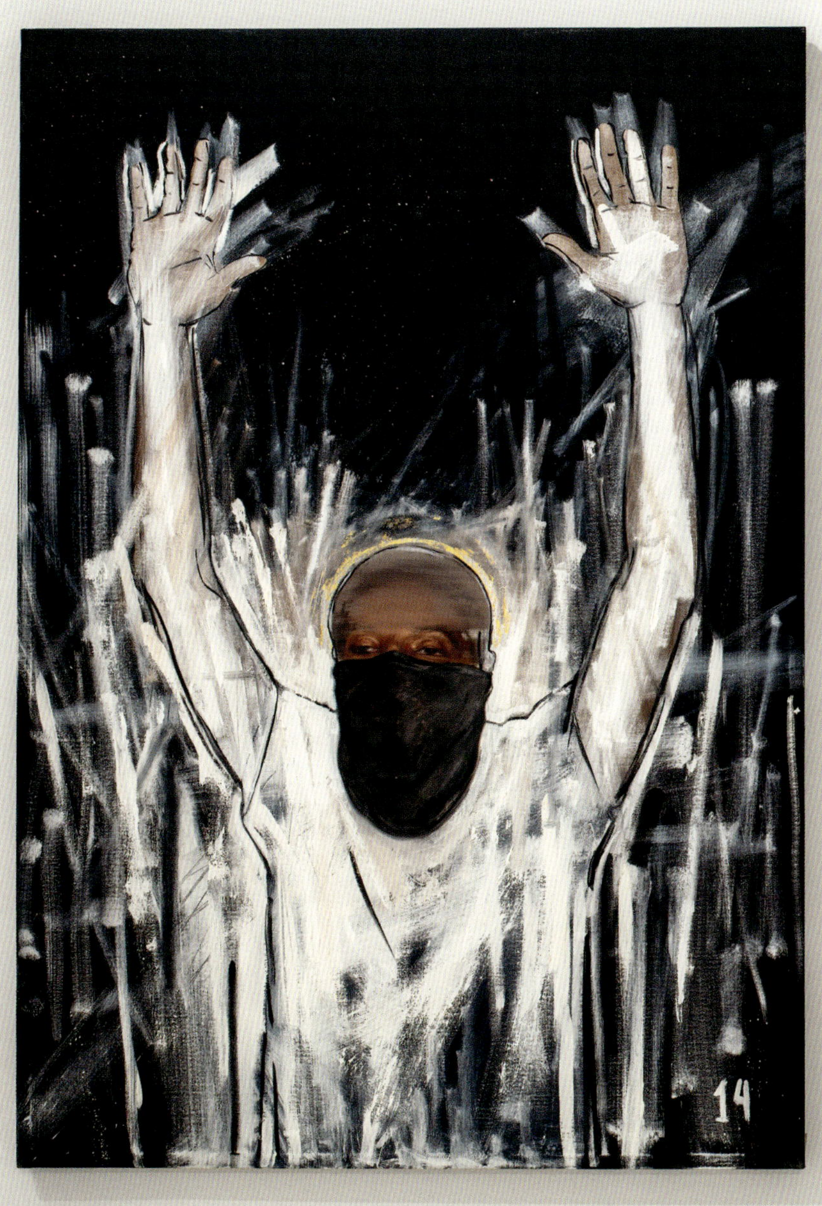

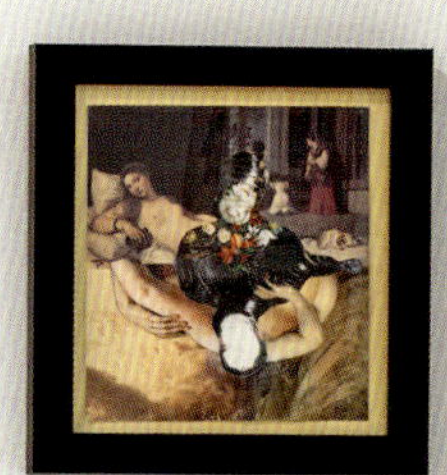

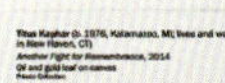

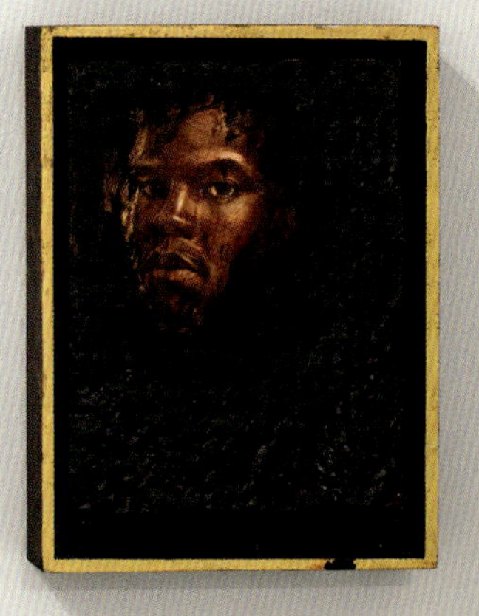

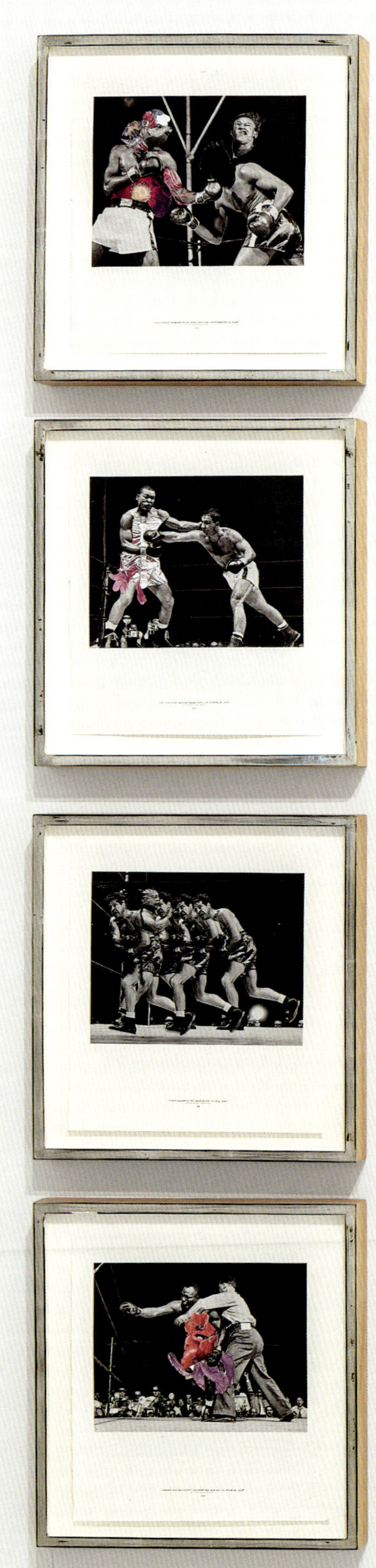 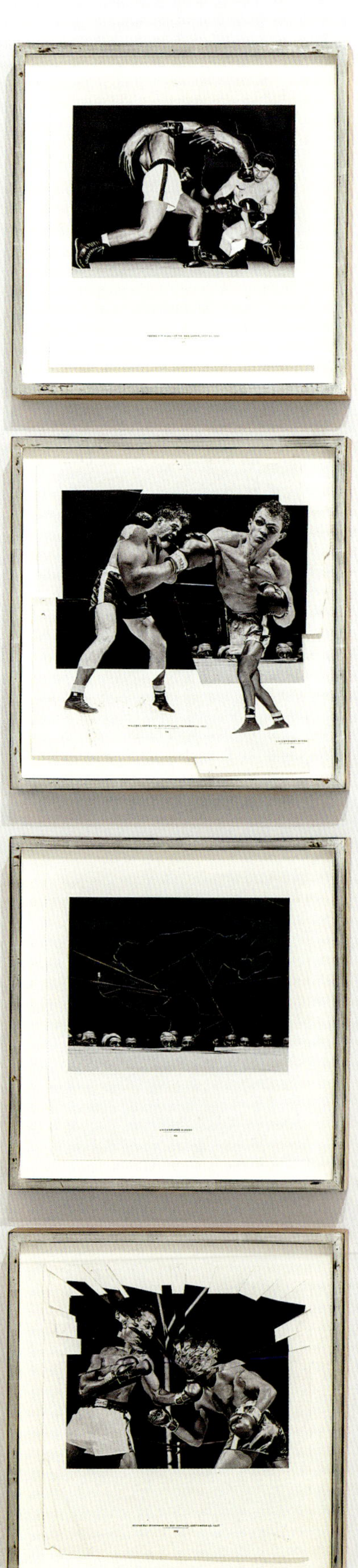

Wardell Milan

Battle Royale, 2007

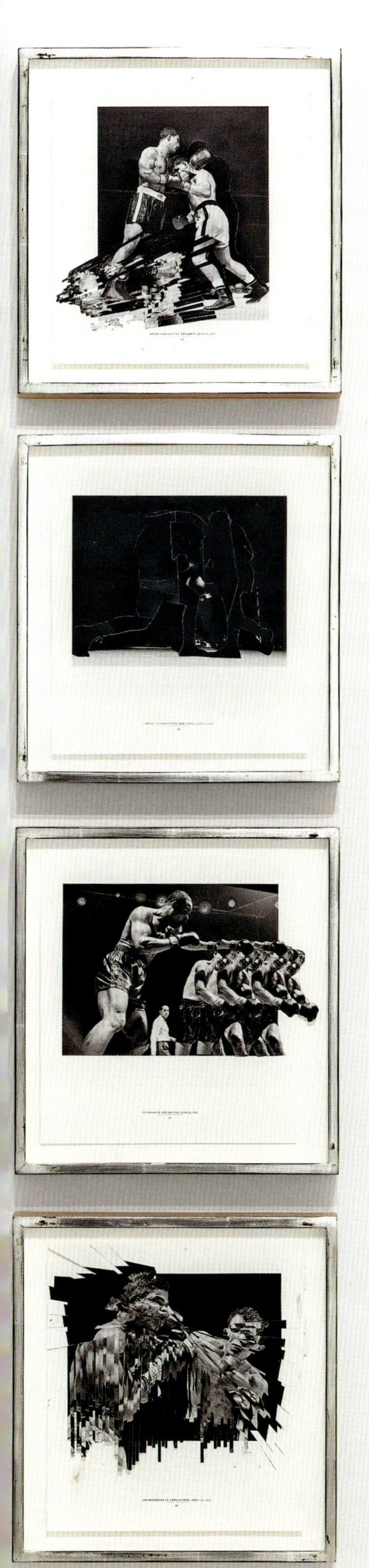
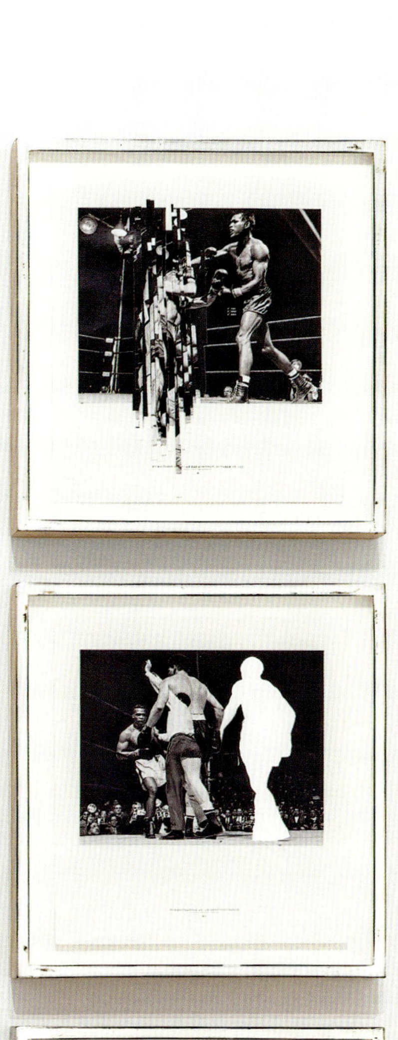
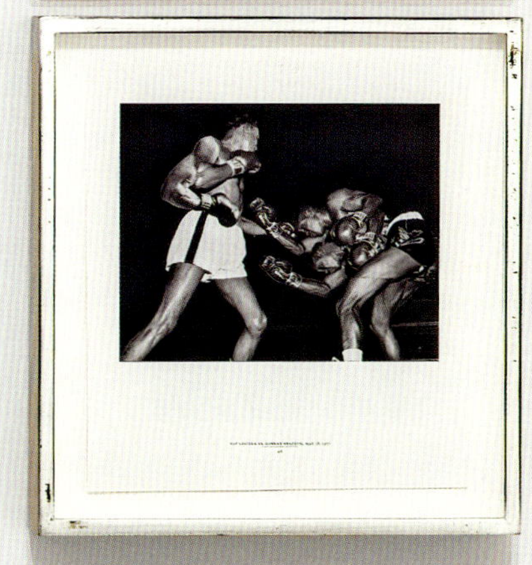
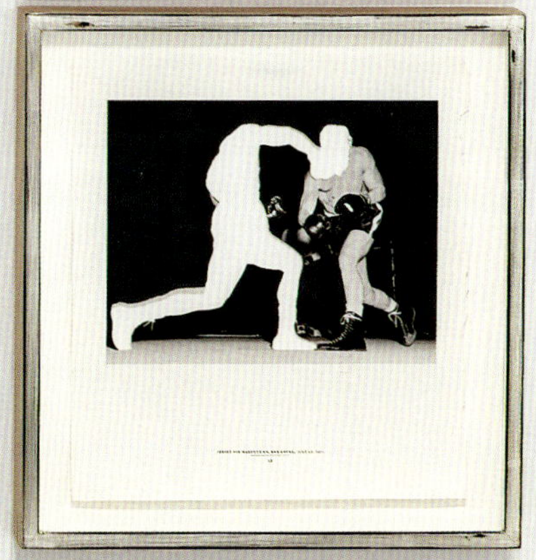
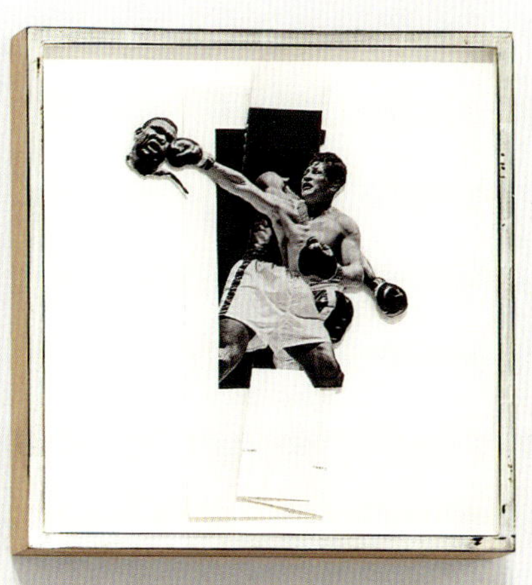
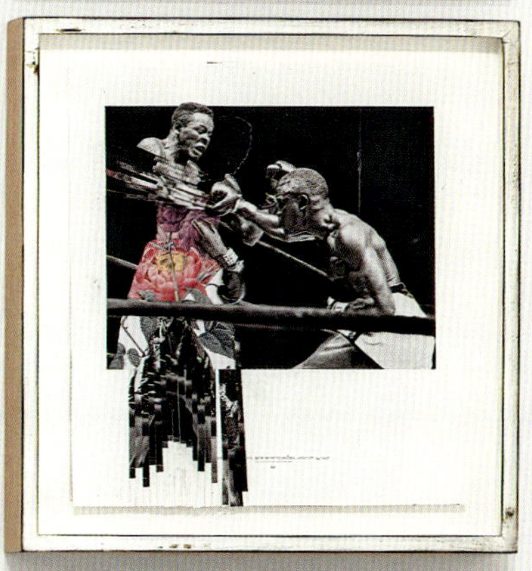
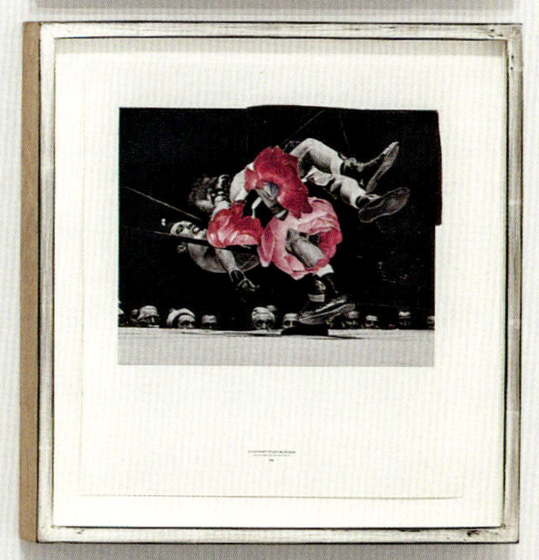
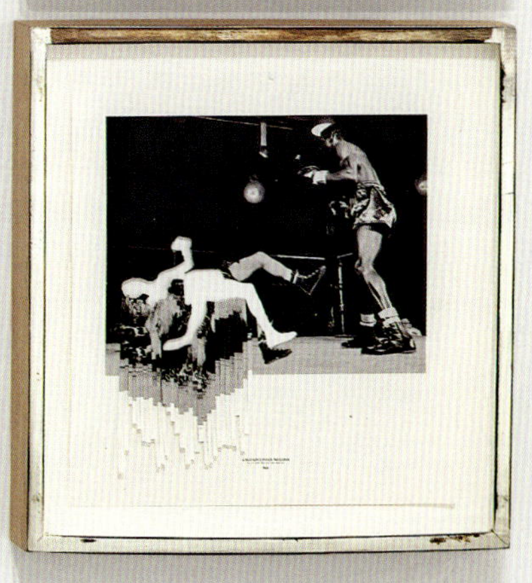

female bodies, the hide-and-seek imagery in Njideka Akyunili Crosby's portraits, Griffin's *The Changing Room* (ill. p. 121) in which viewers cannot escape their reflection, Otsubo's wooden cabinet—*Time Traveler*—with sliding doors that remain shut (ill. p. 118), the locked doors that shield the interiors of Tsouhlarakis' rockets (ill. p. 89), and Hewitt's photograph of the cover of a closed book (ill. p. 110). As with the use of symbols and codes, this condition of controlling access is connected with how much the artists want to show or make evident.

Interrogating and invoking the past is inherent in the work of most of these artists. DeVille, for instance, sites James Baldwin's seminal essay, the "Creative Process" (1962), as her mission statement: "We know… that whoever cannot tell himself the truth about his past is trapped in it, is immobilized in the prison of his undiscovered self. This is also true of nations… the war of an artist with his society is a lover's war, and he does… what lovers do, which is to reveal the beloved to himself and, with that revelation, to make freedom real."[9] cordova has similarly adopted the sentiment of Toni Morrison about myth and folklore: "There is infinitely more past than there is future… So in each step back, there is another world, and another world. The past is infinite. I don't know if the future is, but I know the past is."[10] These artists confront the past through the process of self-reflection in their work so as to move towards a constructive future.

Art School

According to the National Center for Education, the number of Master of Fine Art (MFA) students has been increasing every year since 1991. Originally conceived in the 1940s to confer credentials for teaching, these two-year programs increasingly became an essential degree for professional artists as it afforded them the time to fully immerse themselves in the exploration of making art and to obtain constant feedback from faculty, visiting critics, and their peers so as to sharpen their self-critical skills and to find the means to discuss and defend their work. It also offered the opportunity for students to bond with other artists as a community that could grow over the years beyond graduation. With tuition now averaging in the tens of thousands the value of MFA programs has been scrutinized in recent years and other paths to educating artists are evolving.

There are over 300 accredited fine arts schools in the United States. The Yale School of Art, established in 1864 as the nation's first art school connected with an institution of higher learning, has one of the highest rankings. Its curriculum changed little from the time of its founding until 1950 with the hiring of the German-born Josef Albers as Chair of the Department of Design. Albers, an abstract painter known for his color theory, brought a fresh perspective as a former professor of the German Bauhaus school of design, architecture, and applied arts, and as an influential teacher at the experimental Black Mountain College,

in North Carolina. Under Albers the Yale School of Art was brought current with Modern art with the hiring of new faculty. The legacy of Albers and the Bauhaus utopian agenda were among the subjects explored and analyzed by a number of the artists represented in the *Lux et Veritas* exhibition, such as in cordova's *quotidian palimpsest*, which renders a revolutionary design by Bauhaus architect Le Corbusier (ill. pp. 106–107), Otsubo's minimal wood-crafted cabinet *Time Traveler*, and Mack's application of color theory for his abstract work (ill. p. 137).

The Yale School of Art graduate program consisted of classes taught by faculty and visiting professors and studio visits, culminating in a thesis exhibition.[11] Each student was assigned an advisor. A mainstay of most art schools, including Yale, is the formal critical discussion of the artwork known as the "crit." Group crits were generally held weekly as well as in classes. For Titus Kaphar (MFA Painting 2006), the crits felt "like being on trial, and your work is the evidence… A faculty member will basically say: 'So you say your work means this, but exhibit A shows that'."[12]

Coco Fusco, who witnessed several studio crits while she was a Visiting Associate Professor there (2004–2005), wrote of this experience: "Sitting together in white rooms with a student's art works on display, the discussants were not supposed to stray from what was in front of them. The dominant rhetoric was formalism mixed with heavy doses of bravado and personal opinion… Black students I met there at the time conveyed in private that they felt stifled by the terms of discussion, especially because white students would frequently claim that they were unable to relate to work by students of color because they did not understand their cultural references." Fusco adds "if you were an art student and you spoke up about institutional racism or cultural appropriation, it was quite likely that you would either be socially excluded by peers, reminded that identity politics are 'over,' or admonished by mentors for not realizing that such concerns fall outside the boundaries of the aesthetic appreciation." As visiting faculty and an artist of color from a previous generation, Fusco had students confide in her that "the message being driven home was that for artists of color to succeed they had to avoid talking about racial politics and concede that their presence at the school was sufficient evidence of a post-racial art world."[13]

While many art schools offered a cross-disciplinary education in the late twentieth century, Yale remained committed to the separation of painting and printmaking, sculpture, photography, and graphic design to the extent that the Department of Painting and Printmaking and Department of Sculpture are still housed in separate buildings.[14] Some students considered the concentration on their chosen discipline an advantage, while others found it limiting and chose the more all-encompassing Sculpture department. Although video as a discipline was not part of the graduate school, several of the artists who studied there early in the decade have pursued this medium as part of their practice.[15] These comprised of mostly Sculpture majors Gispert, Mutu and Tsouhlarakis as well as Painting major cordova. Yale's Digital Media Center for the Arts (founded in 1998 by Ken Lovell and Lee Faulkner) made its facilities and technical assistance available for digital video and photography editing and printing. Kellie Jones taught an undergraduate art history class on Latin American cinema, which cordova and Hewitt attended. Moreover, as cordova notes, the graduate faculty of the School of Art did not embrace the making or showing of video or film. cordova recalls being discouraged from discussing the subject at the crits but he persisted, nevertheless. The collaborative nature of filmmaking made these artists' collectives a necessity.

Despite its proximity to New York, the School of Art tended to shelter its students from art dealers and collectors to minimize the influence of the art market. This fortification held until the middle of the decade when the primary gatekeeper, Sue Szary, Secretary, Department of Painting and Printmaking, retired. For several of the artists included in *Lux et Veritas*, this isolation was one of the defining aspects of their school experience that separates them from the subsequent decade in which there was more interaction with the art world and art market.[16]

Each of the departments of the Yale School of Art have their own director and their own admissions selection review process. Between 2000 and 2010 over thirty artists of color attended the graduate program at the School averaging two to three first-year students a year throughout most of the decade. Several chose to attend the School based on its esteemed alumni of previous generations of artists of color who attended Yale since the 1960s, including Barbara Chase-Riboud (MFA 1960),[17] Howardena Pindell (MFA 1967), William T. Williams (MFA 1968), Barkley Hendricks (MFA 1972), Martin Puryear (MFA 1977), Tomas Vu (MFA 1989), Dawoud Bey (MFA 1993), and Candida Alvarez (MFA 1997), among others.

As most of the artists included in this exhibition who attended art school as undergraduates had an immersive core art education, one of the allures of Yale was the opportunity to attend art history courses taught by such eminent faculty as Kellie Jones (1999 to 2006) and Robert Farris Thompson (one of the most prominent scholars of African art), and to audit lectures in a variety of subjects.[18] Although the School of Art's student body became increasingly diverse during the decade (a stated goal of artist and curator Robert Storr, who became Dean in 2006), lack of funding from Yale's administration impeded the hiring of new faculty to broaden the representation of artists of color. The gap in the diversity of the faculty was addressed by inviting artists, curators, critics, and writers of color as adjunct professors, advisors, and guest speakers, rather than engaging them as full-time faculty.[19] In June 2021, Kymberly Pinder (Yale Ph.D. Art History 1999), was hired as the first Black, and only second woman, dean in its 157-year history.[20]

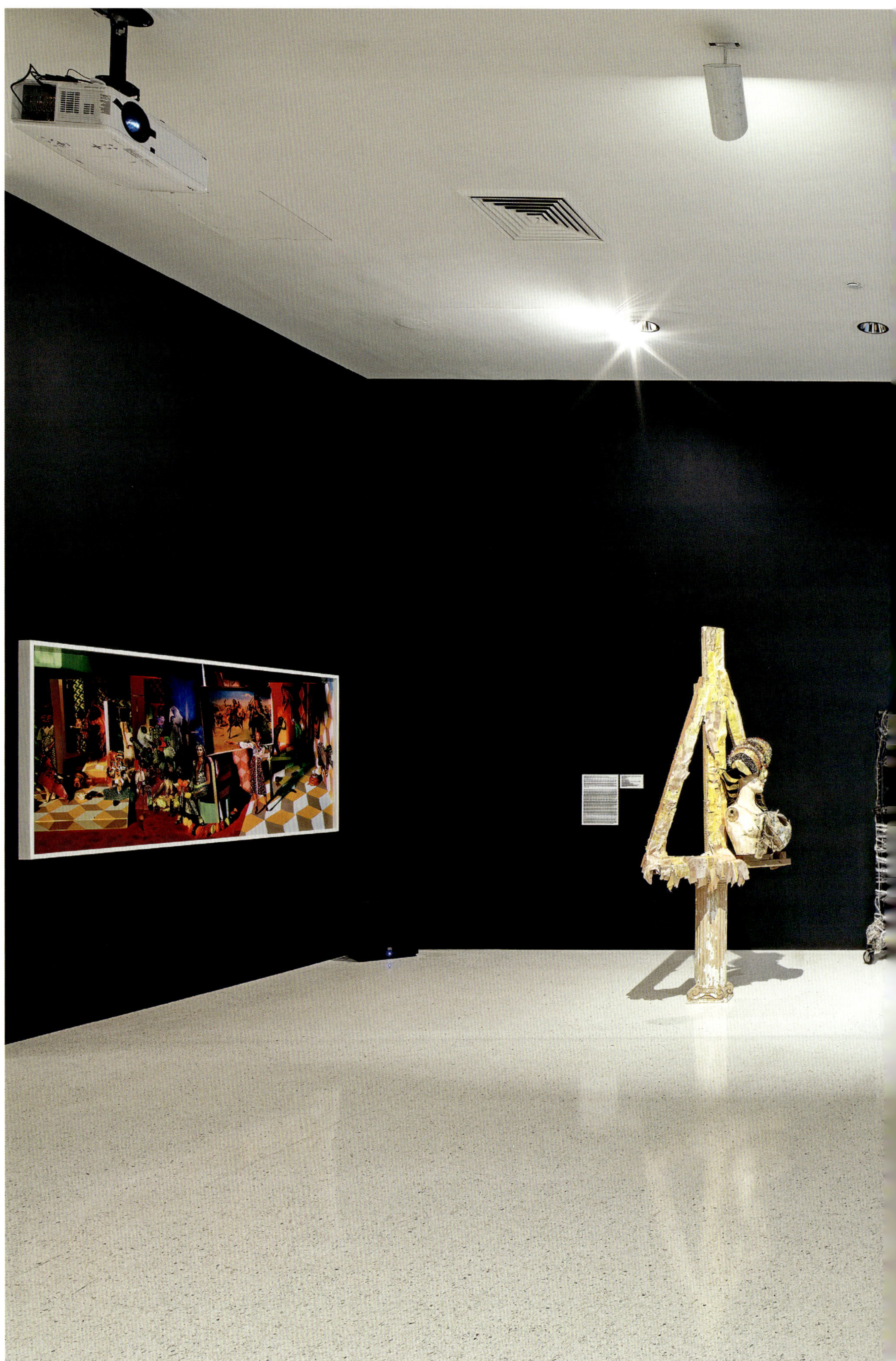

Wardell Milan

I'm trying to keep my faith. But, I'm searching for more. Somewhere I can be safe, 2017–2018

Abigail Deville

Lady Liberty, 2022

Pharaoh March, 2022

Libertas (study in off white), 2022

Loren Holland

The Bathers, 2018

The Shadow Queen, 2018

Bait and Switch, 2018

Luis Gispert, Jeffrey Reed

Stereomongrel, 2005

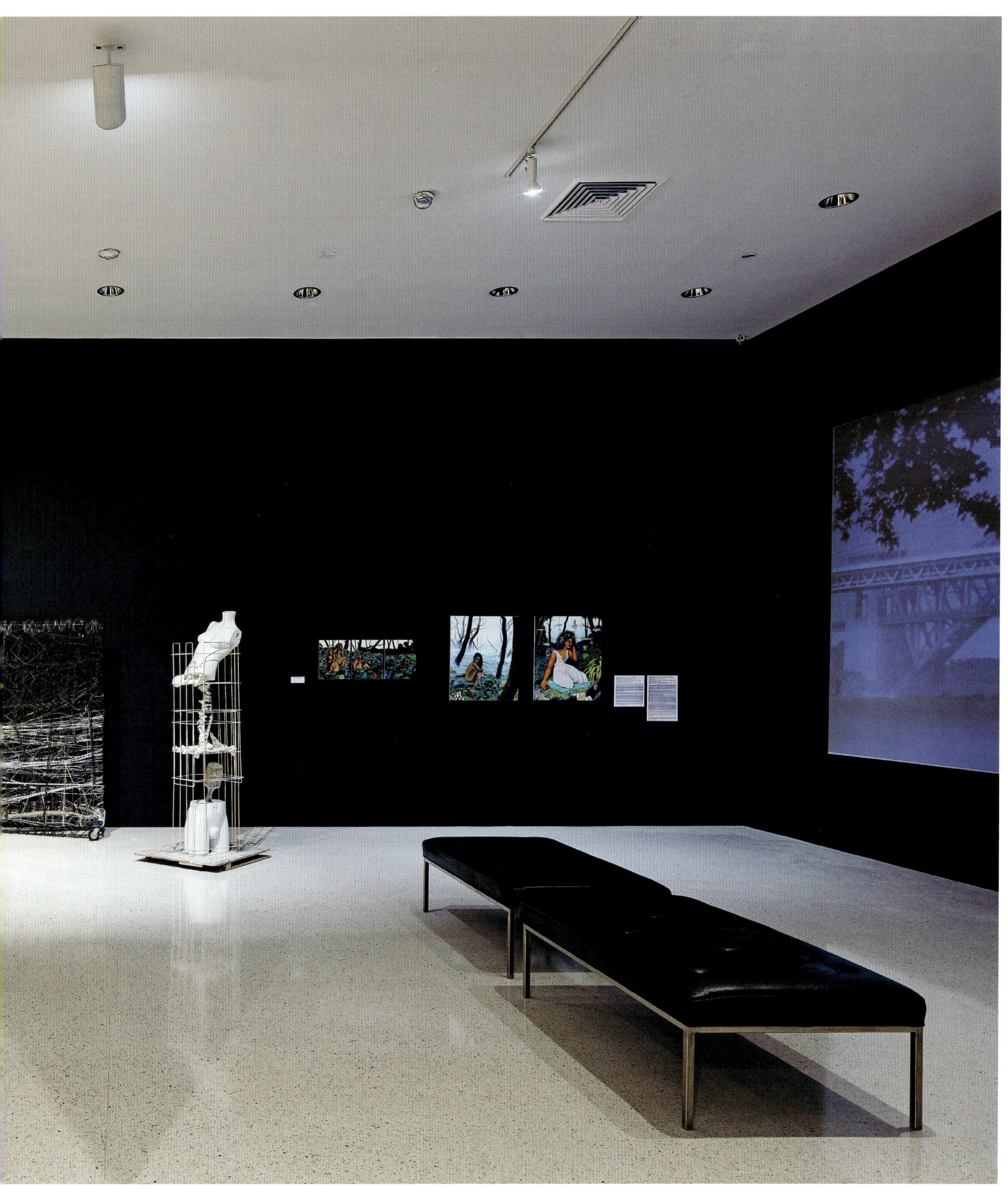

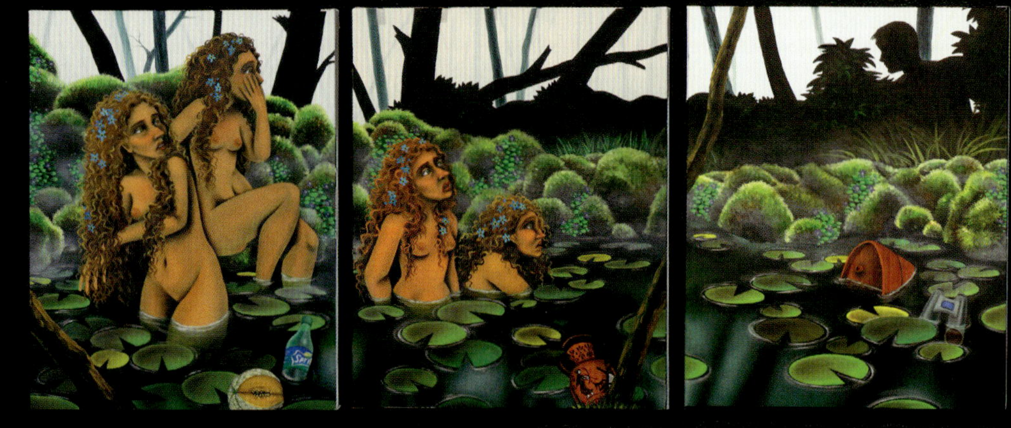

Loren Holland

The Bathers, 2018

The Shadow Queen, 2018

Bait and Switch, 2018

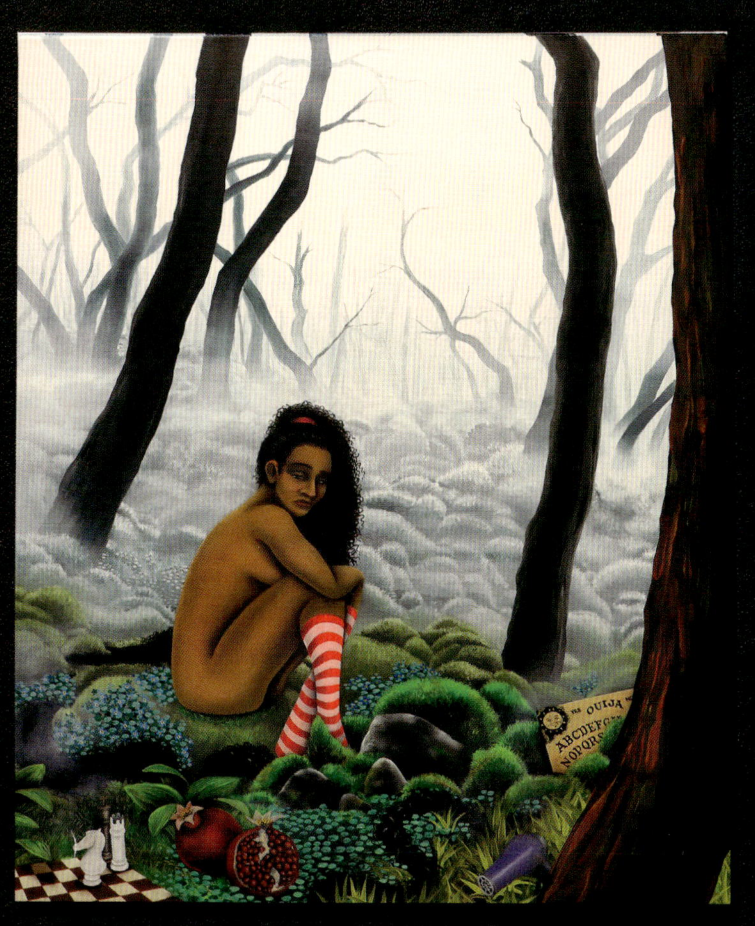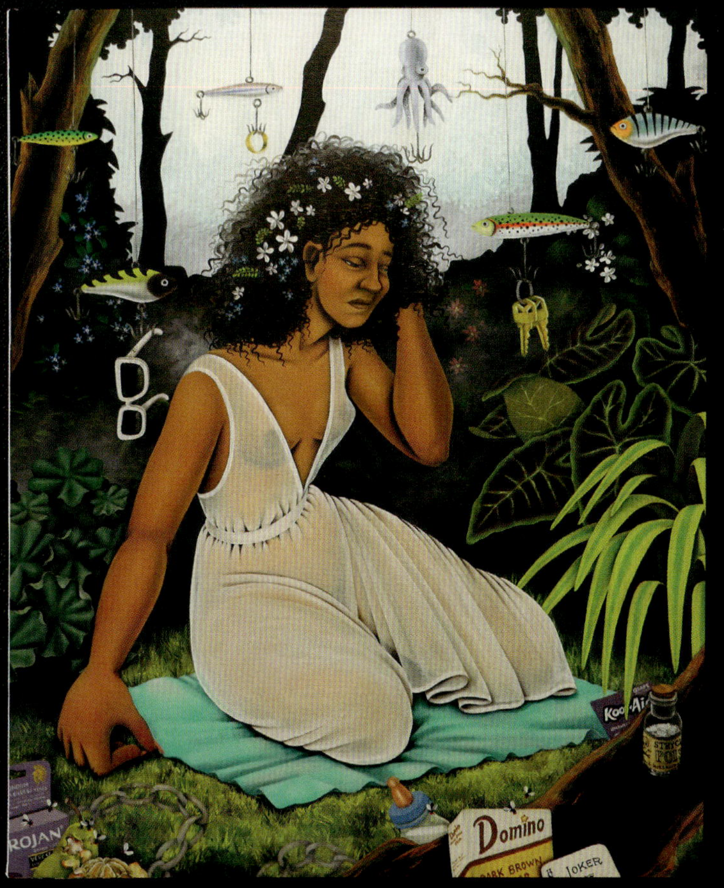

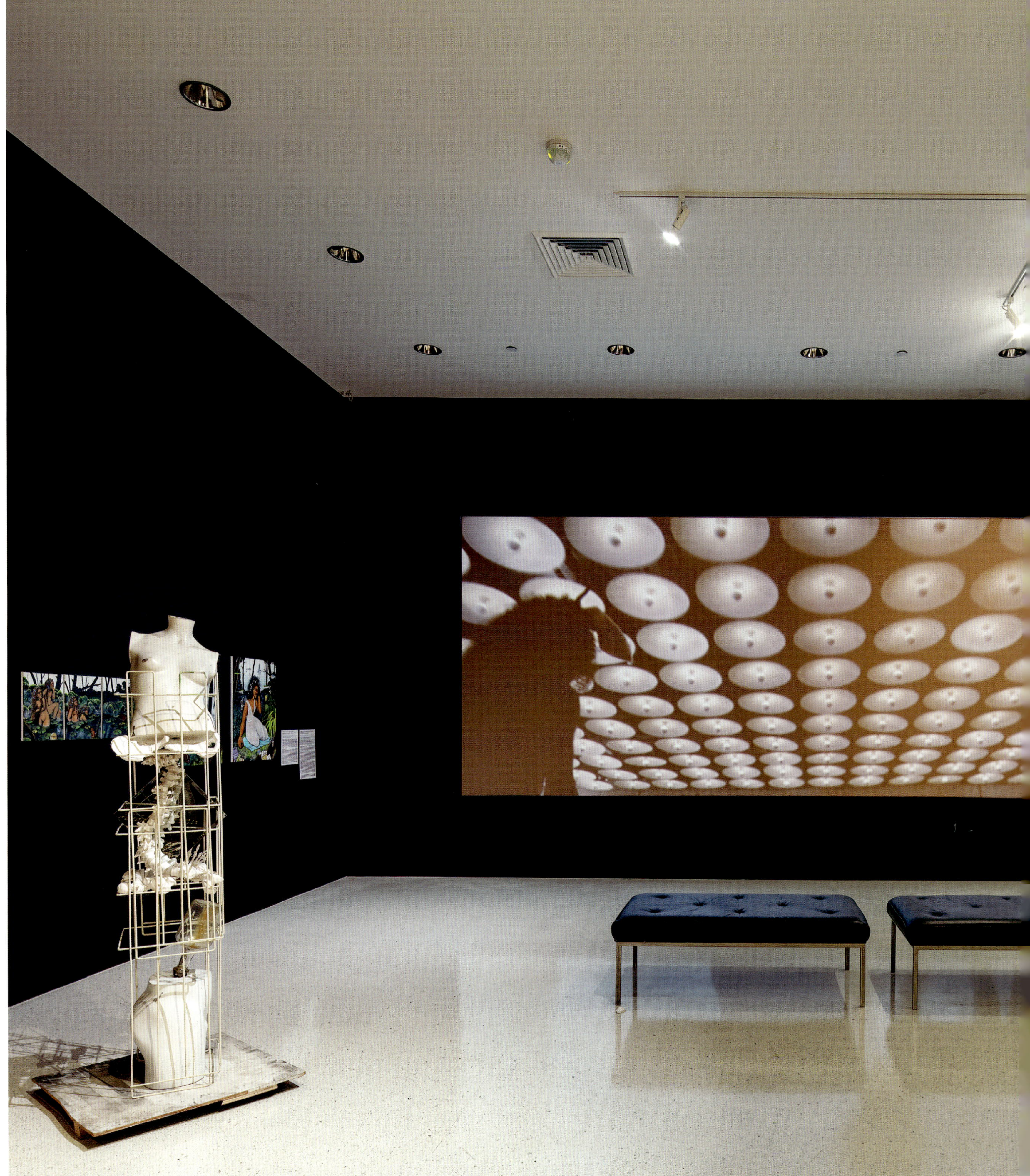

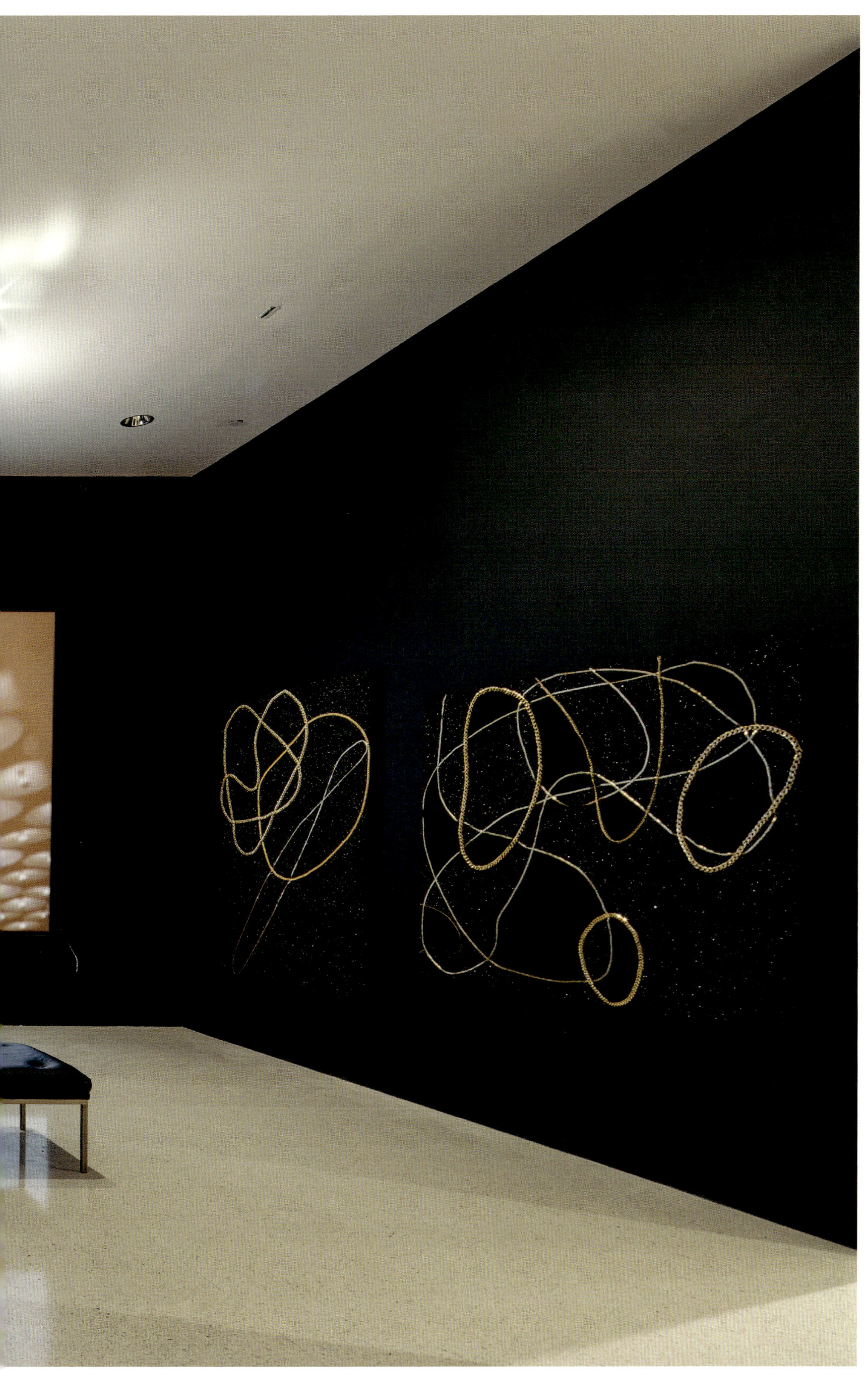

Abigail Deville
Libertas (study in off white), 2022

Loren Holland
The Bathers, 2018
The Shadow Queen, 2018
Bait and Switch, 2018

Luis Gispert, Jeffrey Reed
Stereomongrel, 2005

Luis Gispert
Secret Pilgrim, 2015
Bojangles, 2016

Following pages:
william cordova
quotidian palimpsest, 1983

John Espinosa
People with Eyes, 2004
Rut and Reconstitution, 2001

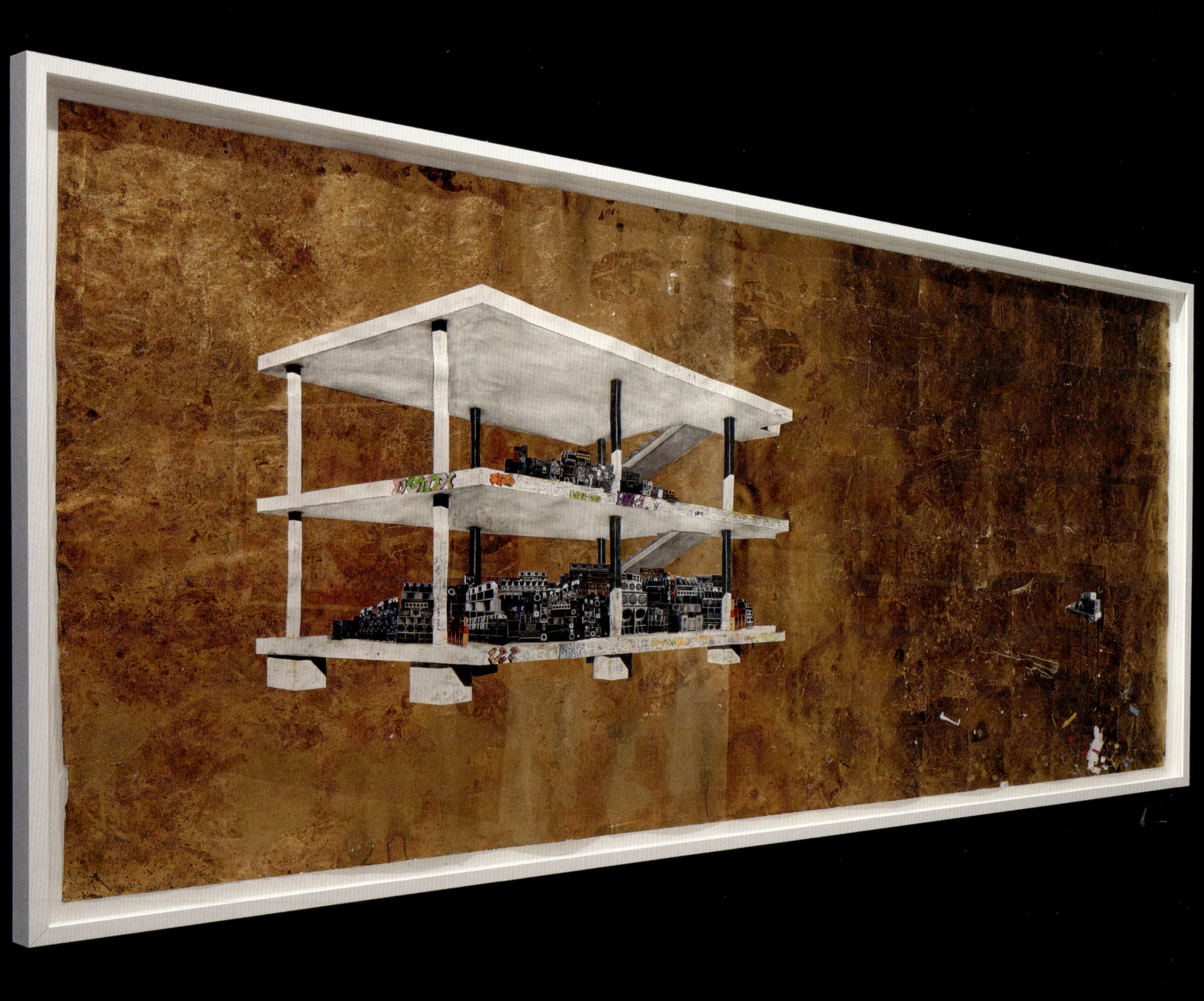

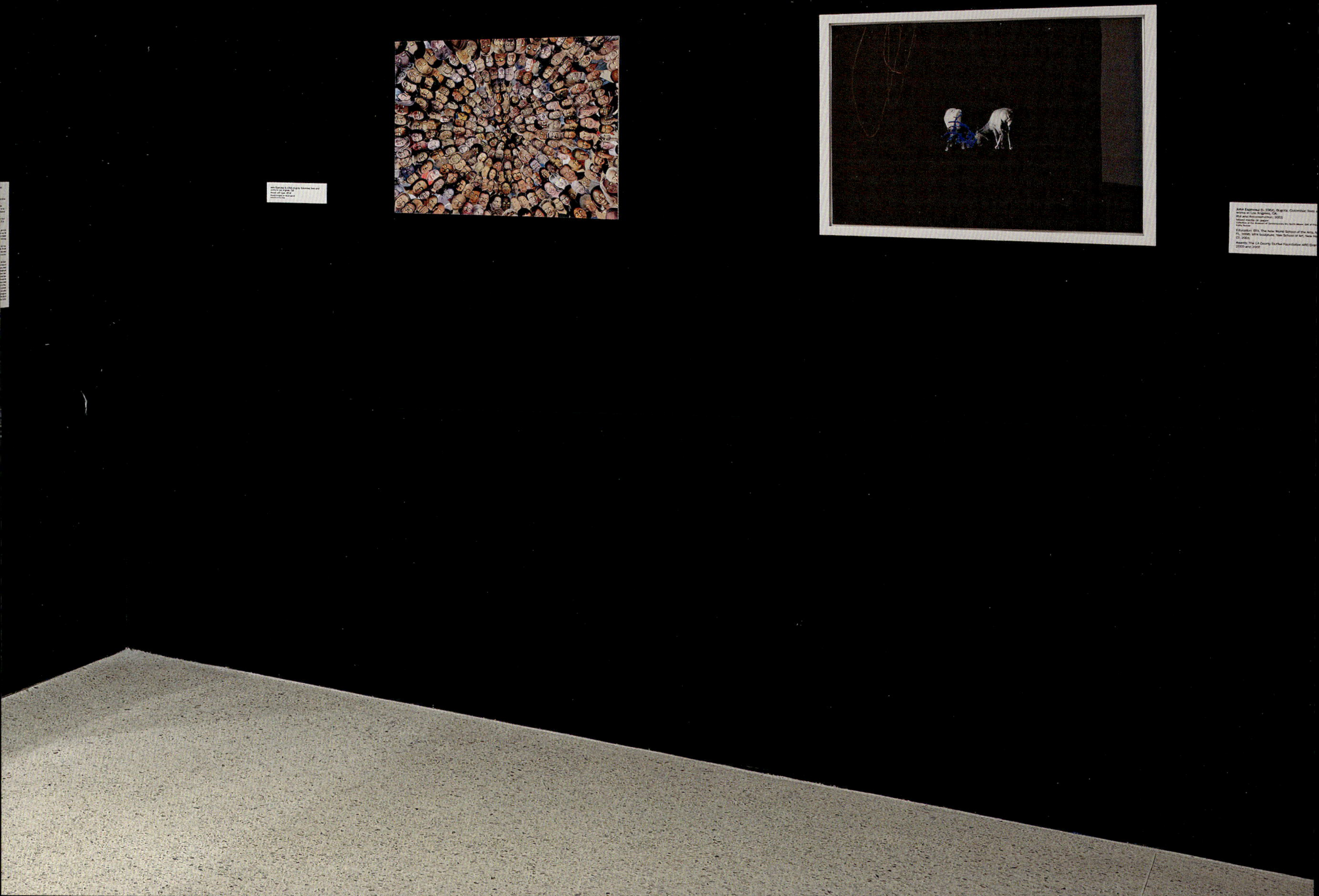

**Beyond the Art School Experience:
Artist-in-Residence Programs**

Although graduate school provided these artists
with a concentrated period to work, most forged
their distinct paths following graduation while
participating in artist-in-residence programs,
where they could continue to concentrate on
their work and establish relationships with fellow
resident artists and arts professionals for feedback
and support. The prestige of these residencies
also conferred art world validation that was
independent of the art market. Chief among
these was the Studio Museum in Harlem's Artist-
in-Residence program (AIR) with the guidance of
Executive Director Lowery Stokes Sims, Director
and Chief Curator Thelma Golden, and Curator
Christine Y. Kim; and Skowhegan School of
Painting & Sculpture, in Madison, Maine.[21]

Rush Arts Gallery and Resource Center, a
New York–based not-for-profit space (directed by
Derrick Adams, 1998 to 2009, and Nico Wheaton,
2007–2010) provided opportunities for many of
these artists to continue developing and exhibiting
their work. As cordova notes, many young art
students would hang out at Rush Arts during this
time and were encouraged by the example of the
Yale graduates to apply to the School of Art
"because they saw that we had a strong bond
among each other." Multiple not-for-profit art
spaces and museums in New York, including Exit
Art, Artists Space, White Columns, and El Museo
del Barrio, and in regions throughout the USA
played key roles in supporting artists of color
as incubators for their work.

Lineage

Curatorial and scholarly art practice has been
significantly reconsidered in the last few
decades, resulting in a reimagined lineage of
art history that diverged from the Western art
canon's emphasis on the perceived progress
from one period to the next. The artists included
here, however, attended the Yale School of Art
during a transitional time when, as Cloud notes,
it was understood "that to be in a lineage, not
only do you have to be inspired by somebody,
but you have to inspire people down the line.
You cannot be part of a lineage unless other
artists recognize your legitimacy." Moreover,
Cloud adds that in regards to women and race
in the art world, "there was this idea that you
could be famous but not significant. You
couldn't be assigned within this symbolic
language of history." Because of this concept
of lineage, Cloud postulated that the faculty
felt like his and the work of his peers operated
in a post-critical space. "We didn't even need
to be critiqued because of the way our work
was going to operate in the world."[22]

Alternatives to this concept of lineage
circulated among the graduate students at
the School of Art. For instance, Tsouhlarakis'
concept stemmed from a Navajo allegory
that recounted the necessity for each new
generation to add their own voice to traditional
songs, "If you don't do it, it's going to die. You
have to keep making songs and know that that's
within you."[23] While Japanese-born Otsubo is
constantly reconciling the clash between her

American experience and the Japanese
adherence to tradition, noting "They don't
blend into each other, they're very distinct
things."[24] The teachings of Yale art history
professors Thompson and Jones linking
contemporary culture to global art, migrations
of people, and the legacy of vernacular forms of
art, also played a valuable role in expanding
these artists' concept of lineage and legacy. As
cordova notes, "the legacy we spoke of in 2000
was not what it is today. Today, people are very
familiar with Barkley Hendricks. Back then, most
people didn't know him. When Kehinde Wiley
started doing his paintings, people didn't
reference Barkley, because they didn't know
Barkley even though he graduated from Yale."[25]
But cordova and other artists in his cohort were
aware of the artists of color who came before
and considered them part of their lineage even
though they were not considered mainstream
at the time. This new millennial generation of
artists of color collectively made it their purpose
to further illuminate the previous generation's
contribution.

Changing Room

The Changing Room is the aptly titled
installation by Rashawn Griffin in the *Lux et
Veritas* exhibition (ill. pp. 120–123). Changing
rooms are private spaces in public places where
people try things on in front of mirrors. The
subject of this work is not the colorful structure
Griffin created with its mirrored interior, rather
it is the person who is changed by experiencing

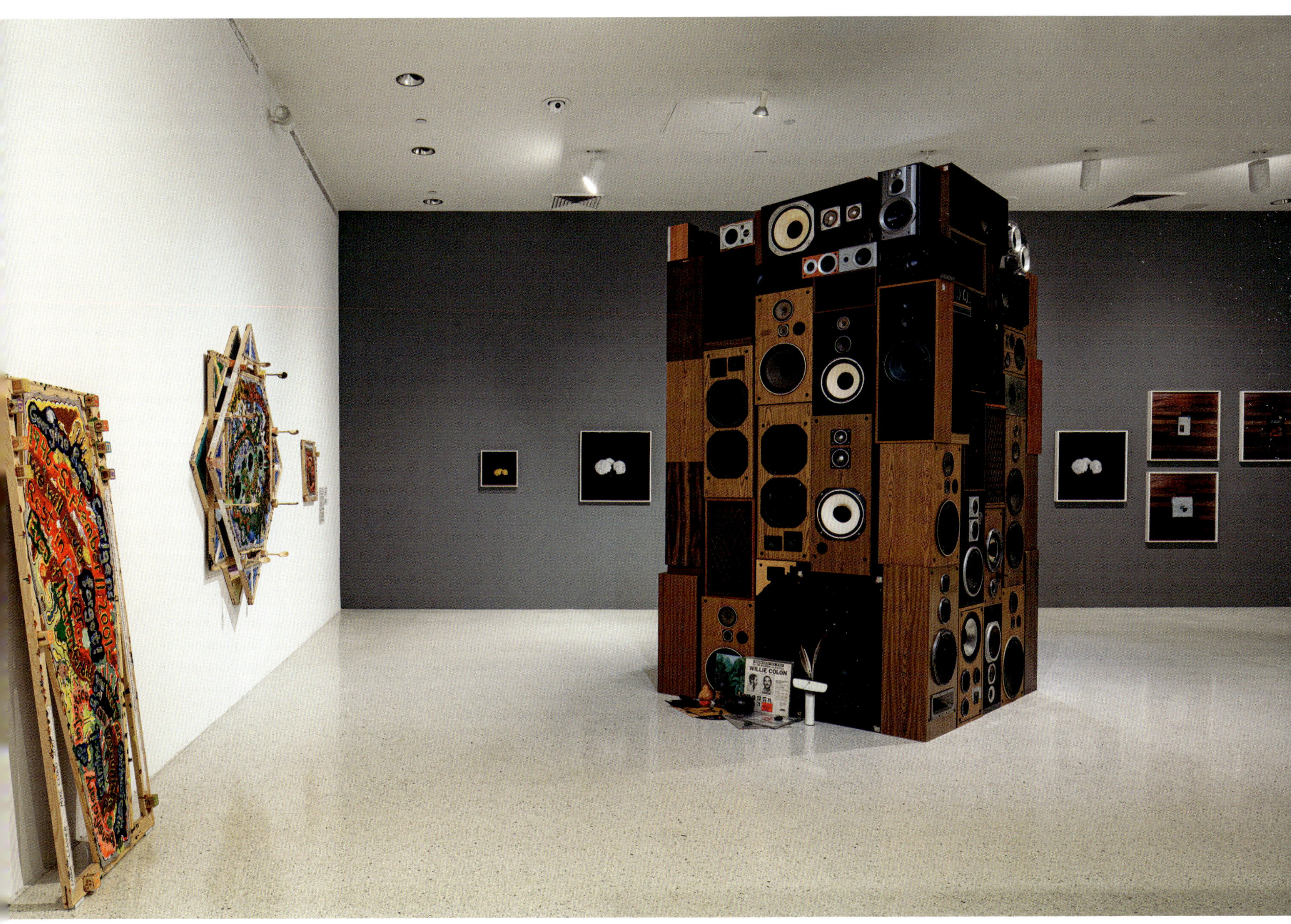

Left to right:

Mike Cloud

Hero Portrait Georgine Carrigan, 2020

Mixed Marriage Dr. Strasser and Balaji Pandian, 2020

Advice Getting Puppy, 2020

Leslie Hewitt

Color Study_01, 2016

Aura, 2016

william cordova

machu picchu after dark (pa' victoria santa cruz, macario sakay y damion thurston), 2003–2014

Leslie Hewitt

Screen, 2016

Object, 2016

Topologies (Veblen with camera shake), 2017

Topologies (folded memory object), 2017

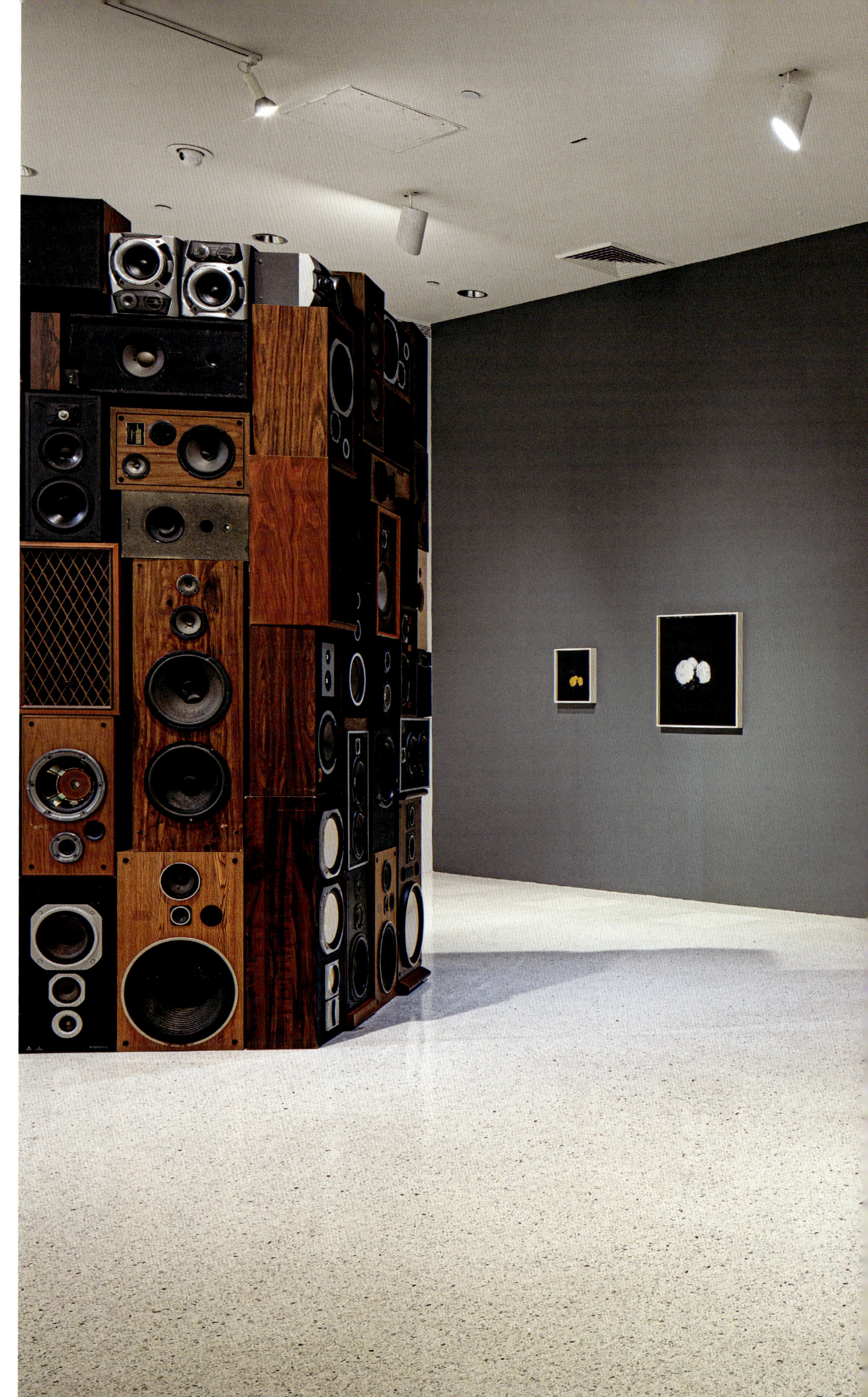

william cordova

*machu picchu after dark (pa' victoria
santa cruz, macario sakay y damion
thurston)*, 2003–2014

Walls from left to right:

Leslie Hewitt

Color Study_01, 2016

Aura, 2016

Screen, 2016

Object, 2016

Topologies (Veblen with camera shake),
2017

Topologies (folded memory object), 2017

Topologies (Fanon mildly out of focus),
2017

On floor:

Leslie Hewitt

Untitled, 2019

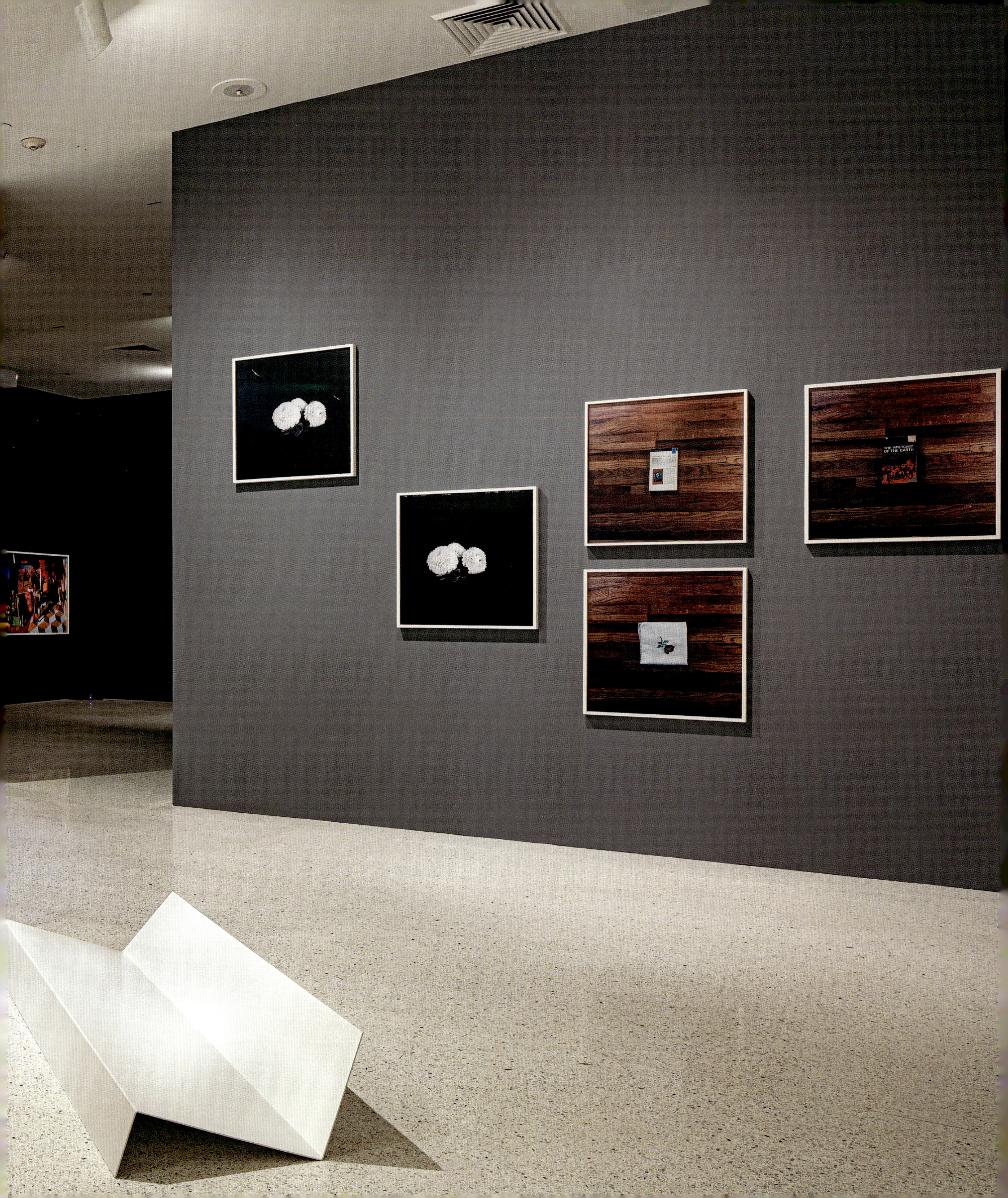

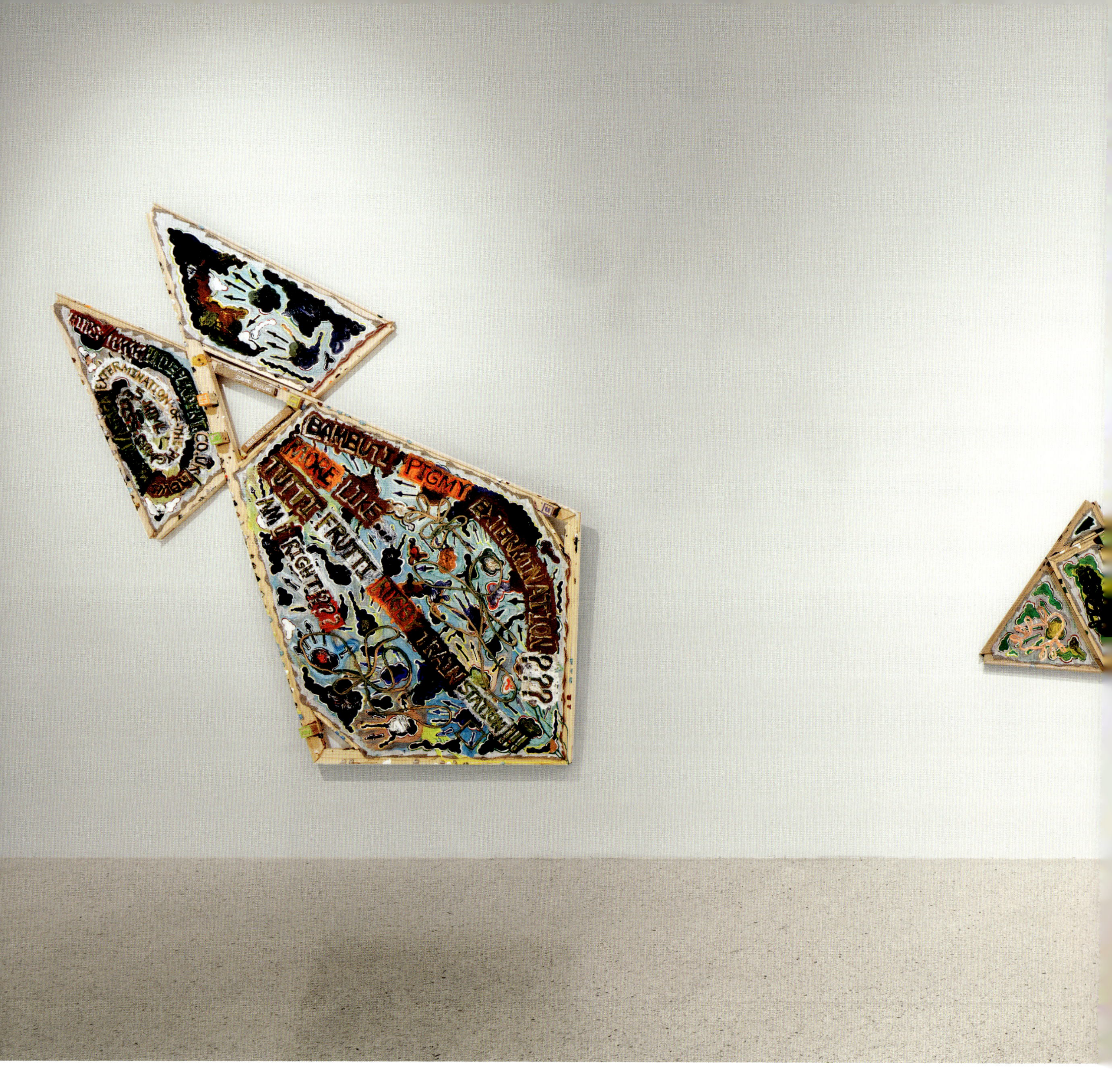

BAMBUTI PIGMY EXTERMINATION???
MORE LIKE...
TUTTI FRUTTI
AM I RIGHT???
RUGBY TRAIN STATION!!!

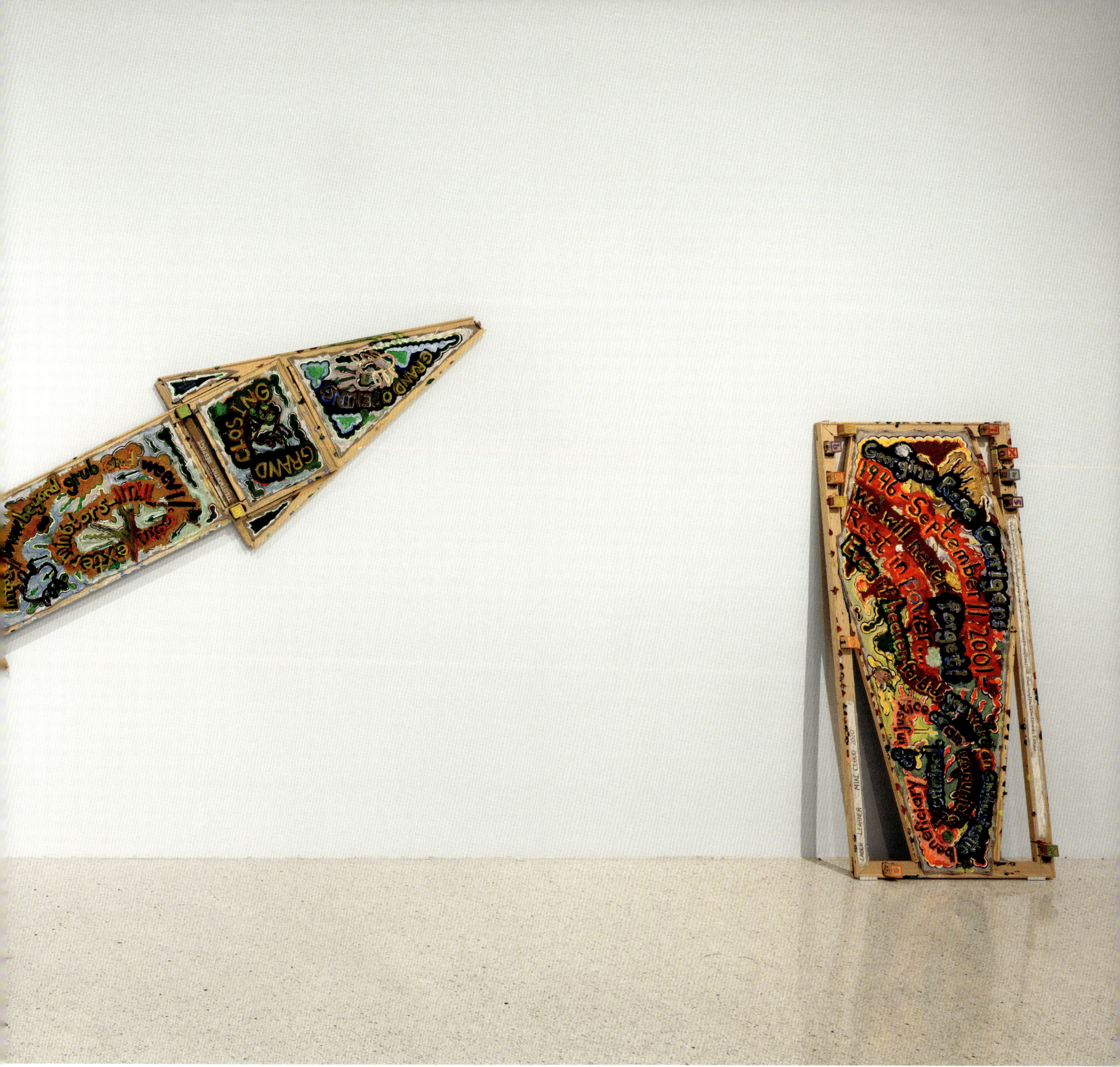

Left to right:

Mike Cloud

Bomb Bambuti Pigmy, 2020

*Business Idea Beyond Grub
and Weevil,* 2020

Hero Portrait Georgine Carrigan, 2020

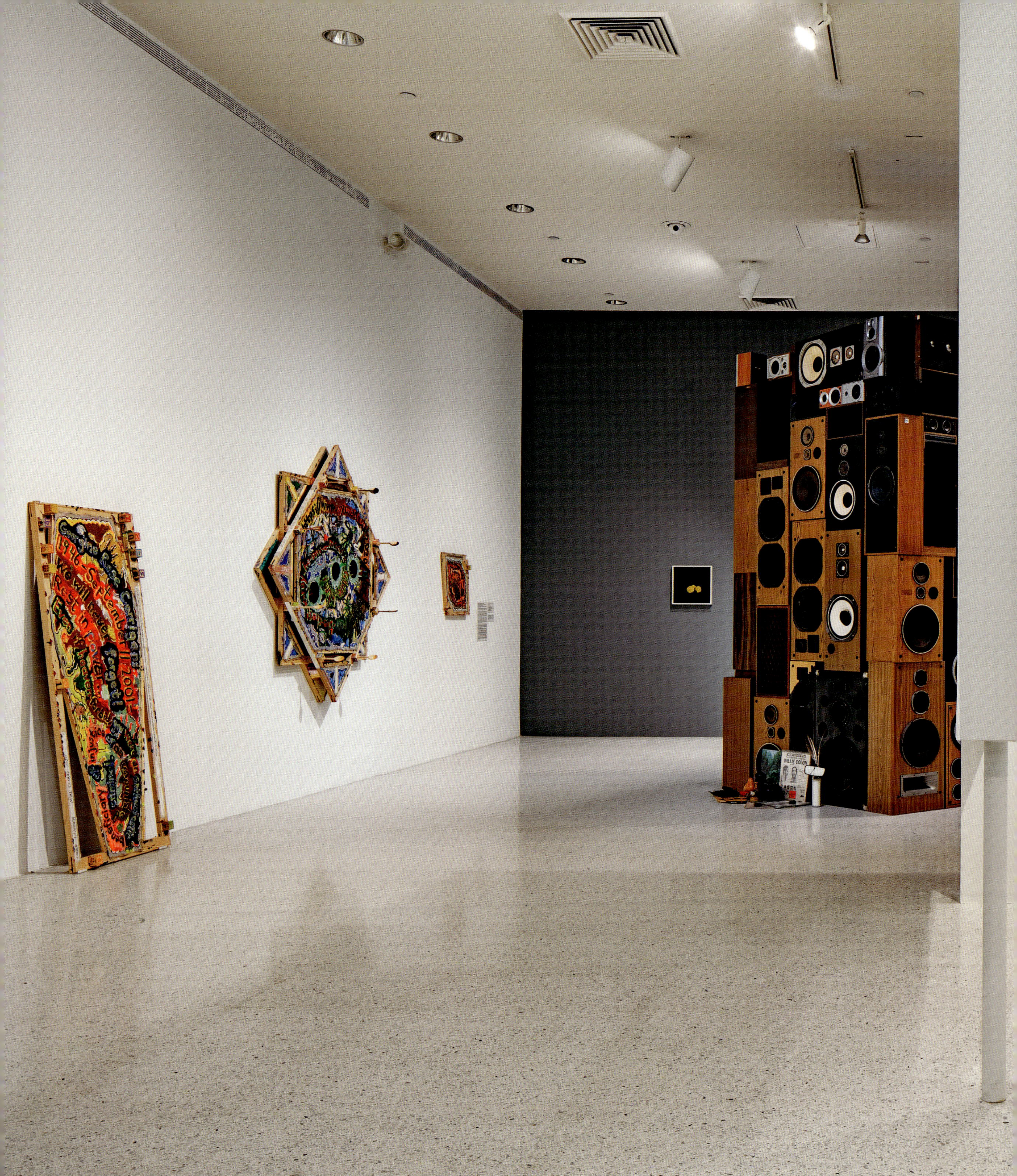

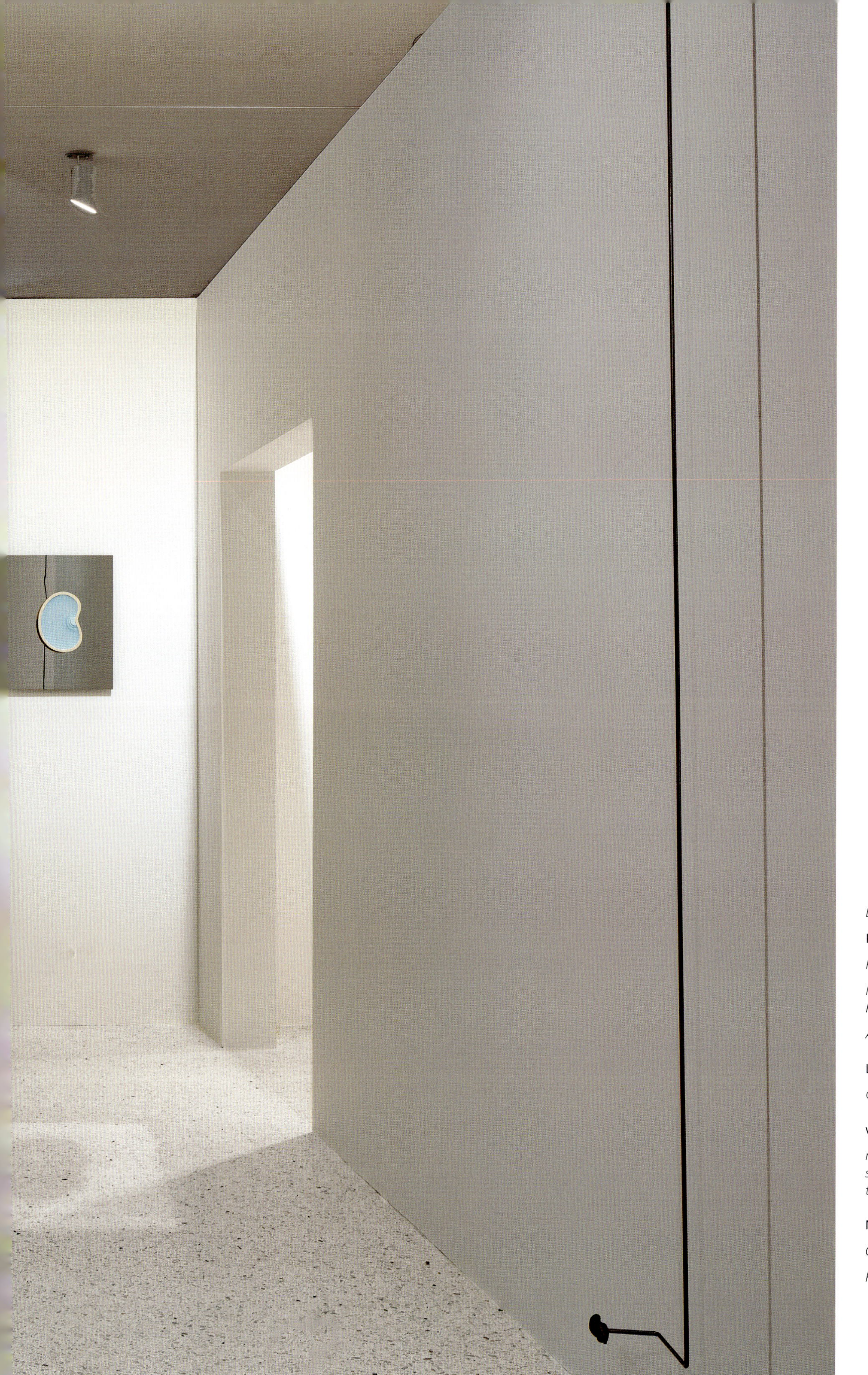

Mike Cloud

Hero Portrait Georgine Carrigan, 2020

Mixed Marriage Dr. Strasser and Balaji Pandian, 2020

Advice Getting Puppy, 2020

Leslie Hewitt

Color Study_01, 2016

william cordova

machu picchu after dark (pa' victoria santa cruz, macario sakay y damion thurston), 2003–2014

Mamiko Otsubo

On the Edge of the Western World, 2022

Keeping Your Ear to the Ground, 2016

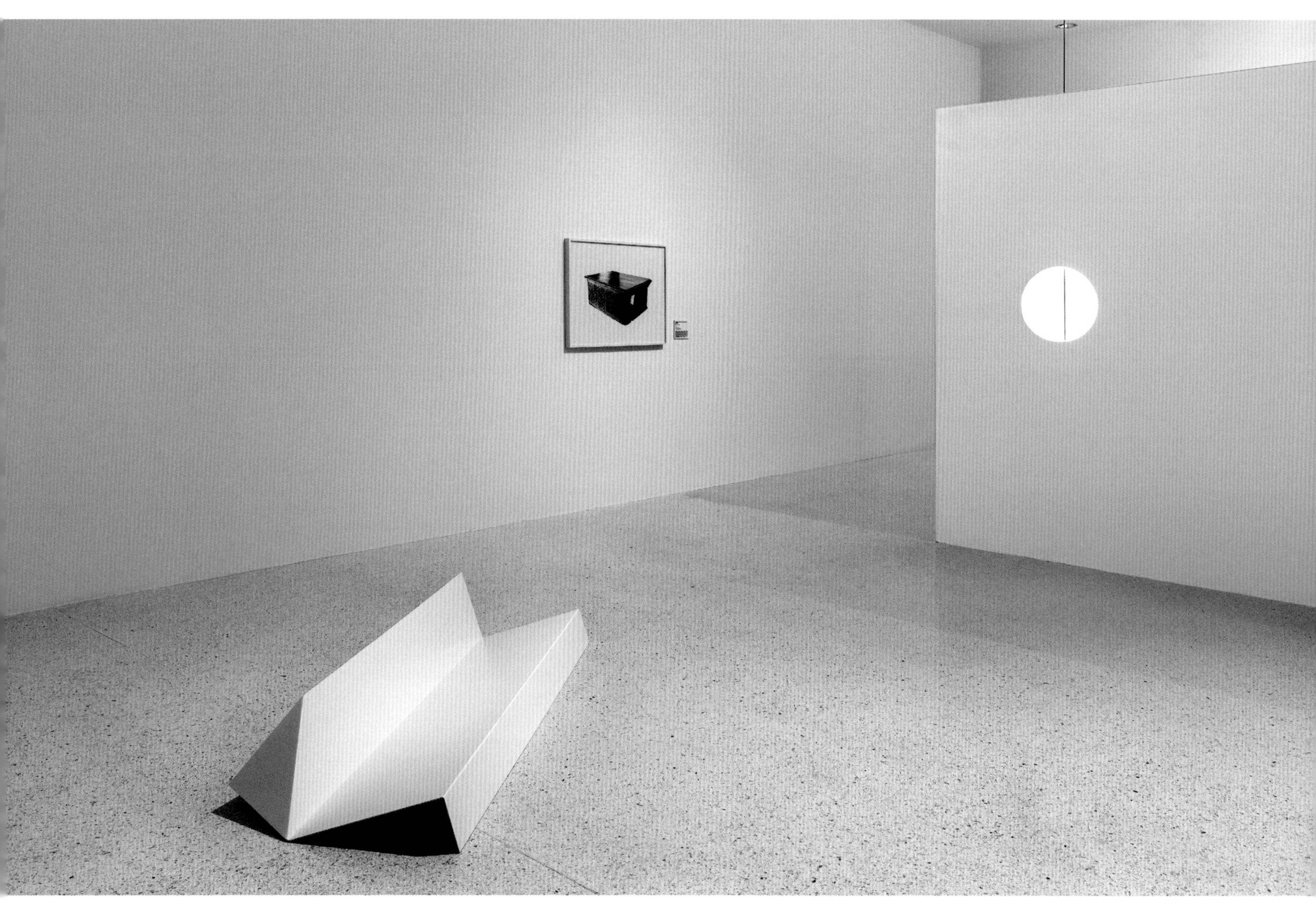

Leslie Hewitt

RAM, 2017

Mamiko Otsubo

Keeping Your Ear to the Ground, 2016

On floor:

Leslie Hewitt

Untitled, 2019

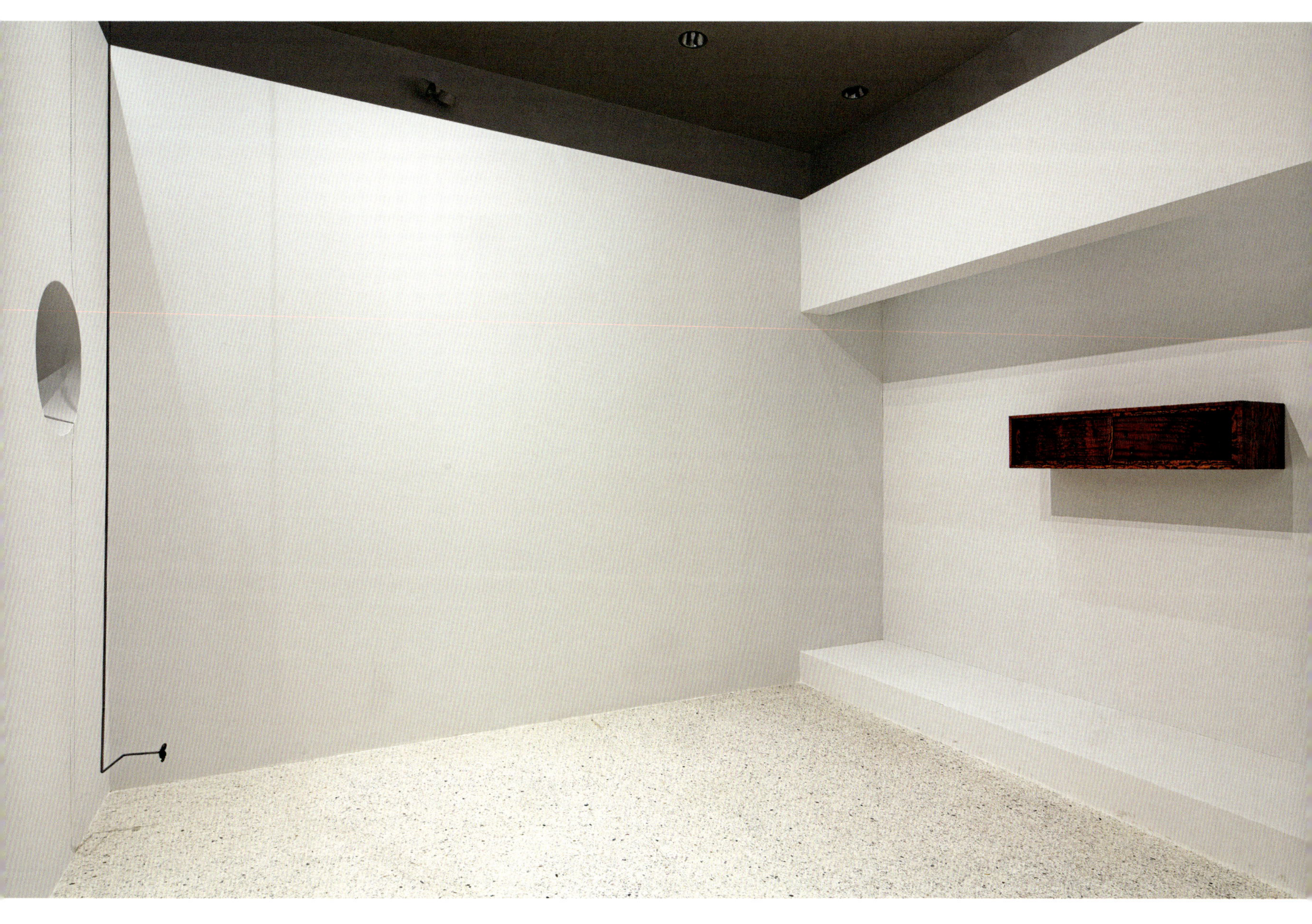

Mamiko Otsubo

Keeping Your Ear to the Ground, 2016

Time Traveler, 2016

the artwork. "Changing room" also describes these artists' praxis, which encompasses educating, curating, writing, and participating in public artworks and events in order to shape public discourse and art history. As cordova notes, this participation is derived from a desire *"to not only sit at the table but transform its meaning."*[26] These artists have adapted bell hooks' proposal to move critical thinking out of academia and into the streets where it can be shared with a larger audience.[27]

Through teaching and mentoring, participating in public art works and exhibitions, writing, curating, and crossing over into mass media forms of music, performance, fashion, and film, these artists have become agents of change. Like James Baldwin, they acknowledge, "the artists cannot and must not take anything for granted, but must drive to the heart of every answer and expose the question the answer hides."[28]

Artist as Teacher:

Many of these artists teach either as full-time faculty or as adjuncts and visiting artists, and some have returned to Yale to teach.[29] They are important mentors to young artists and have opened the door for more artists of color to attend Yale for their graduate studies. Expanding the opportunities for high school art students of color to have access to art school is a goal of several of these artists. Since April 2021, Jamerry Kim (MFA Graphic Design 2005) has directed Cooper Union's Saturday Program, which offers free classes in art and architecture to over 200 underserved New York City public high school students annually to develop competitive portfolios for college applications. Kim herself is an alumnus of this program.

A number of Yale graduates have also created new opportunities for art education and career development for artists. cordova, Hewitt, Kim, Quevedo, and Milan formed the BASE collective in 2005 as "a forum, a response in discourse and design. It is a platform for locality and grounded-ness and includes various artists and community activists."[30] The coffee cup collective (CCC), was formed more organically by cordova around 2006 as an ongoing mentoring platform supporting incoming and outgoing art students of color at Yale and other institutions of higher learning. He considers these activities as an integral part of his studio practice. Wiley established Black Rock Senegal in 2019 as a workplace to explore new ideas and to create work outside of the Western context through his personal relationship with Africa, while inviting international artists to live and work there. His inspiration for Black Rock Senegal was his early experience in The Studio Museum in Harlem's Artist-in-Residence program where "the lion's share of growth and introspection was a direct result of inter-personal communication and friendship with my fellow artists."[31] Titus Kaphar's social engagement has led to the establishment (with Jason Price) of the nonprofit arts organization NXTHVN, in the predominantly Black Dixwell neighborhood of New Haven, close to Yale's campus. Launched in 2019, NXTHVN is a national arts model that empowers high school students, emerging artists, and curators of color by providing intergenerational mentorship, professional development, and cross-sector collaboration to accelerate professional careers in the arts. Kaphar, like cordova, considers this social engagement part of his practice. The active role these artists have played as art educators further establishes an art historical lineage that has extended to the next generation of artists.

Public Works:

Works these artists have produced for the wider public have brought subjects of race, history, and social justice to the fore. The BASE collective organized dozens of projects such as the billboard project *From the Root* (2006) that was activated in various cities over the years. The billboards featured a fragmented list of their predecessors: "an evolving list of activists and martyrs." This list served as a "catalyst for remembering, for asking, for searching and for seeking out information about these individuals." Their stated intent for this project was to "activate public space to speak to people in tangible and historical ways."[32]

Individual projects similarly influenced the public discourse. When Wiley was selected to paint the official portrait of former President Barack Obama in 2018 for the National Portrait Gallery, it was not only a portrait of the first Black president of the United States, it was also the first official American presidential portrait painted by a Black artist. The portrait brought to the public sphere the subjects that have occupied Wiley throughout his career—the absence of Black people from the history of Western art and the representation of Black masculinity. Its marked departure from the staid, traditional presidential portraits sparked widespread commentary while its profusion of symbols launched internet searches during its nationwide museum tour.[33]

Two weeks after the murder of George Floyd, *Time* magazine turned to Kaphar to communicate the pain of the Black experience for its June 15, 2020 cover. He presented the magazine with a portrait of a Black mother clutching a baby to her chest. The infant, however, is cut out of the scene so that it appears as a silhouetted absence, the very essence of loss and sorrow. Kaphar stated in *Time*, "This Black mother understands the fire. Black mothers understand despair. I can change NOTHING in this world, but in paint, I can realize her… I want to be sure that she is seen. I want to be certain that her story is told. And so, this time America must hear her voice. This time America must believe her."[34] This was the second artwork by Kaphar published in *Time;* the first was for an article entitled "The Activists: Ferguson Protesters" for the Person of the Year shortlist (2014).[35] The painting on view in *Lux et Veritas* belongs to this series painted in response to the protests in Ferguson, Missouri, which began August 10, 2014, the day after the fatal shooting in that city of a Black man, Michael Brown, by a white police officer (ill. p. 131). Kaphar, who had immersed himself in criminal justice research, produced a composition of Black male protesters,

with mouths covered and hands raised in the air; their bodies mostly painted out with white paint.

These artists not only have brought widespread awareness to the complicated soft power of public art and monuments, but their actions have had significant results. In 2014, filmmaker Monique Walton (Yale BFA 2004), Quevedo, and cordova, in collaboration with choreographer Monique Moss and the Soul Rebels Band took an unsanctioned public stand against the Robert E. Lee statue in Lee Circle, New Orleans. The action was made into a documentary, *Silent Parade: or the Soul Rebels Vs. Robert E. Lee*, that was later used as a rallying cry to remove all Confederate statues throughout the South. The statue of Lee was finally removed in 2017.

The Statue of Liberty, one of the United States' most potent icons, was the subject of Abigail DeVille's monument *Light of Freedom* (displayed October 27, 2020, in Manhattan's Madison Square Park and The Mall in Washington, D.C., October 15, 2021 to June 2022, ill. p. 156). The Madison Square Park Conservancy commissioned DeVille in 2020 during a time marked by the pandemic, Black Lives Matter protests, and political turmoil. She sought to respond to history's relation to the present condition by shedding light on the original intent of the Statue of Liberty's French creator Frédéric Auguste Bartholdi to commemorate the emancipation of enslaved people, and how the USA's rejection of this subject in favor of dedicating it as a welcoming symbol of freedom to immigrants

arriving to its shores influences social and political beliefs to this day.

Other influential public works include the Greenwood Art Project, an initiative of the 1921 Tulsa Massacre Centennial Commission, for which cordova and fellow artist, Rick Lowe, served as organizers. The project was a catalyst for uniting the city of Tulsa and honoring the Black victims of the Tulsa Massacre. Other projects heralded institutional changes. The Metropolitan Museum of Art signaled its commitment "to expand and amplify dialogues with contemporary artists" and its recalibration towards the global by commissioning Mutu to inaugurate its initiative to fill the vacant niches on its facade for the first time in its building's 117-year history.[36] For this commission, Mutu chose to blend Western and African art traditions to depict strong Black female figures. This prominent commission generated massive media attention that brought wider recognition to Mutu's concerns.

Several of the artists who graduated from Yale between 2000 and 2010 achieved early national and international critical and commercial successes: Wiley and Thomas had solo exhibitions at the Brooklyn Museum within years of graduation, while Gispert was featured in the 2002 Whitney Biennial and had two solo exhibitions at the Whitney Museum of American Art (at its Altria branch) in 2003, and in 2004, with the premiere of his film *Stereomongrel*. (ill. p. 79) The Studio Museum in Harlem's *Frequency* exhibition of 35 emerging Black artists, in 2005, included Cloud, Griffin, Hewitt,

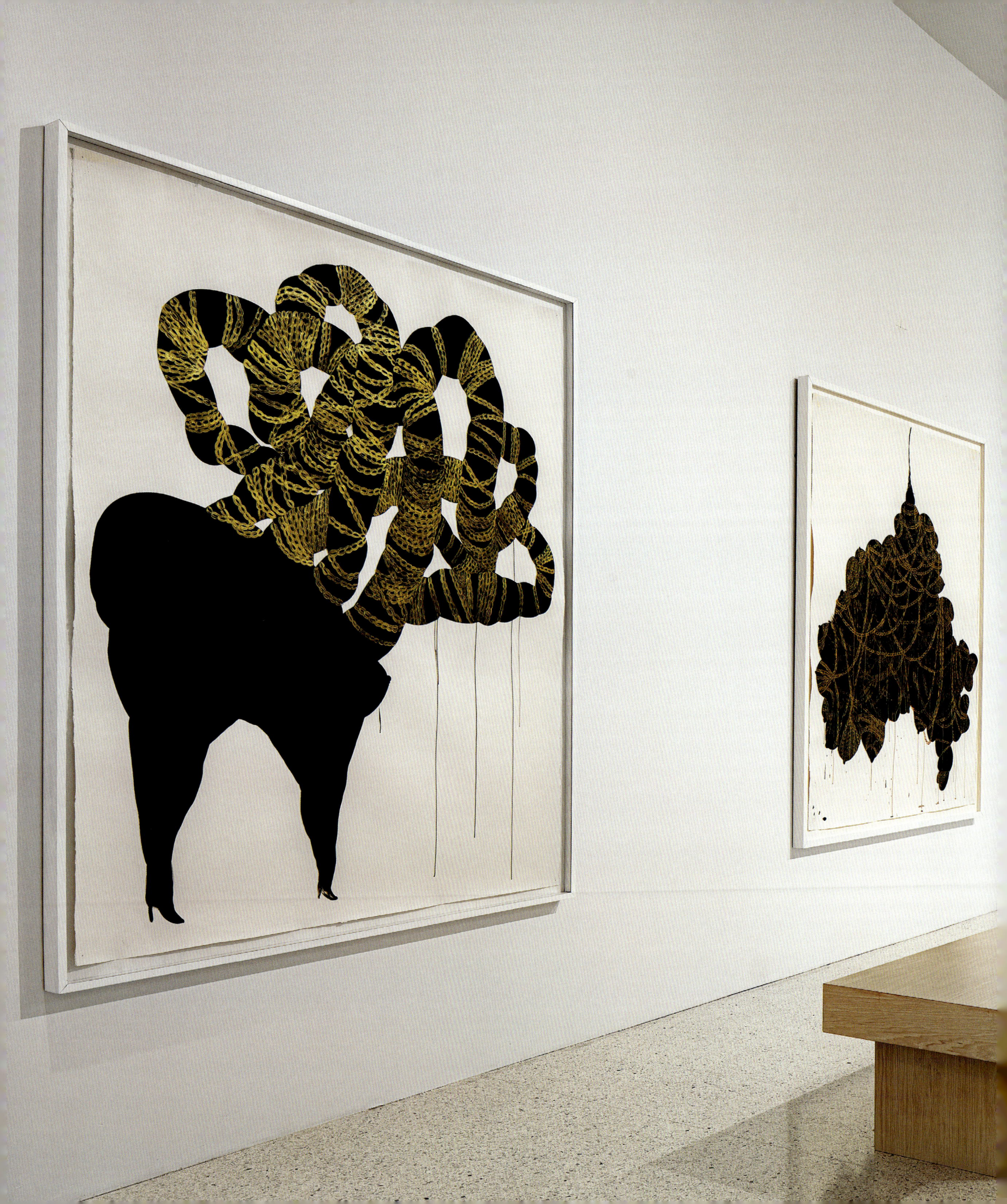

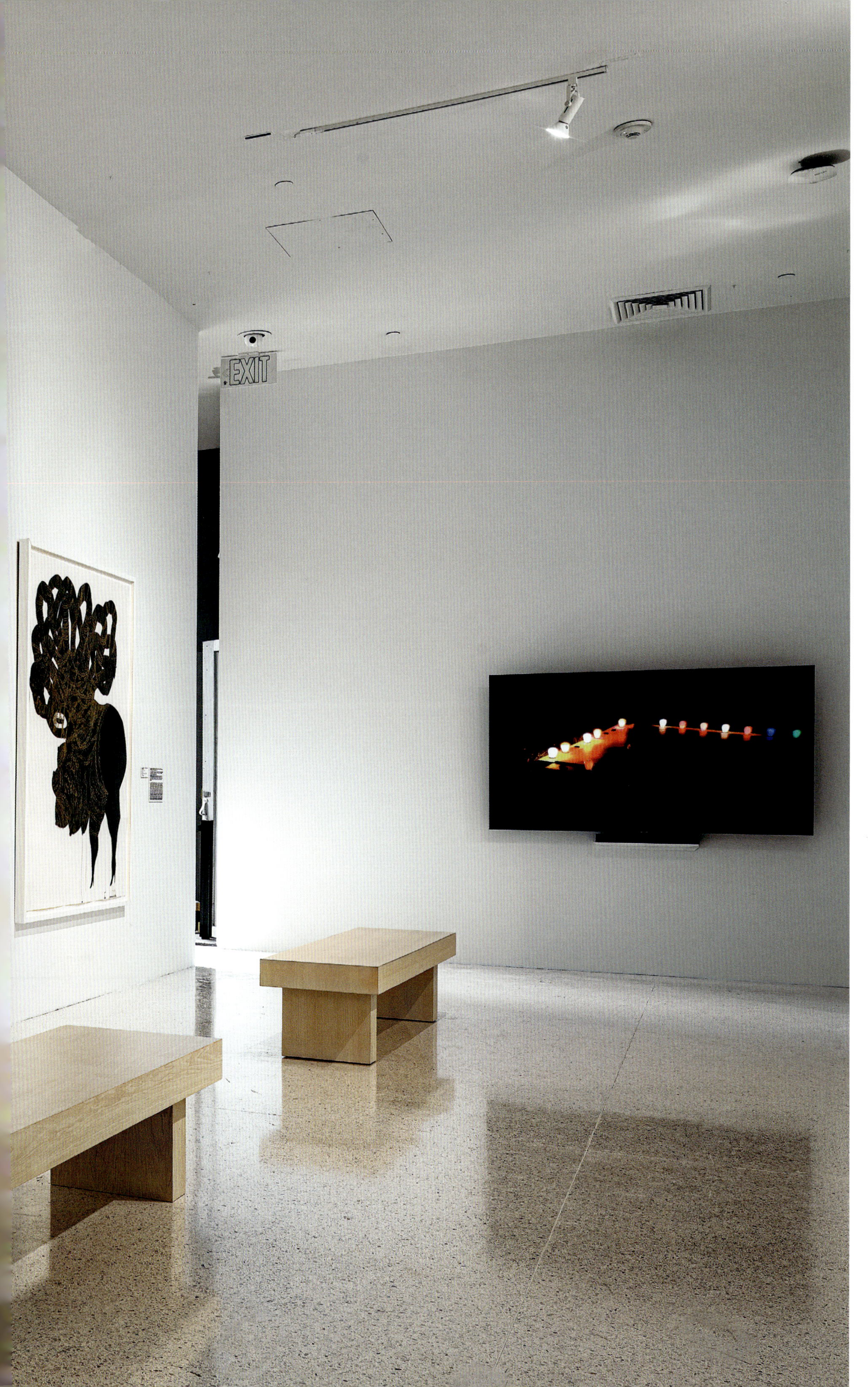

Left to right:

Shoshanna Weinberger

Muffin Top Banana Bottom, 2014

Ménage à Trois, 2013

Potbelly Porn Star and the Rise of Bacon, 2012–2013

Ronny Quevedo

Critical Mass, 2013

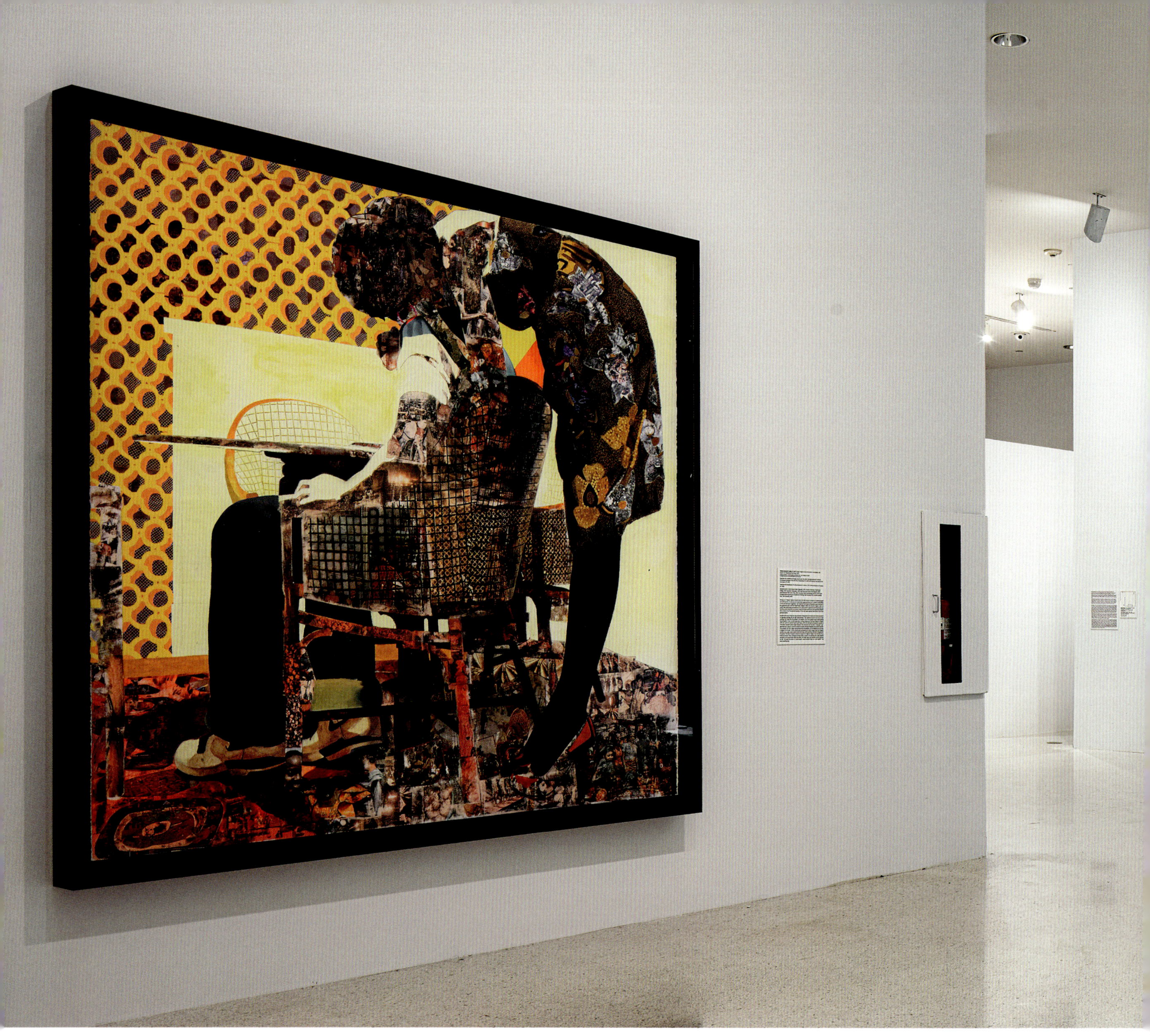

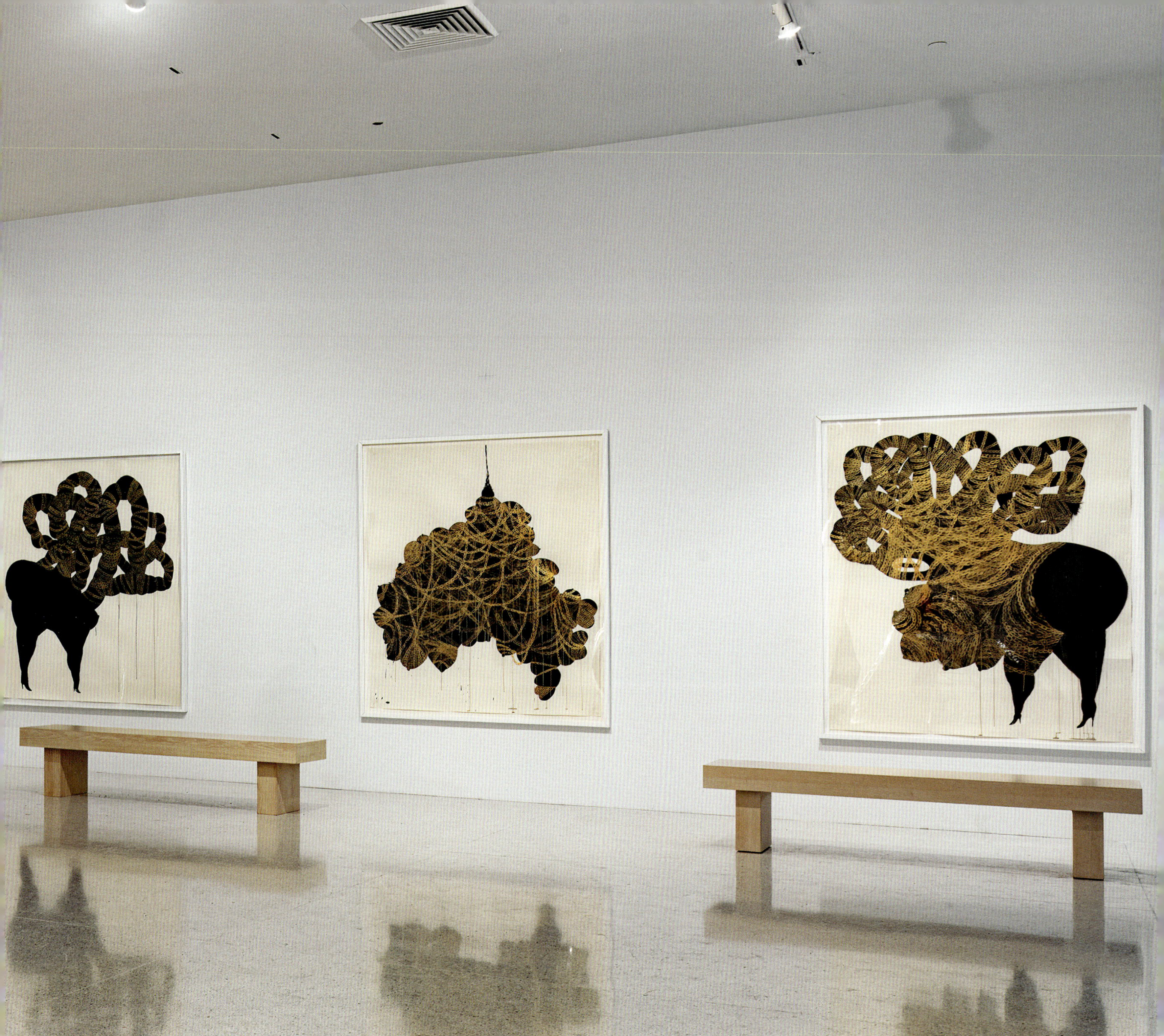

Left to right:

Njideka Akunyili Crosby

Nyado: The Thing Around Her Neck, 2011

Shoshanna Weinberger

Muffin Top Banana Bottom, 2014

Ménage à Trois, 2013

Potbelly Porn Star and the Rise of Bacon,
2012–2013

Milan, and Thomas, while the 2008 Whitney Biennial featured Griffin and a collaboration between cordova and Hewitt (begun in 2004 while they were students at Yale).

As author Khephra Burns proposes, "Perhaps… art is not necessarily an artifact but a process whereby the artist creates something out of a particular social or cultural context, and the community is then changed by it in some way."[37] Through their work and actions these artists drove home the need for greater recognition of and participation by artists of color in cultural institutions and academia and raised awareness to the lack of diversity in all aspects of society as well as to the history that contributed to this disparity. Much as this generation looked to their predecessors as examples, they have established new paths and opportunities for those who embarked on their art studies in the subsequent decade.

Miami Artists at the Yale School of Art

The artists who attended the Yale School of Art for their graduate studies between 2000 and 2010 hailed from throughout the USA and various parts of the world. However, the students who came from Miami in the first years of the decade were distinguished for having bonded as a collective prior to their enrollment at Yale. In 1999 Miami artists Espinosa and Gispert enrolled at the School. cordova, observing how much his friends' work had evolved during their time at Yale, followed suit in 2002, majoring in painting. These artists were part of the 1990s generation of Miami artists who benefited from the city's rapid rise as an international art center with ambitious contemporary art museum exhibitions, strong private collections, the presence of two international art fairs (Art Miami launched in January 1991, and Art Basel Miami Beach in December 2002), a proliferation of art galleries and alternative spaces, access to affordable studio space, and local and international media attention.

By 2000, the Miami art world had reached a turning point. Although it had long been home to artists and a supportive and active local art scene, the city experienced unprecedented growth of a community of emerging artists. This was the first generation of artists to benefit from the burgeoning Miami art world and the art enrichments available locally, including the Miami-Dade Public Schools art magnet programs, Miami-Dade Community College's regional campuses and The New World School of the Arts for high school and college students. Their mentors, including Robert Thiele, Carol K. Brown, Pat Johnson, Karen Rifas, Elmer Craig, Kabuya Pamela Bowens-Saffo, Roland Woods Jr, Robert Huff, Salvatore La Rosa, Gene Tinnie and other members of the Miami Black Arts Workshop, were Miami-based artists with substantial careers. Miami is also home to internationally recognized artists from Latin America and the Caribbean who play a major role in the local art community.

cordova, Espinosa, and Gispert were friends and constant collaborators in Miami along with artist Gean Moreno who also curated over a dozen exhibitions between 1998 and 1999. Gispert and cordova took foundation art classes at Miami-Dade Community College before enrolling in the School of the Art Institute of Chicago. Espinosa was accepted into Yale after completing his Bachelor of Fine Art degree at The New World School of the Arts. These artists drew influences from the Miami environment of their youth, which was a broad spectrum of landscapes that included urban vernacular architecture and historic spiritual sites, southern hip-hop, and cinema. Some of these sources were exquisitely natural and others, outlandishly artificial. Peruvian-born cordova, Colombian-born Espinosa, and first-generation Cuban American Gispert also brought the immigrant perspective to their work. All three were in the early stages of their art careers before they decided to attend Yale in order to have unencumbered time to develop their work and expand their perspectives. They were included in the group exhibition *Making Art in Miami: Travels in Hyperreality* (Museum of Contemporary Art North Miami, 2000), curated by Bonnie Clearwater (curator of *Lux et Veritas*). Like *Lux et Veritas*, *Making Art in Miami* focused on a transformative generation of artists who actively contributed to the art community and shared distinct ideas, influences, and experiences. Gispert and Espinosa had post-graduate solo exhibitions at the Museum of Contemporary Art North Miami, while cordova took the opportunity of his solo project there to create the first iteration of his installation *machu picchu after dark* in 2003, which he further developed as his MFA exhibition at Yale in 2004.[38] While Gispert now lives in New York and Espinosa in Los Angeles, cordova continues to live in Miami as well as New York and Lima, Peru, and is an essential catalyst who consistently mentors and collectively networks with alumni of the Yale School of Art, The Art Institute of Chicago, and Miami-Dade Community College, and other artists and writers. His dedication to breaking down barriers and building an expansive art community significantly contributed to the development of the exhibition *Lux et Veritas* and this publication.

Author's note
Artist statements are based on interviews and correspondence with the author unless otherwise noted.

[1] Coco Fusco, "One Step Up, Two Steps Back?," *The Brooklyn Rail*, May 2014. william cordova, in discussion with Fusco when she was writing this article, brought up the fact that the only critically successful artists to come out of Yale during the decade between 2000 and 2010 have been artists of color.

[2] Fred Wilson's project, *Mining the Museum,* was commissioned in 1994 by The Contemporary, Baltimore (a museum-without-walls) and the Maryland Historical Society. It was curated by Lisa G. Corrin. This project went beyond institutional critique by implicating the viewer's perspective and interpretation of these objects. Wilson's project expanded the boundaries between the objects on display, the museology of museum curators, and the role of visitors. For example, Wilson displayed rough slave manacles, identified in the text label as having been made in Baltimore circa 1793–1872, displayed alongside elaborately worked repoussé silver vessels, dating from a similar period (1830–1880) with origins in the same city. These two artifacts "trace back to the same geography, and the brutal conditions of enslavement that enabled the acquisition of wealth represented in the silver." Laura Raichivich, "What Happened When Fred Wilson Dug Beneath a Museum's Floorboards," *Hyperallergic*, August 16, 2019.

[3] "Black Male (1994–95)," interview with Thelma Golden as told to Thomas J. Lax, *Artforum*, Summer 2016.

[4] Leslie Hewitt in "Leslie Hewitt and Eva Respini in conversation," *Leslie Hewitt*, ed. Cay Sophie Rabinowitz (New York: Osmos Books, 2018), p.120.

[5] "What Else You Should Know About the Latin American Art Market, from Cecilia Fajardo-Hill," *Artsy*, November 12, 2013.

[6] Correspondence with the author.

[7] William Pope.L performed a piece in which he painted on drywall with peanut butter at the Yale School of Art in 2003.

[8] Kellie Jones, *Energy/Experimentation: Black Artists and Abstraction 1964–1980* (New York: The Studio Museum in Harlem, 2006).

[9] James Baldwin, "The Creative Process," *Creative America,* ed. Adolph Suehsdorf (New York: Ridge Press, 1962), p. 21.

[10] Toni Morrison, *Conversations,* ed. Carolyn C. Denard (Jackson, Mississippi: University Press of Mississippi, 2008), p. 27.

[11] As reported by william cordova, one required class in the Department of Painting and Printmaking was with faculty member Mel Bochner, who would address art world topics. Another mandatory class was printing with Rochelle Feinstein, who, cordova recalls, was open to experimentation. Studying with Bochner was one of Kehinde Wiley's strongest memories. He recalls, "one of the things that I took from Mel specifically was his ability to look at oneself and one's relationship to the history of art and the practice of art at arm length, the ability to sort of clinically and coldly remove oneself from the picture and see it simply as a set of rules, habits, systems, moving parts." (Smithsonian Archives of American Art, Oral History with Kehinde Wiley, September 29, 2010, conducted by Anne Louise Bayly Berman.) Unlike other MFA programs, Yale did not require students to write a thesis for graduation. For a list of faculty members, visiting artists and students, and courses see the Yale School of Art Annual Bulletins.

[12] Jori Finkel, "Tales From the Crit: For Art Students, May is the Cruelest Month," *New York Times*, April 30, 2006.

[13] Fusco, "One Step Forward, Two Steps Back?", cit.

[14] In 2000 the Department of Painting and Printmaking moved from Paul Rudolph's Brutalist designed Art and Architecture Building to its new modernist headquarters, Holcombe T. Green, Jr. Hall, designed by Deborah Berke. It would be another eight years before the Department of Sculpture moved out of its ramshackle building into its new home, designed by Kieran Timberlake. The physical disparity between the two buildings contributed to the students' perception that the school favored painting over the other disciplines.

[15] The focus of Yale's Film School was on theory as it lacked film and video editing equipment. As cordova reports, the one hands-on film/video faculty member was D. A. Pennebaker, who generously shared his practical, technical, and theoretical information.

[16] The school was still strict about students participating in exhibitions in 2006, when Kaphar was scrutinized for his participation in the student art show, *School Days*, held at the Jack Tilton Gallery in New York just before his final critique of his last year of graduate school. See Finkel, "Tales from the 'Crit'," cit.

[17] First known African American woman to receive an MFA from what was then the Yale School of Architecture and Design.

[18] Hewitt, Milan, Holland, and cordova attended most of Kellie Jones' classes, including History of Latin American Photography, Black Daguerreotype Photography, and Black British Art. Jones hired cordova as a contributing researcher for the 2005 Jean-Michel Basquiat exhibition at the Brooklyn Museum. Robert Farris Thompson first covered hip-hop as a topic in 2003 (cordova and Hewitt attended a session of the class.) As cordova reports, Thompson focused on parallels between sanding a djembe drum and scratching a vinyl record.

[19] The list of visiting artists in the *Yale Annual Bulletin is* incomplete. Among those who visited either through invitation from the faculty or students were: Coco Fusco and Pope.L in 2004. (Invited by Hewitt, Milan, and cordova). Hewitt, Milan, Holland, Griffin, and cordova invited curators Franklin Sirmans and David Hunt to visit Yale and see their

thesis show in 2004. Otsubo recalls additional Visiting Artists and Critics who came to lecture at the Sculpture department: Libby Lumpkin, Hirsch Perlman, Dan Peterman, Rita McBride, Miwon Kwon, Andrea Zittel, Tom Friedman, Roni Horn, Ralph Rugoff, Dave Hickey, Sue de Beer, Martin Kersels, and Robert Gober, among others.

[20] Curator, writer, and academic Marta Kuzma was the first woman Dean of the Yale School of Art (2016–2021).

[21] The Studio Museum in Harlem Artist-in-Residency attendees included: Njideka Akunyili Crosby (2012), william cordova (2005), Abigail DeVille (2014), Rashawn Griffin (2006), Leslie Hewitt (2008), Titus Kaphar (2007), Eric N. Mack (2015), Wardell Milan (2007), Wangechi Mutu (2004), Mickalene Thomas (2003), and Kehinde Wiley (2002). Skowhegan School of Painting and Sculpture attendees included: Abigail DeVille (2007), Leslie Hewitt (2001), Eric N. Mack (2014) Wardell Milan (2003), Ronny Quevedo (2013), Anna Tsouhlarakis (2002).

[22] See Mike Cloud, Appendix, p. 147.

[23] See Anna Tsouhlarakis, Appendix, p. 151.

[24] See Mamiko Otsubo, Appendix, p. 152.

[25] cordova, conversation with the author.

[26] Correspondence with the author, September 20, 2022.

[27] bell hooks, *Outlaw Culture: Resisting Representations* (Abingdon-on-Thames: Routledge, 2006).

[28] Baldwin, *The Creative Process*, cit., p. 134.

[29] During their graduate studies students had the opportunity to gain teaching experience as Teacher Assistants.

[30] Statement in the printed tabloid text for the *From the Root* project, copyrighted by william cordova and Leslie Hewitt, and designed by Ronny Quevedo/BASE 2007. This statement included the BASE collective manifesto: "BASE is a forum, a response in discourse and design. It is a platform for locality and grounded-ness and includes various artists and community activists."

[31] Scott Indrisek, "Inside Kehinde Wiley's Vibrant New Artist Residency in Senegal," *Artsy.net*, April 22, 2019.

[32] Statement in the printed tabloid for *From the Root* project, cit.

[33] Katie White, "Kehinde Wiley's Presidential Portrait of Barack Obama Is Arriving in New York. Here Are 3 Things You Might Not Know About It," artnet.com, August 16, 2021.

[34] *Time*, June 4, 2020.

[35] *Time*, December 10, 2014.

[36] Nancy Princenthal, "Wangechi Mutu: A New Face for the Met," *New York Times*, September 5, 2019.

[37] "Conversation between Thelma Golden and Khephra Burns, *Harlem Fine Arts Show Magazine*, 2013, p. 25.

[38] The exhibitions of these artists' works that were organized by the Museum of Contemporary Art North Miami and curated by Bonnie Clearwater are: *william cordova: No More Lonely Nights* (November 29, 2003 – February 8, 2004); *John Espinosa: Standing Still as We Move Across the Land* (November 25, 2004 – January 30, 2005); *Luis Gispert* (MOCA at Goldman Warehouse, April 11 – June 27, 2009).

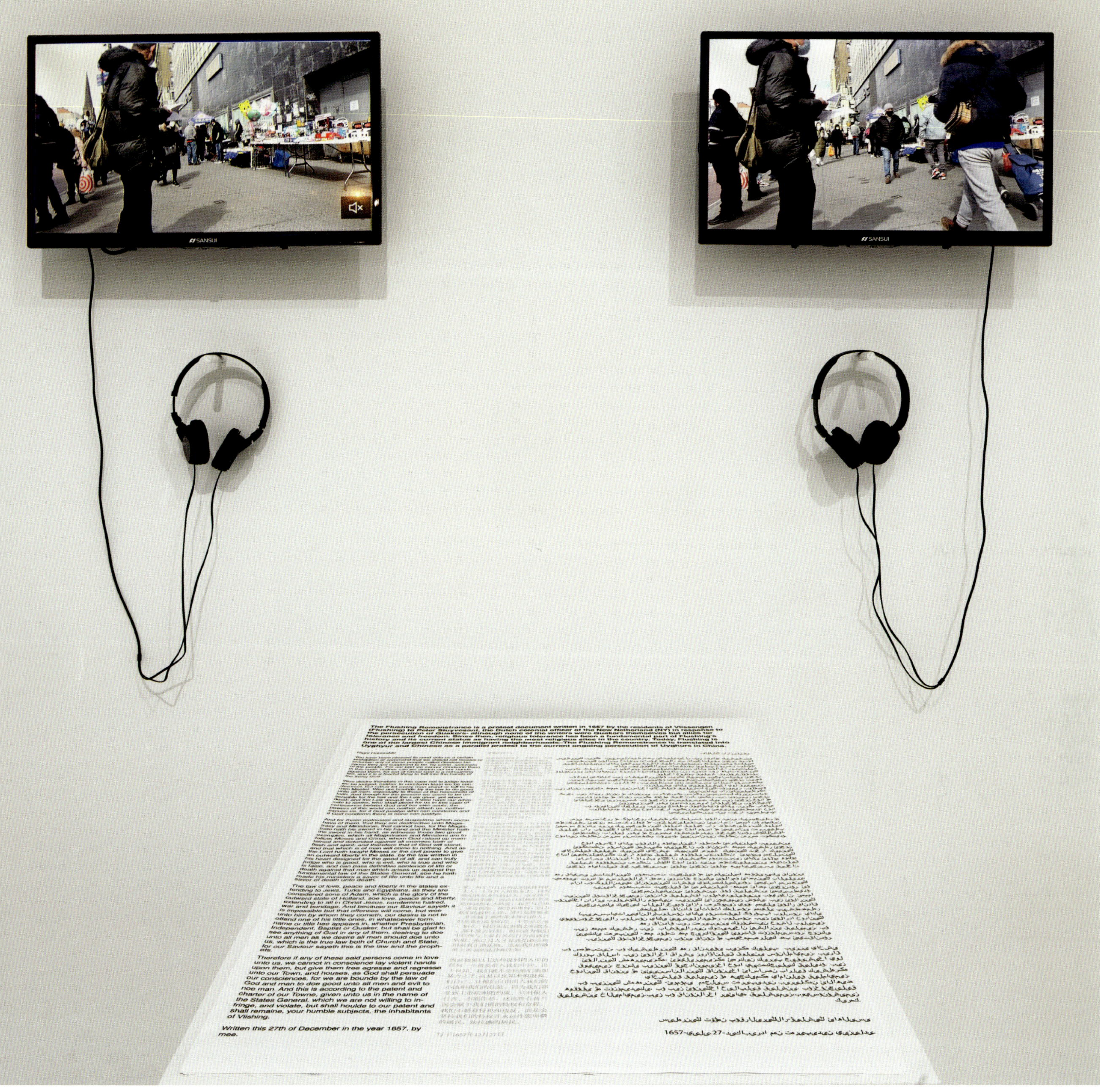

The Flushing Remonstrance is a protest document written in 1657 by the residents of Vlissengen (Flushing) to Peter Stuyvesant, the Dutch colonial officer of the New Netherland (NY) in response to the persecution of Quakers; although none of the writers were Quaker themselves but pitch for tolerance and freedom. Since then, religious [...] history and its current status as having the most religious ethos in the country. Today, Flushing is one of the largest Chinese immigrant neighborhoods. This Flushing Remonstrance was translated into Uyghur and Chinese as a parallel protest to the current persecution of Uyghurs in China.

Right Honorable,

You have been pleased to send unto us a certain prohibition or command that we should not receive or entertain any of those people called Quakers, because they are supposed to bee, by some, seducers of the people. For our part we cannot condemn them in this case, neither can we stretch out our hands against them, for out of Christ God is a consuming fire, and it is a fearful thing to fall into the hands of the living God.

Wee desire therefore in this case not to judge least we be judged, neither to condemn least we be condemned, but rather let every man stand or fall to his own Master. Wee are bounde by the law to do good unto all men, especially to those of the household of faith. And though for the present we seeme to be unserviceable for the law and the Law giver, yet when death and the Law assault us, if wee have our advocate to seeke, who shall plead for us in this case of conscience betwixt God and our own souls; the powers of this world can neither attach us, neither excuse us, for if God justifye who can condemn and if God condemn there is none can justifye.

And for those jealousies and suspicions which some have of them, that they are destructive unto Magistracy and Ministerye, that cannot bee, for the Magistrate hath his sword in his hand and the Minister hath the sword in his hand, as witnesse those two great examples, which all Magistrates and Ministers are to follow, Moses and Christ, whom God raised up maintained and defended against all enemies both of flesh and spirit, and therefore that of God will stand, and that which is of man will come to nothing. And as the Lord hath taught Moses or the civil power to give an outward liberty in the state, by the law written in his heart designed for the good of all, and can truly judge who is good, who is evil, who is true and who is false, and can pass definitive sentence of life or death against that man which arises up against the fundamental law of the States General: soe he hath made his Ministers a savor of life unto life and a savor of death unto death.

The law of love, peace and liberty in the states extending to Jews, Turks and Egyptians, as they are considered sons of Adam, which is the glory of the outward state of Holland, soe love, peace and liberty, extending to all in Christ Jesus, condemns hatred, war and bondage. And because our Saviour sayeth it is impossible but that offences will come, but woe unto him by whom they cometh, our desire is not to offend one of his little ones, in whatsoever form, name or title hee appears in, whether Presbyterian, Independent, Baptist or Quaker, but shall be glad to see anything of God in any of them, desiring to doe unto all men as we desire all men should doe unto us, which is the true law both of Church and State; for our Saviour sayeth this is the law and the prophets.

Therefore if any of these said persons come in love unto us, we cannot in conscience lay violent hands upon them, but give them free egresse and regresse unto our Town, and houses, as God shall persuade our consciences, for we are bounde by the law of God and man to doe good unto all men and evil to noe man. And this is according to the patent and charter of our Towne, given unto us in the name of the States General, which we are not willing to infringe, and violate, but shall houlde to our patent and shall remaine, your humble subjects, the inhabitants of Vlishing.

Written this 27th of December in the year 1657, by mee.

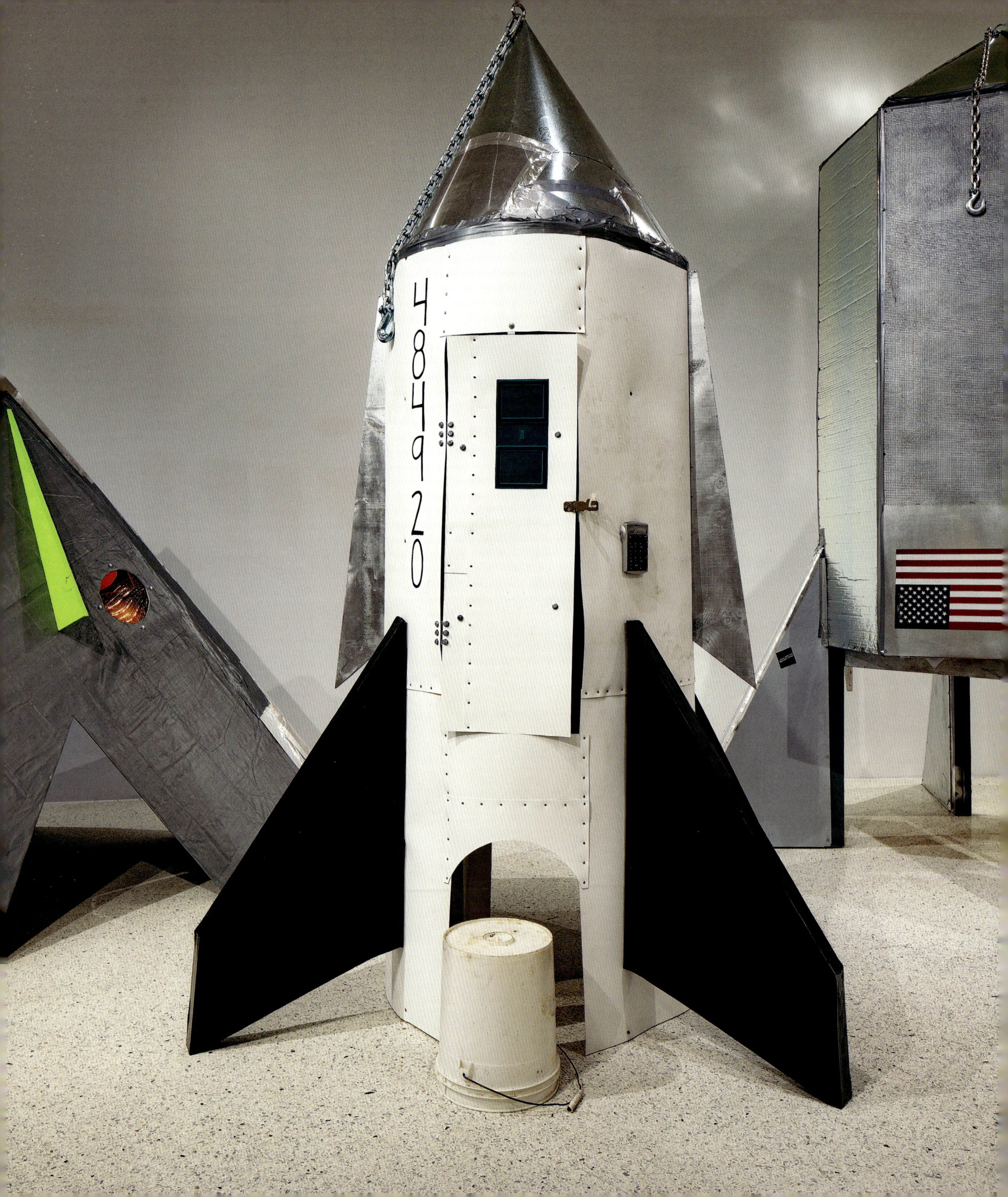

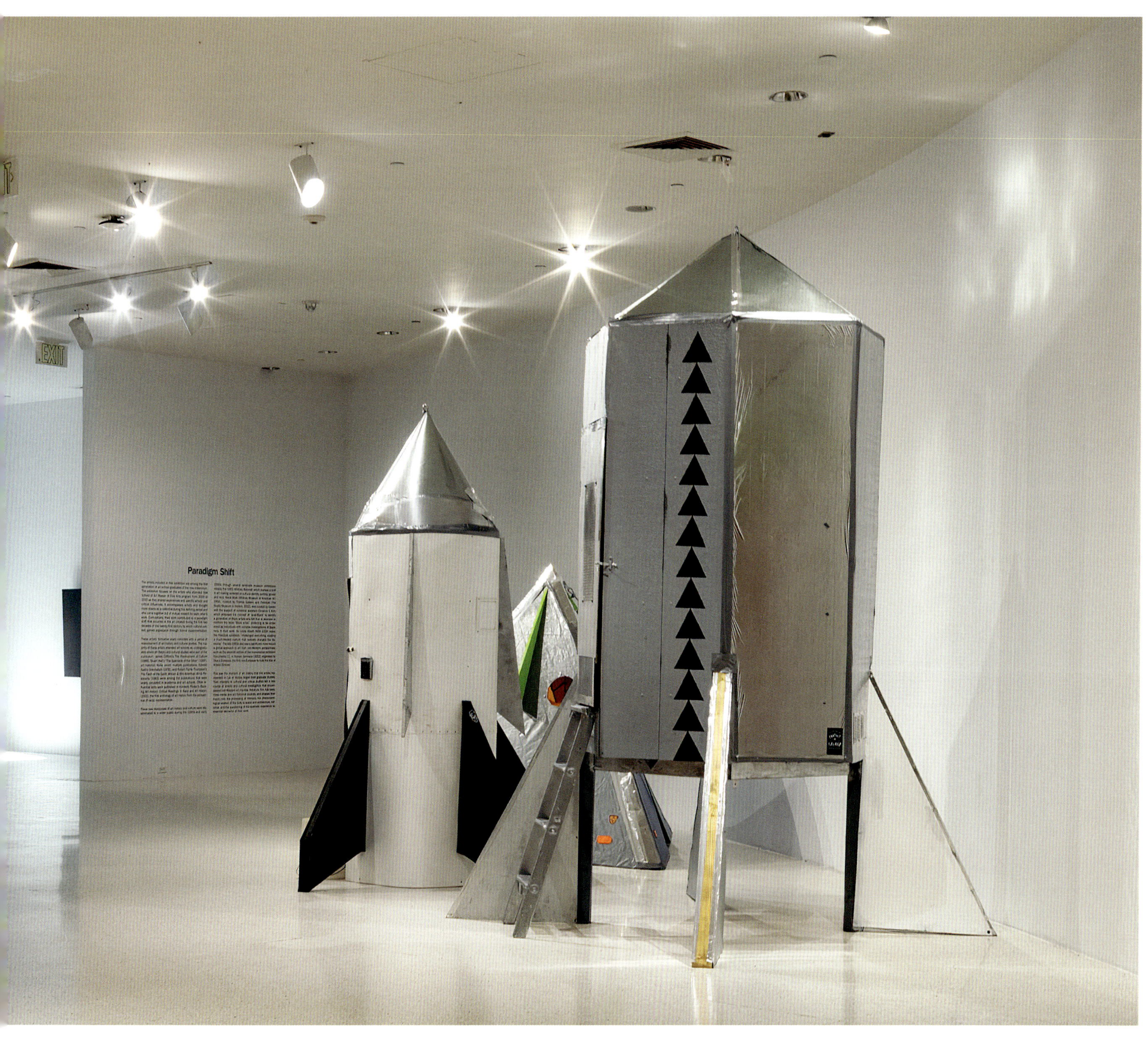

Anna Tsouhlarakis

Rocketship 3/4, 2002–2022

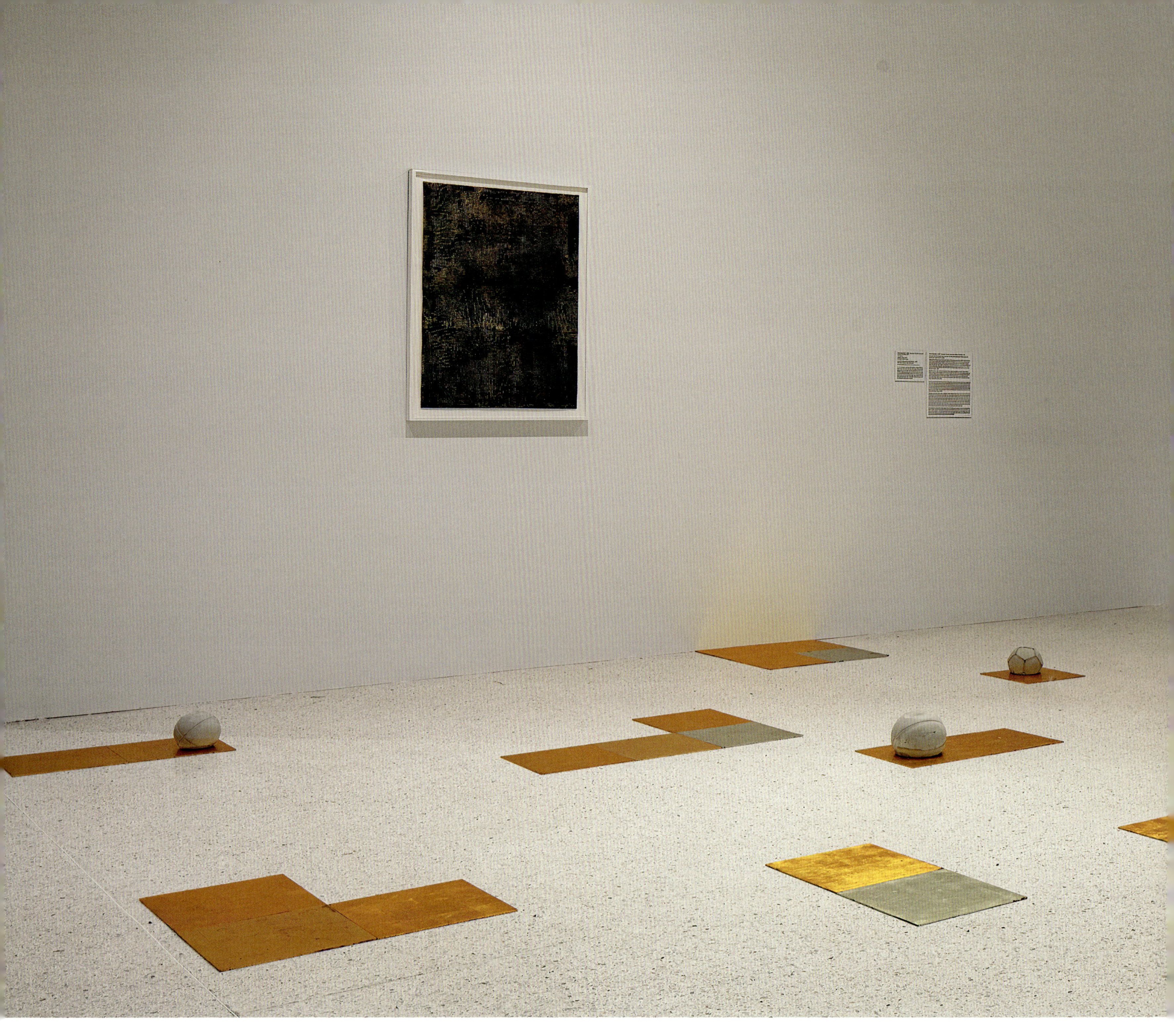

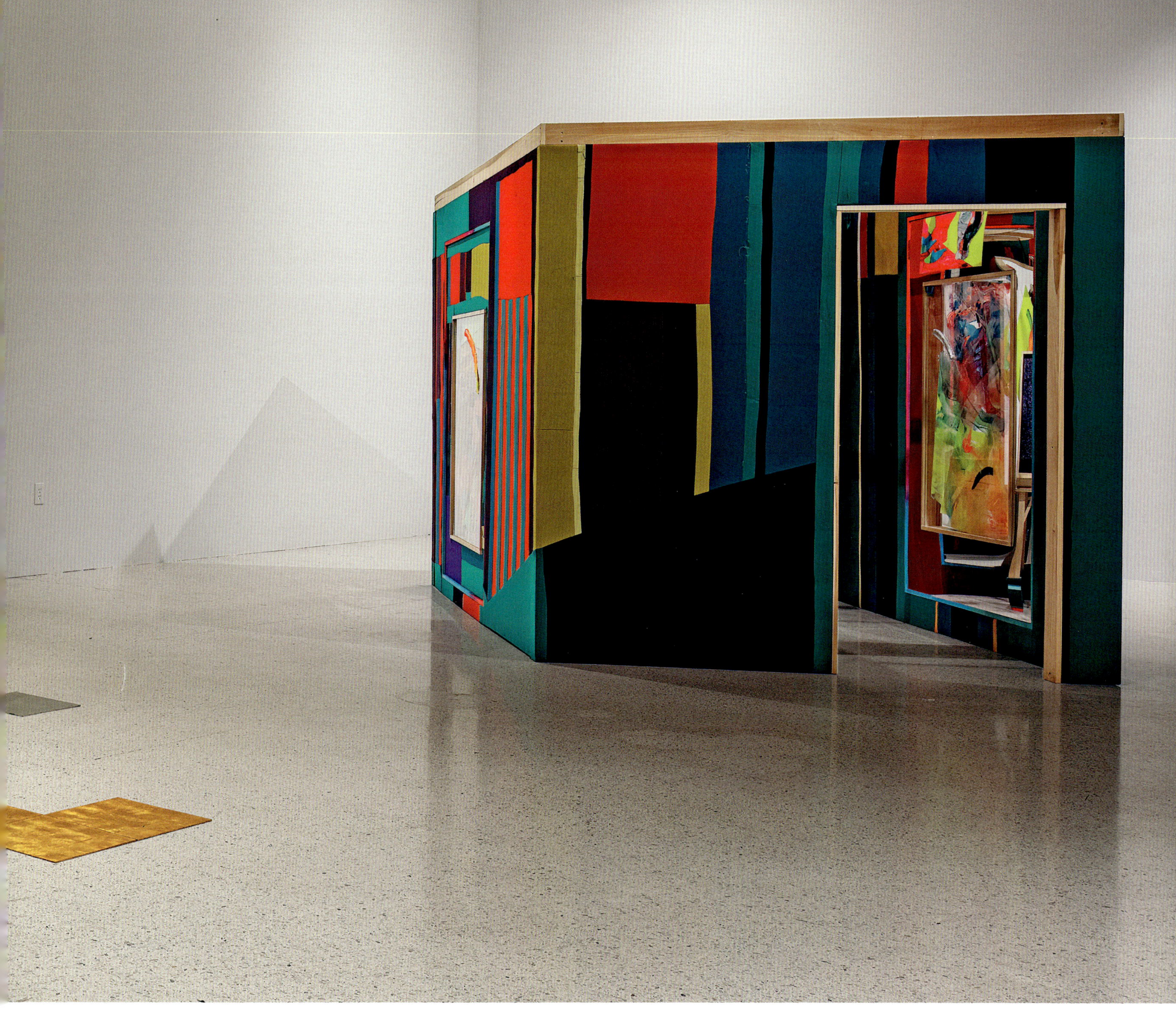

Left to right:
On wall:
Ronny Quevedo
migration lines, 2019

On floor:
errantry (the benefit of being offsides),
2019

Rashawn Griffin
The Changing Room, 2022

Following pages:
Left to right:
Anna Tsouhlarakis
Rocketship 3/4, 2002–2022

Eric N. Mack
Tessuti Raponi (Ciao Milano), 2018

On floor:
Ronny Quevedo
errantry (the benefit of being offsides),
2019

Lux et Veritas

The exhibition *Lux et Veritas* explores a transformative period in contemporary art by focusing on a generation of artists of color who attended Yale School of Art for graduate studies between 2000 and 2010. The exhibition's title alludes to Yale University's motto, *Lux et Veritas*, which translates from Latin to "Light and Truth." In the context of this exhibition, the title references how these artists thought with critical complexity about their work and their movement through institutional structures.

As with similar programs, Yale School of Art, in New Haven, Connecticut, had not been historically diverse, which spurred these art students to form affiliations across the departments of painting, graphic design, sculpture, photography and art history. They filled gaps in the school's curriculum and counteracted the lack of diversity among the faculty by inviting artists, curators and writers of color as advisors and guest speakers, developing an interdisciplinary forum, publishing art journals, organizing exhibitions and documenting their experiences in video and photography. The relationships they formed at school evolved into communities that networked and provided essential support and feedback for one another, often passing on these efforts beyond graduate study. Their reevaluation of the Western art canon, and commitment to the method and practice of teaching has contributed to a greater recognition of artists of color, challenged stereotypes and

enriched the overall shared spaces of learning and thinking about art and the art praxis.

Lux et Veritas provides a public forum in which to address the directions these artists took based on the explorations that began in graduate school and were instilled thereafter in their practice. The exhibition is curated by Bonnie Clearwater, Director and Chief Curator, NSU Art Museum, Mike Cloud (Yale, MFA 2003), william cordova (Yale, MFA 2004), Leslie Hewitt (Yale MFA 2004) and Irene V. Small, Associate Professor, Contemporary Art & Criticism, Princeton University (Yale, Ph.D. 2008) are advisors on the exhibition. Oral histories with the artists who attended the School of Art provided significant insight into their experiences, relationships, and work.

We extend our deep appreciation to the essential contribution of the advisory committee, the participating artists and lenders to the exhibition, the museum staff and Board of Governors, and the sponsors who have made this exhibition possible.

Presenting sponsor: S. Donald Sussman

Additional support provided by Funding Arts Broward, Inc.

Major support for NSU Art Museum Fort Lauderdale is provided by the David and Francie Horvitz Family Foundation, the City of Fort Lauderdale, Community Foundation of Broward, the Broward County Cultural Division, the Cultural Council, and the Broward County Board of County Commissioners, and the State of Florida, Department of State, Division of Arts and Culture and the Florida Council on Arts and Culture.

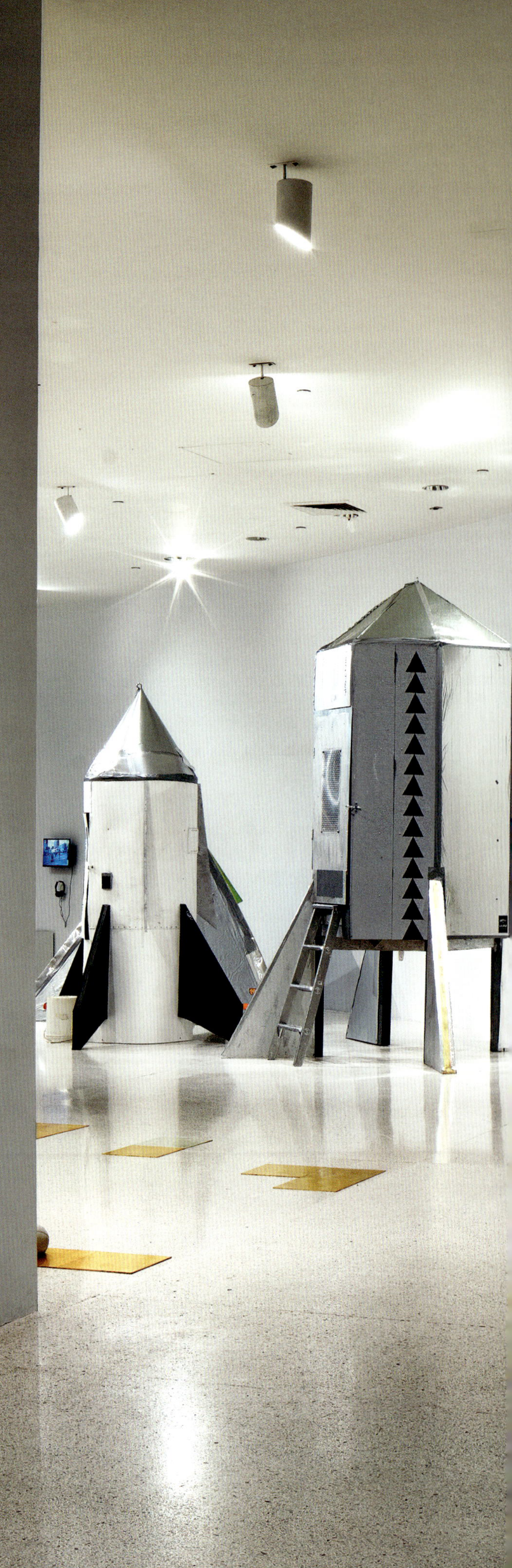

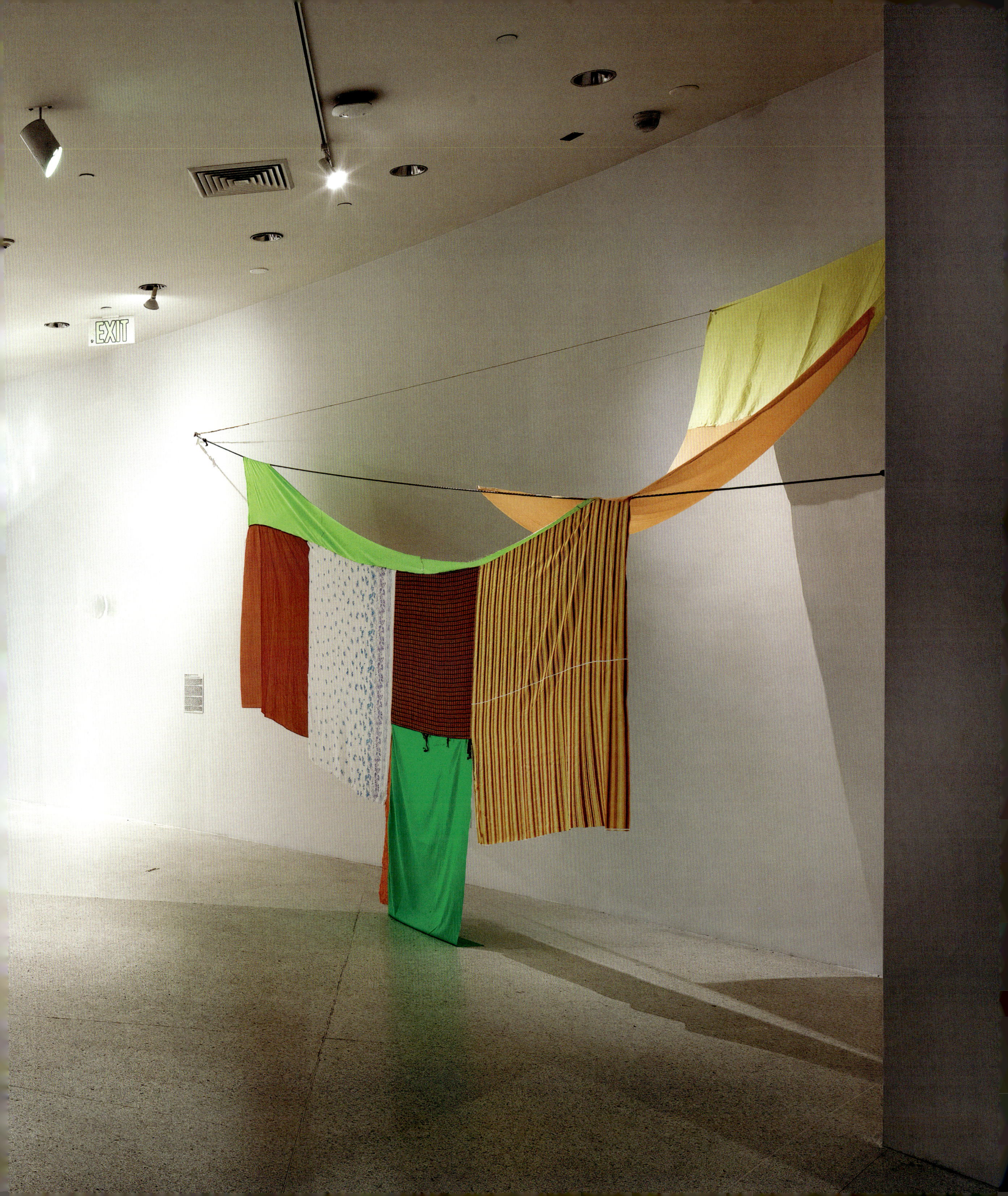

Plates

Plate section is arranged chronologically by date of the artists' completion of their MFA. Text by Bonnie Clearwater. Artist statements are based on interviews and correspondence with the author or their participation in NSU Art Museum's public programs, unless otherwise noted

Wangechi Mutu
MFA 2000

Wangechi Mutu (b. 1972, Nairobi, Kenya; lives and works in Nairobi, Kenya, and New York, NY)[1]

Wangechi Mutu enrolled in the Department of Sculpture in 1998 as an African international student from Kenya. Despite the Yale School of Art's distinction as the oldest art school affiliated with a college in the United States, Mutu discovered that the teaching had not evolved beyond the narrow view of art history and criticism from only a Western perspective. There were four other international students in the small program whilst she was there, from: Korea, Poland, New Zealand, and Denmark; additionally, an Egyptian-American. That first year was disrupted by a major shake-up in the department and the absence of a director. While Mutu's interests were broad and global, the school was "extremely Americancentric." She credits the critical conversations she had over the years with many of the artists in the *Lux et Veritas* exhibition and students from diverse backgrounds from other departments for fortifying her education and growth. Mutu's second year at Yale overlapped with Wiley and Gispert, who brought such richness, criticality and rigor to the program by widening and challenging the pedagogy of art history and opening it up to the multiplicity of art histories.

Mutu enhanced her studies by attending classes with leading thinkers whose work was disrupting notions of Eurocentric singularity in the arts, music, history, including John Szwed (professor and former Director of Graduate Studies in Anthropology and Acting Chair of African American Studies), Michael Veal (Henry L. and Lucy G. Moses Professor Music Department and Professor of African American Studies and American Studies), and Kellie Jones. Her readings included bell hooks, James Clifford's *The Predicament of Culture*, Paul Gilroy's *The Black Atlantic*, Kwame Anthony Appiah, and publications by Yale art historian Robert Farris Thompson, who revolutionized the study of the cultures of Africa and the Americas.

Mutu has a deep interest in artists whose notions of home and history have been ruptured and remade, like the Cuban artist Ana Mendieta and her research into the rituals and deities of the African and Indigenous inhabitants of the Caribbean. Looking at Mendieta's art played an important part in how she positioned her own work in relation to Africanity, art, ritual, and female representation. Mutu was also deeply inspired by the work of Jean-Michel Basquiat, Derek Walcott, David Hammons, Carrie Mae Weems, Alison Saar, Maya Daren, Kerry James Marshall, Ralph Lemon, and Katherine Dunham. Known for her skillful penchant for dissecting images and creating elaborate collage-paintings and drawings, Mutu has recently built a strong new body of sculpture that centers around the female body, bringing her back to her focus on multidimensional figurative object-based studies at Yale.

[1] Trevor Schoonmarker, *Wangechi Mutu: A Fantastic Journey* (Nasher Museum of Art at Duke University, June 2013)

Seeing Cowries
2020
Soil, charcoal, paper pulp, wood glue, soil, emulsion paint, ink, synthetic hair, wood, and shells
39 × 39 ⅜ × 23 ⅝ in / 99.1 × 100 × 60 cm
Courtesy of the artist and Gladstone Gallery
© Wangechi Mutu

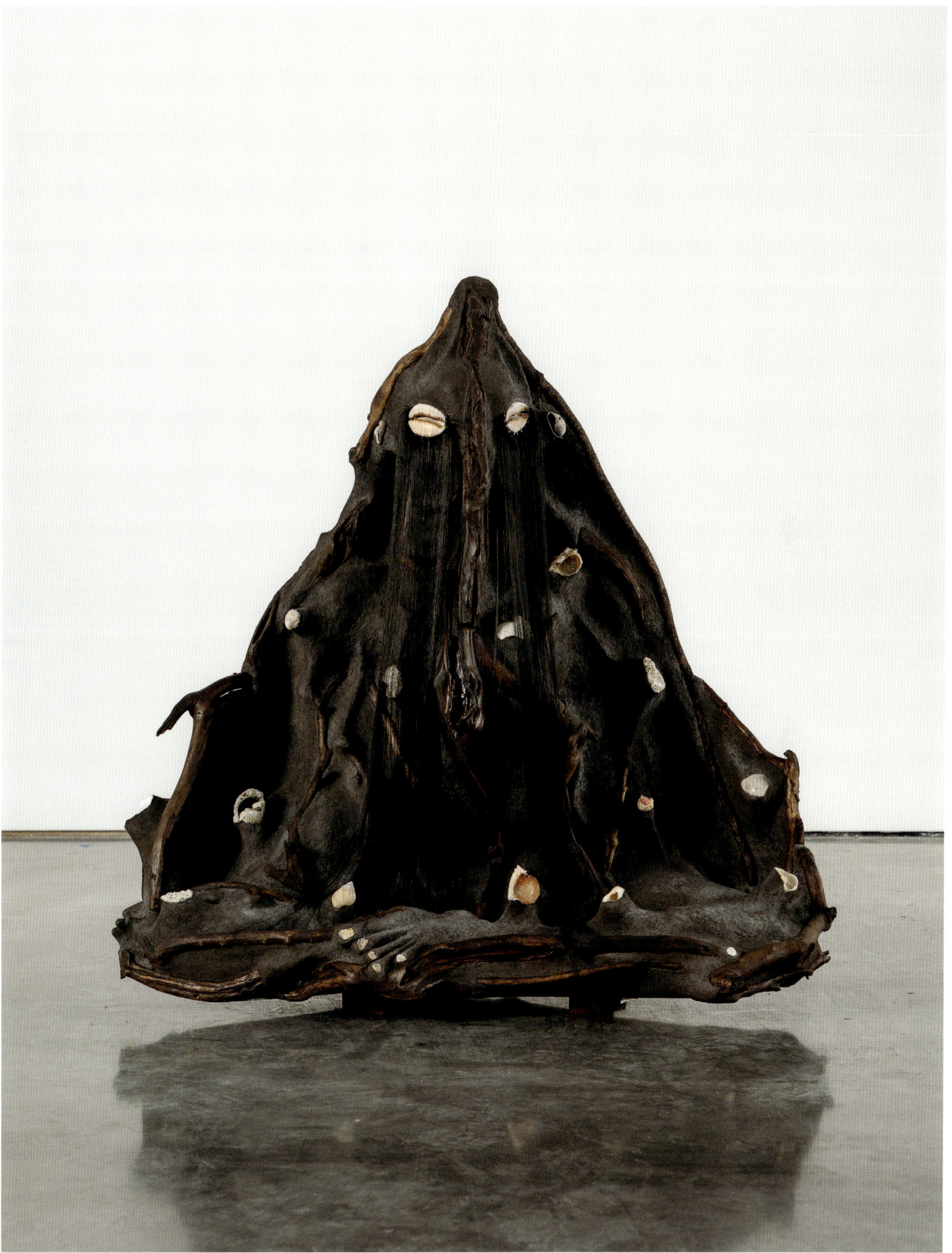

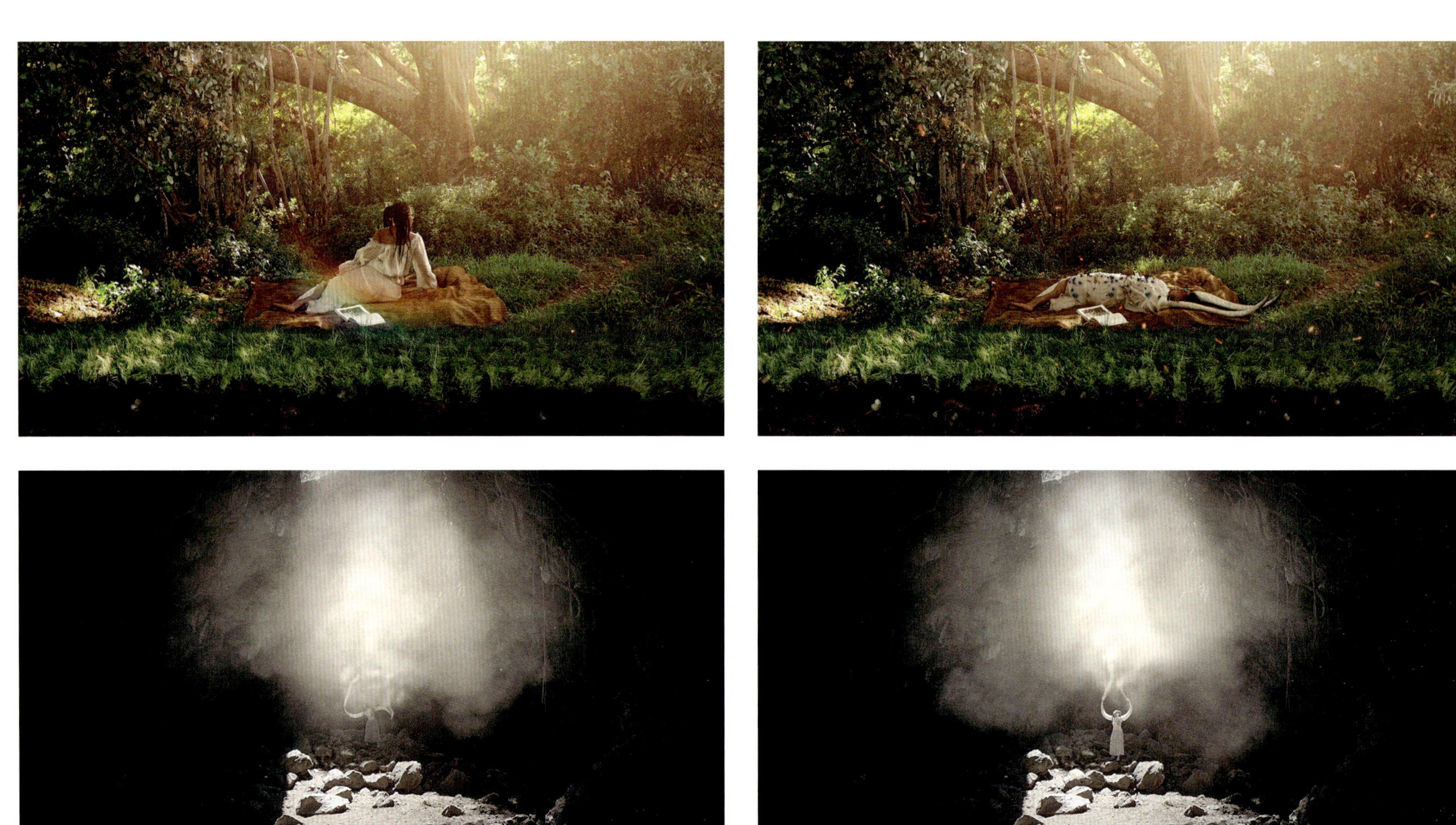

My Cave Call
2021
Digital film (2K HD)
Courtesy of the artist and Gladstone Gallery
© Wangechi Mutu

Sentinel VI
2022
Red soil, paper pulp, wood glue, emulsion
paint, coral bean (Erythrina herbacea),
dead base rock, gourd, brass ornament,
plastic bead, tiger cowry (Cypraea tigris),
jawbone, chiffon, and brass bell
90 ¾ × 35 ⅛ × 36 ⅛ in /
230.5 × 89.2 × 91.8 cm
Courtesy of the artist and Gladstone Gallery
© Wangechi Mutu
Photo by Steven Brooke

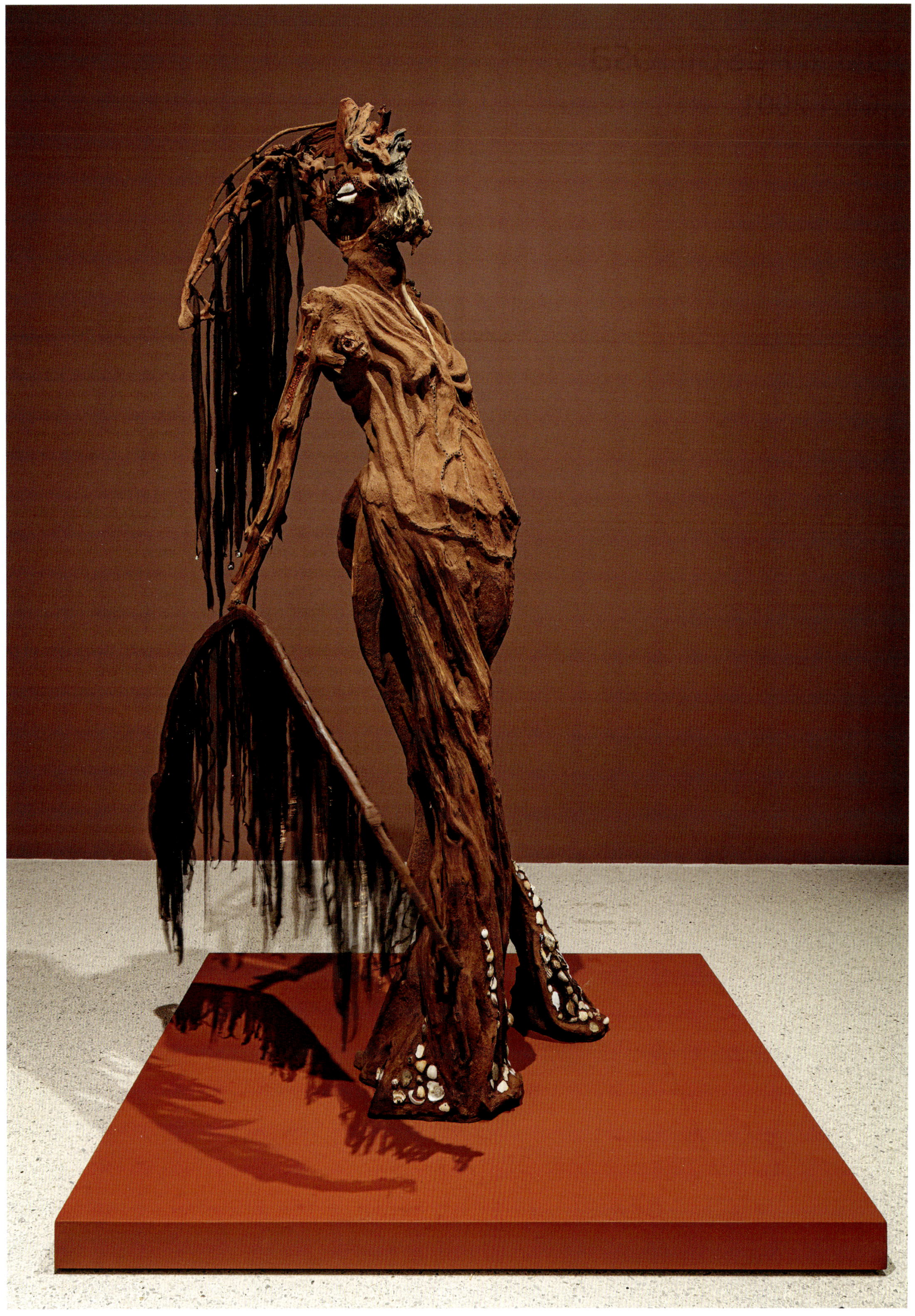

John Espinosa
MFA 2001

John Espinosa (b. 1966, Bogota, Colombia; lives and works in Los Angeles, CA)

Miami artists John Espinosa and Luis Gispert attended the Yale School of Art at the same time. Both artists embraced popular culture in their work without the irony of previous generations of conceptual artists. Espinosa moved with his family from Colombia to the United States in 1970. He grew up in Orlando, a region where Florida wilderness blurred with the hyperreal landscapes of Disney and the tourism industry. His childhood environment created a frame of reference that vacillated between the physical and psychological, the surreal and the spiritual. In his late teens he immersed himself into the surfing community that had a spiritual-like relationship and unique engagement with the natural world. It was within the surfing community that he first met artists and creatives who exposed him to the creative process. Espinosa attended Miami's New World School of the Arts, which offered a primarily post-studio practice, in contrast to Yale's program which was materials oriented. Prior to attending Yale, Espinosa had his work fabricated for him, but during his graduate studies he learned how to construct his own work from foam, plaster, wood, and metal. One of his earliest studio visits was with Tom Friedman, which had a profound impact on his studio practice. Prior to this visit, Espinosa would sit in his empty studio and stare at a single object for a prolonged time until he knew how to develop it. Friedman suggested he do the inverse and fill his studio to the point of over saturation so that ideas would seep into his subconscious.

Although Espinosa's studio practice changed at Yale, his vision was fully evolved prior to entering the Yale School of Art for his graduate studies in 1999. His works embraced recurring narratives of animals and beings in solitary moments of revelation (or delusion) such as in *Rut and Reconstitution*, or in groups locked in a collective trance such as the mandala-like collage on paper *People with Eyes*, with its sea of faces in spiritual rapture, staring out through hypnotic yellow eyes. For Espinosa *People with Eyes* is a "thought on human impulses to assimilate, to believe, and to dissolve into pattern." Both works embody his childhood experiences as a once devout Jehovah's Witness intent on saving souls from the apocalypse, and raised amidst the fantastic landscapes of Central Florida. Both of these works were included in Espinosa's solo exhibition *Standing Still While We Move Across Land* at the Museum of Contemporary Art North Miami, 2004 (curated by Bonnie Clearwater).

Immediately after his graduation from Yale in 2001, Espinosa moved to Los Angeles. From there he maintained a dialogue with fellow classmates on the east coast and kept close ties with the South Florida arts community (including Gispert and cordova); these relationships prompted a cross-country exchange of exhibitions. In 2012 Espinosa joined gallerist Annie Wharton, an artist he had known in Miami since the mid-1990's, in co-curating her gallery space inside West Hollywood's Pacific Design Center, which evolved into Agency, Espinosa's own artist-run project space (2013–2015).

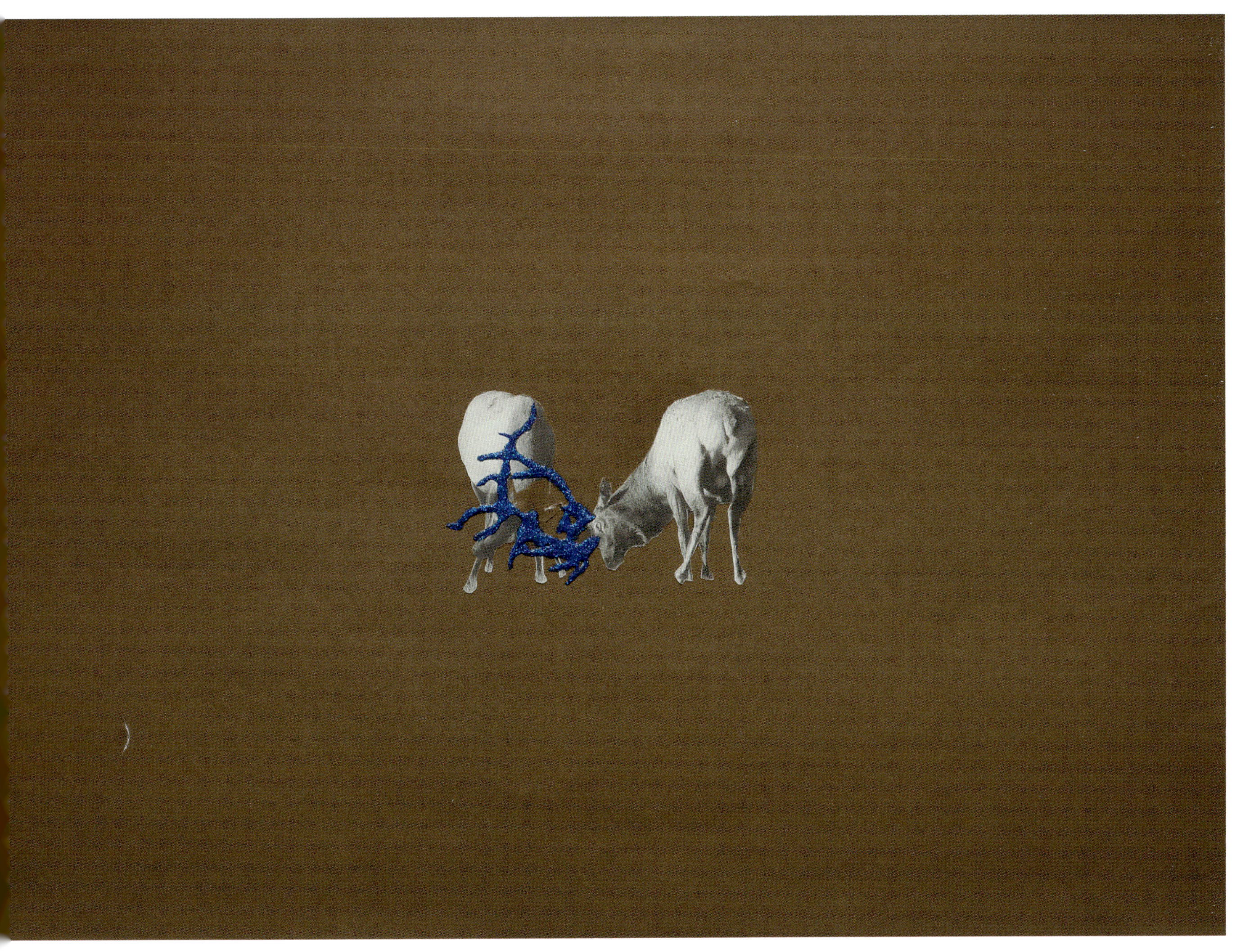

Rut and Reconstitution
2001
Mixed media on paper
20 × 25 ¾ in / 5.8 × 65.4 cm
Collection of the Museum of
Contemporary Art, North Miami
Gift of Fredric and Kathy Snitzer
© John Espinosa
Photo by David Guidi

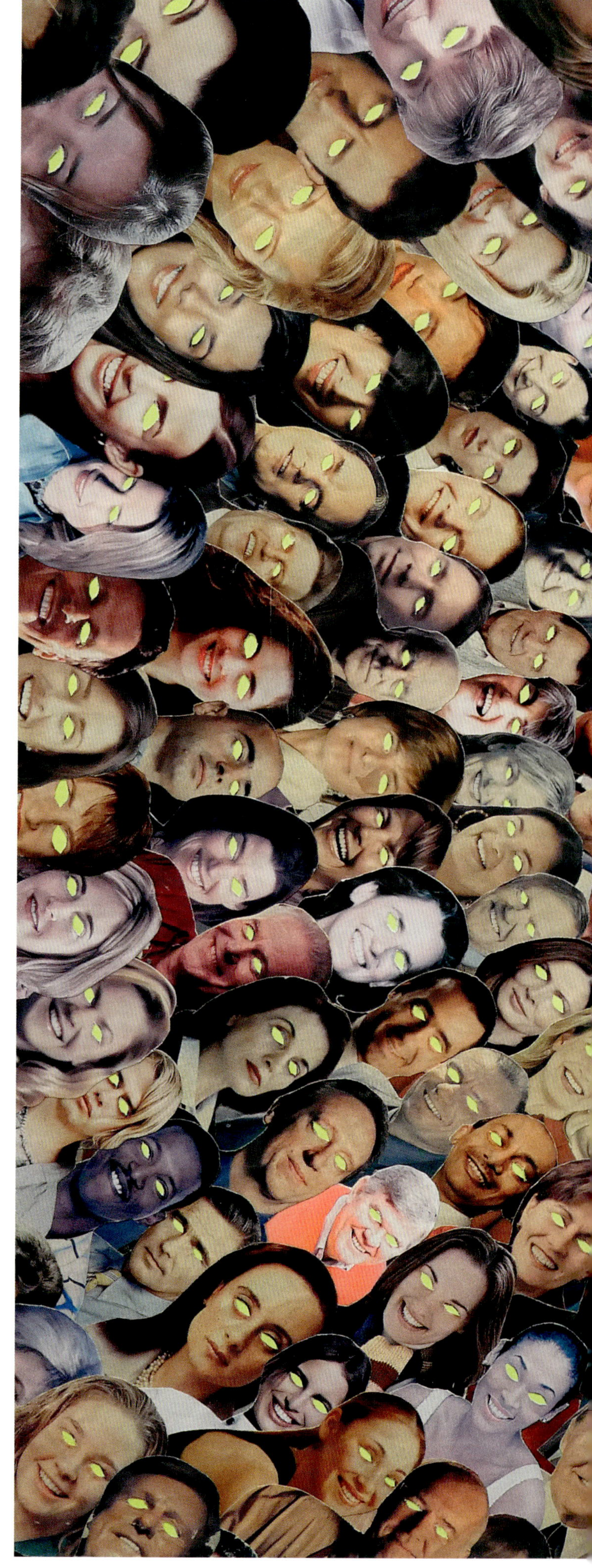

People with Eyes
2004
Magazine clippings and fluorescent
paper on wood
17 ¾ × 22 ⅜ in / 45.1 × 56.8 cm
Collection of Paul Berg
© John Espinosa
Photo by David Guidi

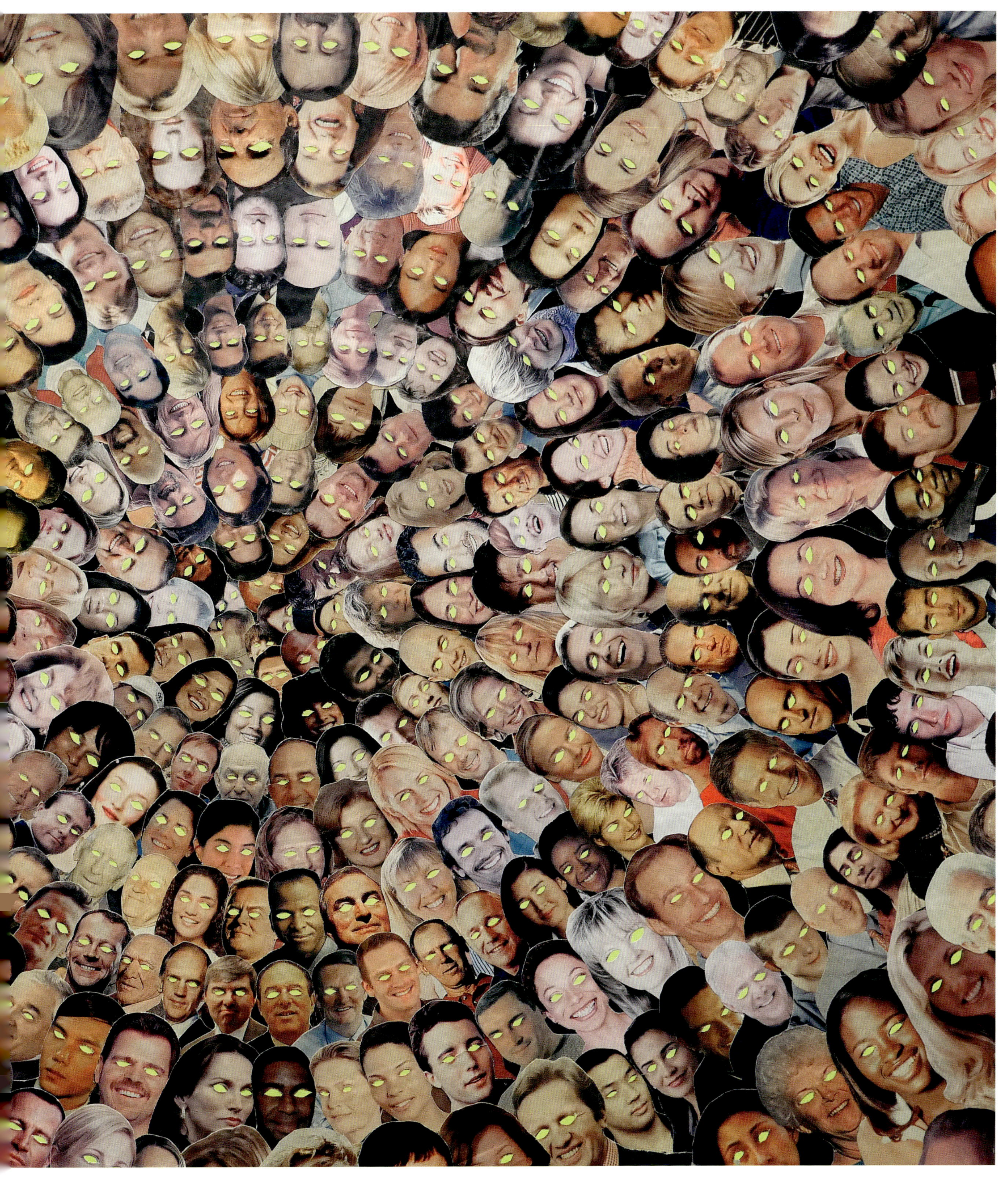

Luis Gispert
MFA 2001

Luis Gispert (b. 1972, Jersey City, NJ; lives and works in Brooklyn, NY)[1]

Among Luis Gispert's earliest childhood memories are watching foreign films with his mother, including the films of Federico Fellini and Luis Buñuel, which she had seen in Cuba before emigrating. Gispert attended South Miami Senior High School's film magnet program where he was introduced to the work of filmmakers Stanley Kubrick, David Lynch, Martin Scorsese, Spike Lee, and Orson Welles, among others. After high school he enrolled in the Miami Dade College south campus art department, which opened up the world of fine art. From there he transferred as an undergraduate in the Film department of the School of the Art Institute of Chicago, where he immersed himself in the world of underground experimental film. Vernacular culture also shaped his aesthetic. As a teenager in Miami, Gispert was involved in customizing cars, participating in a subculture in which the customers, mostly men, aspired to establish their individuality by modifying mass-produced objects. The task required him to make aesthetic decisions long before he was aware of art history or what constitutes a work of art. After graduating he returned to Miami where a critical mass of young artists had convened. Dialogue and friendships established with these artists greatly influenced how his work developed, and led to several film collaborations with cordova and Gean Moreno. For his earliest sculptures, he tapped into this experience to create highly customized race-karts that were so extreme they were nonfunctional as vehicles.

His interest in art history connected his everyday environment and interest in film and became his source for a collective memory. The art of the past provides conventions, sensations, and expectations for the creation of new work. He was especially fascinated with how the intense, ecstatic experience of CinemaScope movies was rooted in the theatricality of seventeenth- and eighteenth-century Baroque paintings, and spent a summer during graduate school photographing Baroque paintings during a visit to Europe. This image bank served as an essential resource for his first major photographic series, "Cheerleaders," in the early 2000s. Although donning contemporary uniforms and bejeweled with the heavy neo-Baroque gold chains and charms associated with hip-hop and gang culture, the cheerleaders, photographed in front of the ambiguous space of a green screen, assume poses that are reminiscent of figures in Baroque allegorical paintings.

Shortly after completing his MFA at Yale, Gispert achieved recognition for both his cheerleader photographs and sculptures inspired by customized cars when they were included in the 2002 Whitney Biennial. He was the subject of two solo exhibitions at the Whitney Museum of American Art, the first at its Altria Branch in New York in 2004 and the second for the premiere of his first major film, *Stereomongrel*, co-directed with Jeffrey Reed in 2005. Although there is a suggestion of a narrative in this film—as the young girl unleashes her superhuman powers and enters a hyper-real world—it is composed of sequences of unforgettable fragmented moments, one of which includes a glimpse of a painting by Wiley. The cheerleaders once again appear in the film in hip-hop regalia. They, along with a giant boom box, are a source for the film's enchantment and mystery. As in the earlier photographs, the figures levitate and fly. In one sequence, the girl wanders through the Whitney. None of the works hanging in the Whitney's galleries are by Latin American artists, which Gispert acknowledged made his presence as filmmaker as exotic as the film's bare-chested Indigenous Latin American security guard singing a 1940s Cuban ballad by Cuban bandleader Beny Moré among the American paintings and sculptures.

Gispert's recent works, included in *Lux et Veritas*, continue the hip-hop and art historical references, in which gold-plated chains embedded in two-dimensional slabs of asphalt (associated with street paving) create arabesques formed by drips of paint in Jackson Pollock-esque abstractions or the calligraphic graffiti tags of street art.

[1] Bonnie Clearwater, *Luis Gispert* (North Miami: Museum of Contemporary Art, 2009).

Luis Gispert and Jeffrey Reed
Stereomongrel
2005
Super 35mm film, color, sound, 12 mins, transferred to video
Courtesy of Lundgren Gallery
© Luis Gispert and Jeffrey Reed
Commissioned by the Whitney Museum of American Art

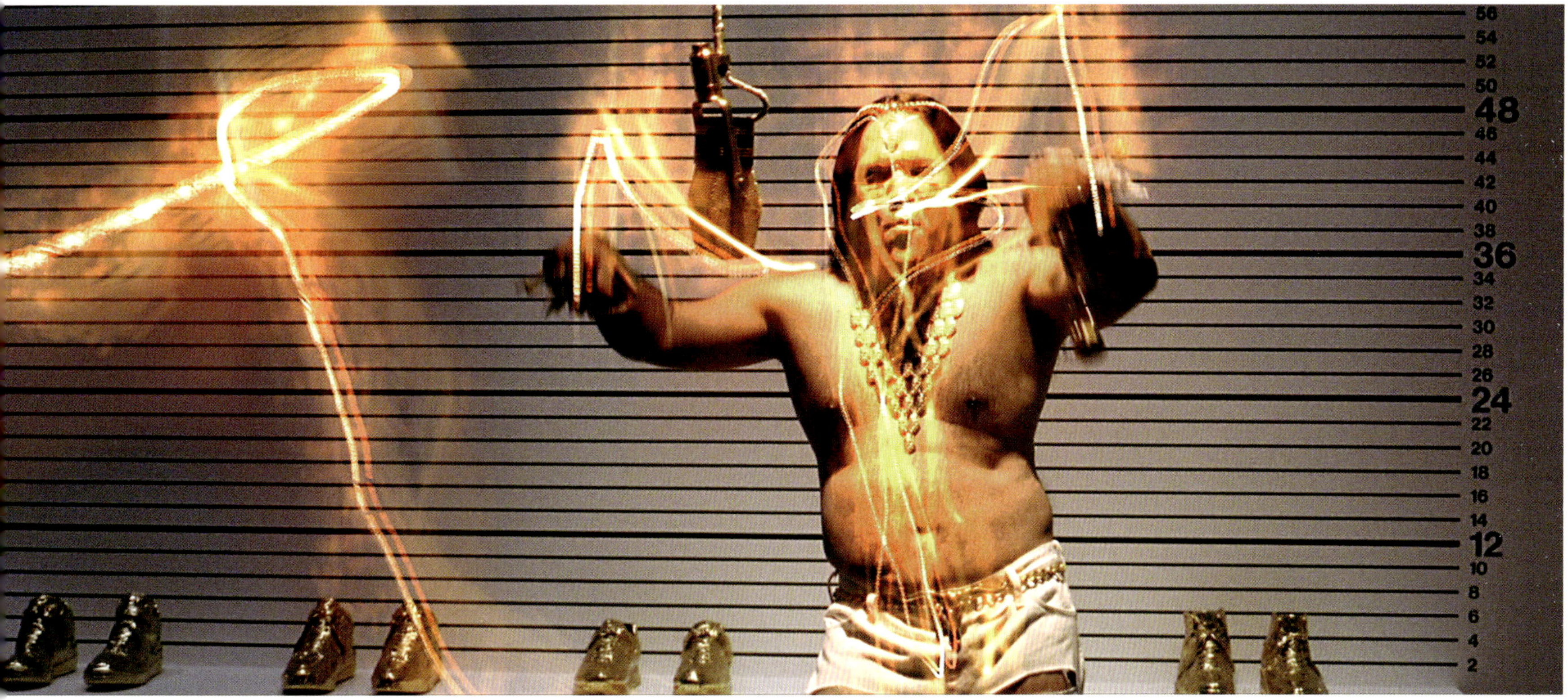
56
54
52
50
48
46
44
42
40
38
36
34
32
30
28
26
24
22
20
18
16
14
12
10
8
6
4
2

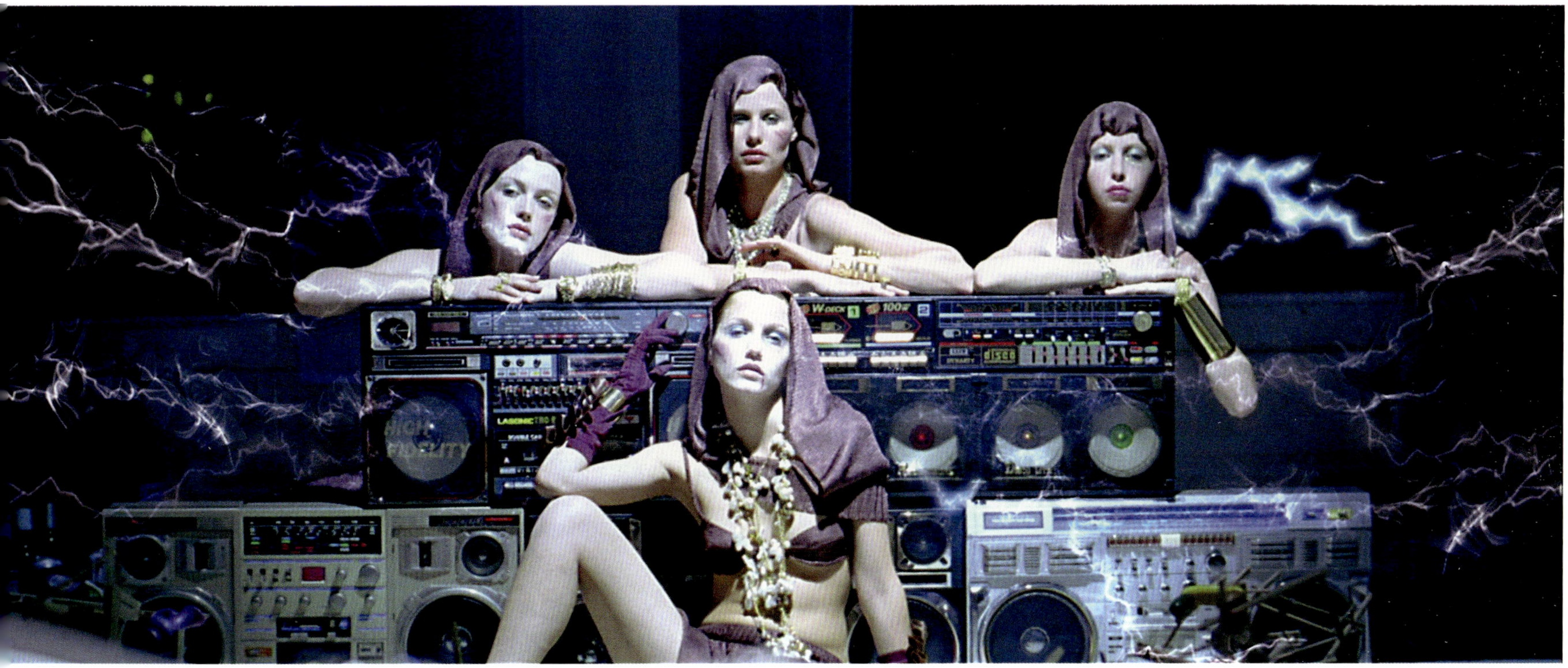

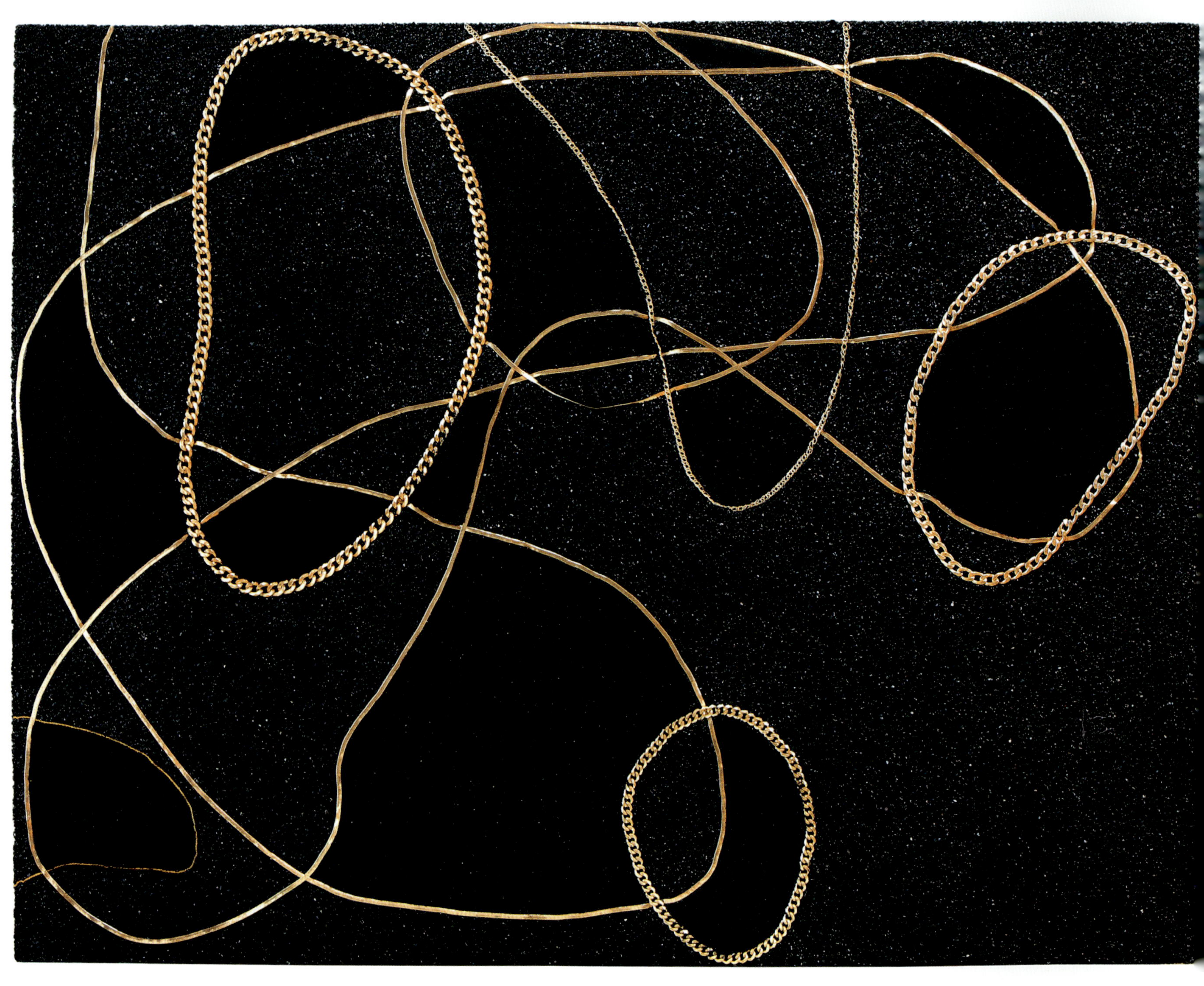

Bojangles
2016
Emulsified bitumen, gold chains
Framed: 61 ½ × 77 ½ in / 156.2 × 196.8 cm;
Object: 61 ¼ × 71 ¾ in / 155.6 × 182.2 cm
NSU Art Museum Fort Lauderdale
Gift of Dr. Robert B. Feldman
Image courtesy of Morán Morán Gallery
© Luis Gispert

Secret Pilgrim
2015
Emulsified bitumen, gold chains
Framed: 77 ½ × 61 ½ in / 196.8 × 156.2 cm;
Object: 71 ¾ × 61 ¼ in / 182.2 × 155.6 cm
NSU Art Museum Fort Lauderdale
Gift of Dr. Robert B. Feldman
Image courtesy of Morán Morán Gallery
© Luis Gispert

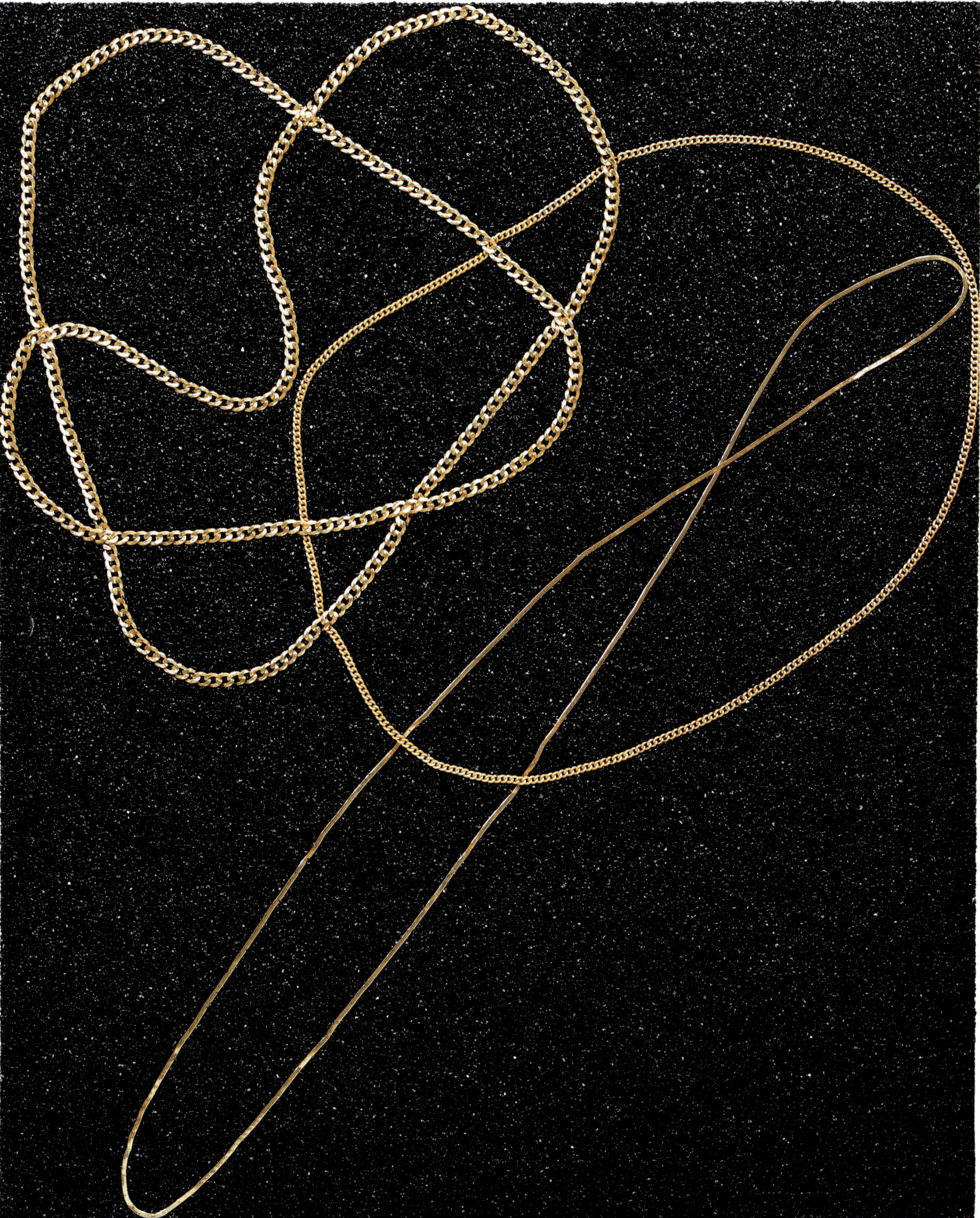

Kehinde Wiley
MFA 2001

Kehinde Wiley (b. 1977, Los Angeles, CA; lives and works in Brooklyn, NY)

The reconsideration of the canon of Western art history informed the practice of several of the artists who attended the Yale School of Art for their graduate studies from 2000 to 2010. Kehinde Wiley played a pivotal role in advancing this theme into the discourse and opening a path for investigation for subsequent Yale graduate students.

Wiley showed artistic talent as a child growing up in Los Angeles, which his mother encouraged by enrolling him in art classes and taking him to museums. Among the Los Angeles museums the family visited was the Huntington Library, Art Museum, and Botanical Garden, with its impressive collection of eighteenth-century British painting by the likes of John Constable, Joshua Reynolds, and Thomas Gainsborough, whose masterwork *The Blue Boy*, 1770, was the star attraction. While he marveled at the technique and realism of these paintings, he also felt alienated from these works, which did not feature Black or brown faces like his. This experience was counterbalanced by his visit to the Los Angeles County Museum of Art where Kerry James Marshall's major painting of a Black barbershop

was on view. Wiley recalls: "There was something absolutely heroic and fascinating about being able to feel a certain relationship to the institution. The fact that these people happen to look like me on some level."[1]

After graduating from Los Angeles County High School for the Arts, Wiley completed his undergraduate degree at the San Francisco Art Institute. Most of his training in painting was copying Old Master paintings, which, as he notes, meant that he "spent a lot of time at museums staring at white flesh."[2]

Wiley's thoughts about portrait painting changed at Yale. As he recalls, "At Yale it became much more about arguments surrounding identity, gender, and sexuality, painting as a political act, questions of post-modernity, etc." During his time at Yale, he was drawn into the language and history of power—its use of, and its potential promise for Black figurative painting.[3] It was during his artist residency at the Studio Museum in Harlem—following the completion of his MFA—that he began his series of portraits based on photographs he took on the streets of young Black men. His subjects assume the poses of the colonial masters, royalty or aristocrats of the Old World, and each painting is typically titled after the subject of a classical European

portrait. As in traditional portraiture, Wiley often incorporates symbols and attributes that reference the sitter's identity, influence, power, character or profession. The most obvious is the large key held by the young man in the painting *The Apostle Peter*. Since at least the fourth century, Saint Peter has been portrayed holding the key to Heaven; it is also a symbol of his papal authority. The pattern formed by the teeth of the key, however, resembles West African symbols. Wiley's use of symbols in his paintings is indicative of how most of the artists included here use icons, codes, and emblems to convey the social, political, and identity subjects of their work. In 2021, the Yale University Art Gallery and the Yale Center for British Art jointly acquired Wiley's portrait of British artist Lynette Yiadom-Boakye, 2017, the first time the two museums teamed up to purchase a work.

[1] Kadish Morris, "Artist Kehinde Wiley: The new work is about what it feels like to be young, Black and alive in the 21st century," *The Guardian*, November 21, 2021.
[2] Finn Blythe, "Kehinde Wiley: interrogating historical portraiture and reframing black identity," *Hero*, June 17, 2020.
[3] Tessa Solomon, "Kehinde Wiley's Portrait of Lynette Yiadom-Boakye Gets Acquired by Yale Museums," *ArtNews*, November 11, 2021.

Following pages

Karl Spindler
2017
Oil on linen
72 × 60 in / 233.7 × 208.3 cm
Courtesy of S. Donald Sussman
© Kehinde Wiley

The Apostle Peter
2006
Oil on canvas
96 × 72 in / 243.8 × 182.9 cm
Courtesy of Laurie Karen
Silverman, N.Y.C.
© Kehinde Wiley

Sir Richard Owen 1804–1892
2013
Oil on canvas
48 × 36 in / 121.9 × 91.4 cm
Courtesy of Laurie Karen
Silverman, N.Y.C.
© Kehinde Wiley

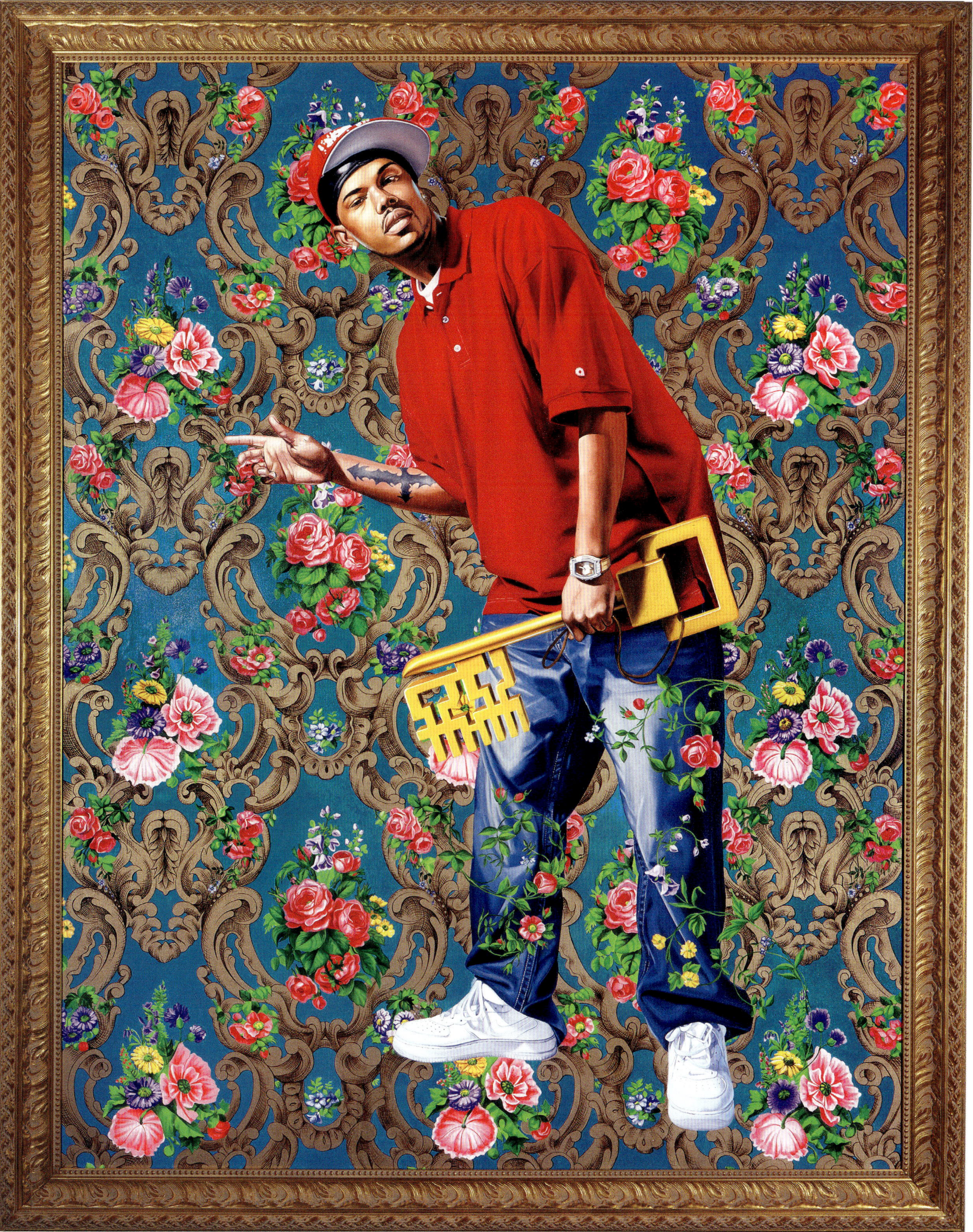

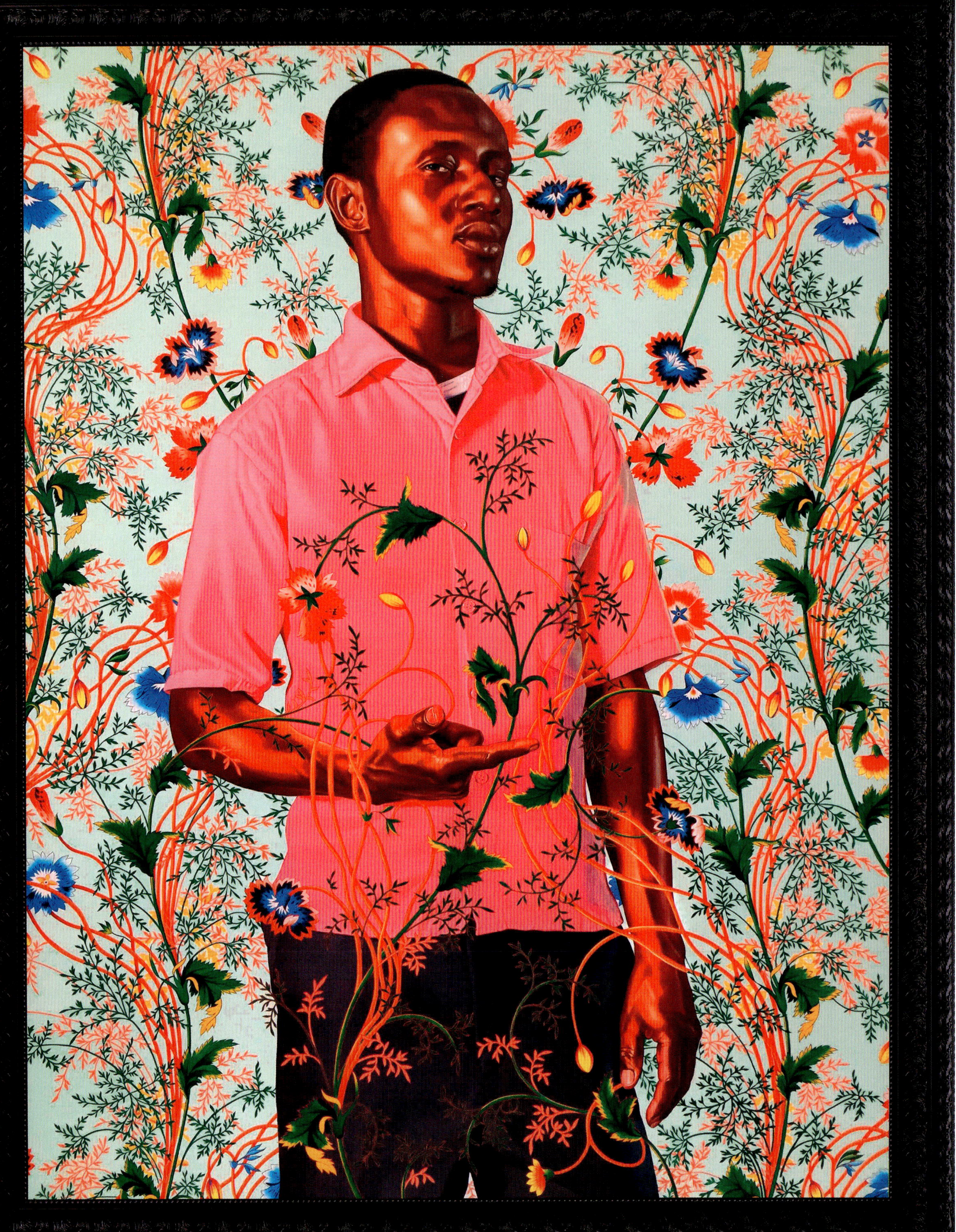

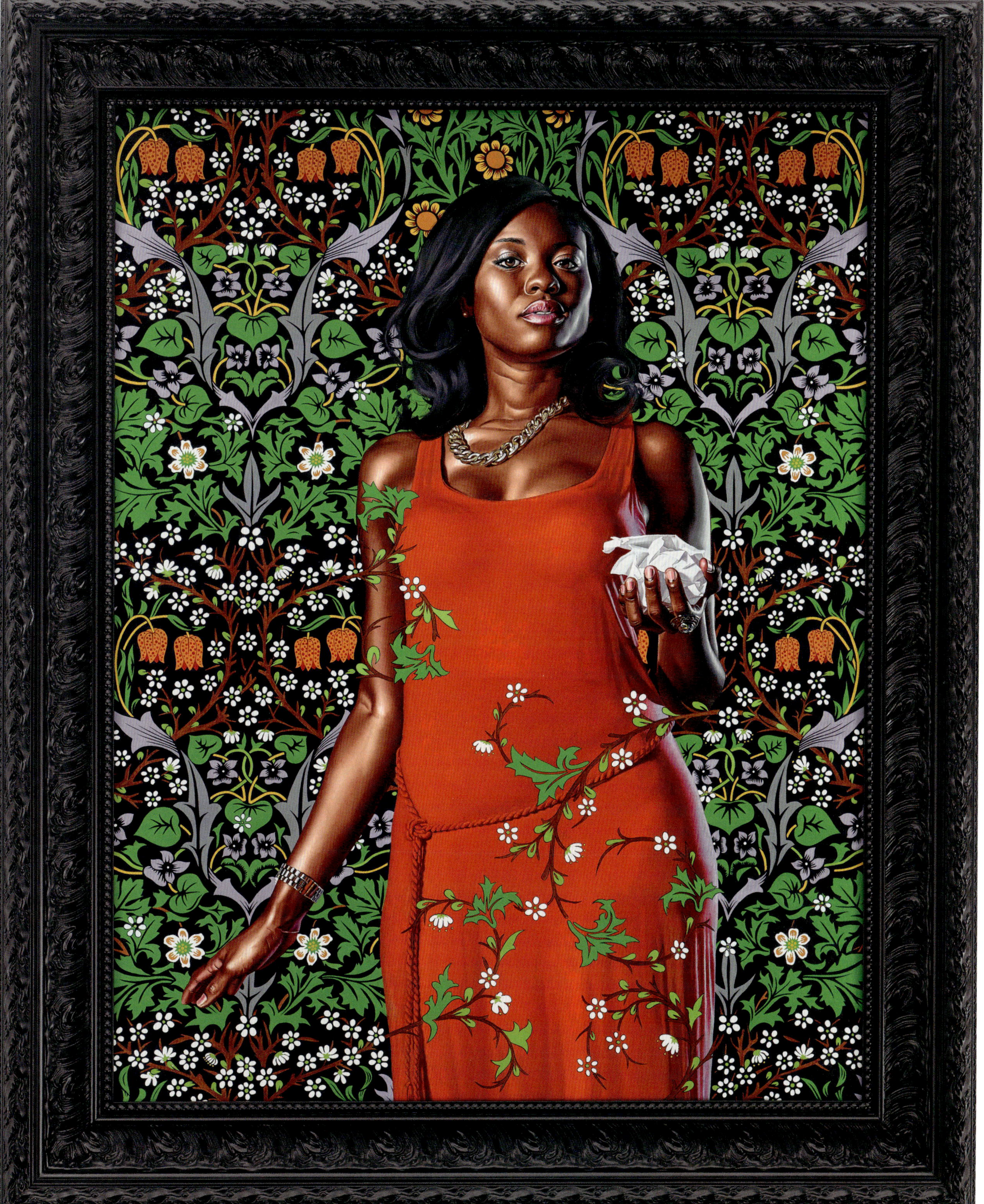

Mickalene Thomas
MFA 2002

Mickalene Thomas (b. 1971, Camden, NJ; lives and works in New York, NY)

While an undergraduate at Pratt Institute, Mickalene Thomas enrolled in Yale's Norfolk School of Art Summer Residency program, where she met Yale painting instructor Sam Messer and painter Lisa Yuskavage.[1] Both artists encouraged her to apply, with Yuskavage writing a letter of recommendation. Thomas used her time at Yale to experiment and explore photography and collage, which served as the foundation of her painting practice.

While matriculating through the university, Thomas met Wiley, a fellow student and artist who would go on to become a close friend. He recommended that after graduation she apply to the Artist-in-Residence program at The Studio Museum in Harlem, which he personally had found so beneficial. Thomas credits her year-long residency there as providing her the opportunity to transition from graduate school to a more professional environment.

Thomas' interest in African art and mid-twentieth-century artists Romare Bearden, Faith Ringgold, and Jacob Lawrence influenced her approach to space and color, as seen in her portraits of Black women accoutred with gems. Photographer Carrie Mae Weems was another artist she studied early in her career. Weems' *Kitchen Table Series* of photographs of mother-daughter relationships in domestic settings encouraged Thomas to consider using her own personal history as a source for her work.

The painting *October 1950*, 2021, is part of a new series in which Thomas engaged with vintage photographs of Black women depicted in the Black-owned magazine *Jet* that were originally the subject of a performance project she presented as a graduate student in Kellie Jones' class at Yale. Thomas described the return to this subject: "Now, at this point in my life, after my journey, after collaborating with muses, working with various sitters and models, it makes sense to look back at the pivotal moment where the first images provided a sense of validation, in beauty and recognition. These images created a platform of agency and became the central point of focus to why the concepts in my work are related to desire, beauty, and erotica." Although she has long been fascinated with photographs in *Jet*, she only discovered the "Jet Calendar Girl" pinups in 2015.[2]

[1] The Yale Norfolk School of Art, located on the Ellen Battell Stoeckel Estate, Norfolk, Connecticut, was established in 1948. It is an intensive six-week undergraduate summer residency program. According to the description on the Yale website, it "seeks to bring together a diverse group of students who have demonstrated a passion in art making and are exemplary community members to participate in a rigorous environment of artistic practice, learning and growth."

[2] Katy Donoghue, "Mickalene Thomas Goes Beyond the Pleasure Principle," *whitewall*, January 13, 2022. https://whitewall.art/art/mickalene-thomas-goes-beyond-the-pleasure-principle.

October 1950
2021
Rhinestones, glitter, acrylic, and oil on canvas mounted on wood panel with mahogany frame
106 × 90 × 8 in / 269.2 × 228.6 × 20.3 cm
Courtesy of Mickalene Thomas
© Mickalene Thomas

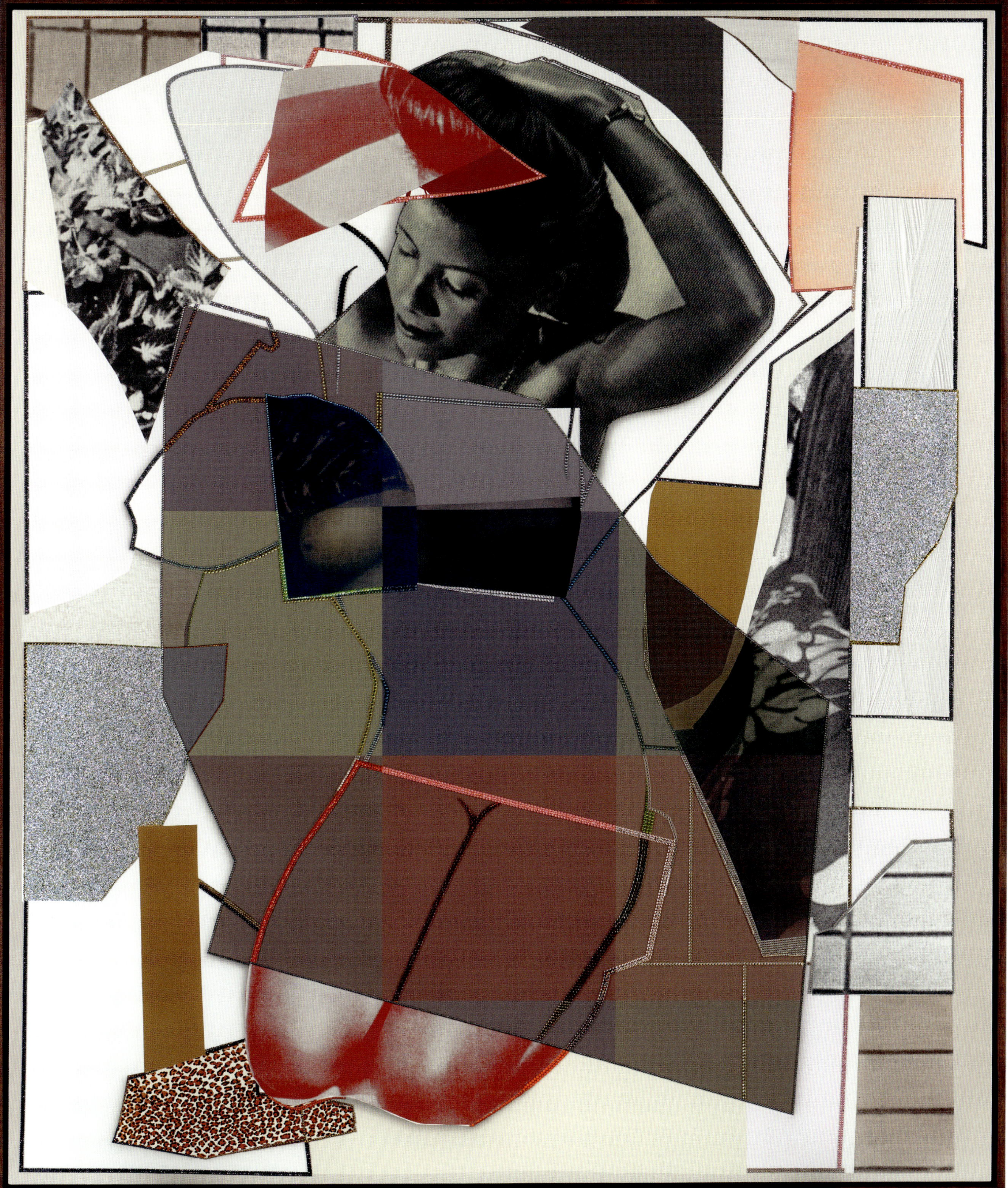

Anna Tsouhlarakis
MFA 2002

Anna Tsouhlarakis (b. 1977, Lawrence, KS; lives and works in Boulder, CO)

Anna Tsouhlarakis, a Native American artist of Navajo, Creek, and Greek descent, attended Dartmouth College in Hanover, New Hampshire, as an undergraduate. As stated in its charter, the college was founded in 1769, "for the education and instruction of Youth of the Indian Tribes… and also of English Youth and any others." Although Dartmouth fell short of its goal for its first 200 years, the College recommitted itself to its purpose in the 1970s, establishing a Native American program at the College and actively recruiting Native students. By the time Tsouhlarakis attended Dartmouth, it had the highest percentage of Native American students at a top-tier school.

At Dartmouth, she was accustomed to associating primarily with Native students. Her decision to attend the Yale School of Art was a strategic decision based on her observation of the way her father, an accomplished jeweler in Native design, as well as other Native artists were treated when selling their more traditional artworks. While their work was desired, they were often spoken to in a condescending and patronizing manner. She reasoned that acquiring two Ivy League degrees would confer indisputable validation of her credentials. At the Yale School of Art, she was the only Native student, and while she aligned with students of color there, she sought out the Native community at Yale Law and the School of Forestry.

The admission policy varied for each department of the School of Art. The Department of Sculpture, under the direction of Jessica Stockholder, included first-year graduate students on the admissions committee. Mutu was on the committee that accepted Tsouhlarakis. As Stockholder was a painter who worked three-dimensionally, she encouraged her students to push boundaries. Tsouhlarakis took the opportunity to explore contemporary performance art, video, and installation.

Tsouhlarakis' concern for the future of the Earth was the impetus behind her rocket ship project that she first created at Yale. She had read an article that suggested that with the imminent demise of the planet, everyone would need to escape Earth and go elsewhere. Assuming that the Natives would be left to make their own rockets,

Tsouhlarakis designed her own. She submitted her rocket ship project to Skowhegan School of Painting & Sculpture as part of her successful application to its residency program after completing her MFA. For the *Lux et Veritas* exhibition, she recreated the original rocket ship along with two additional ones for her children.

Tsouhlarakis recited the following text at her performance for *Rocketship* at the Yale School of Art in 2002:

> When the natural resources of Earth start becoming scarce, many people will look towards the option of leaving this planet in hope of finding another planet that will sustain life. While most people will be in the fancy, sophisticated NASA-type space shuttles there will be people, such as Indians, who cannot afford such luxury and will have to build their own ships. These less complicated rocket ships will not be able to take off on their own and will have chains that hook onto the larger rocket ships. But one thing each of those shoddy rocket ships will have is an escape hatch in the floor. As all of the larger spaceships begin their countdown to take off, all the Indians will be slipping out of their escape hatches. The Indians will be putting their feet on the ground while everyone else is on their way out of here.

Concerning the rockets Tsouhlarakis created for *Lux et Veritas* she states:

> When I say these works are fully functioning rocket ships, they are fully functioning rocket ships. Each of them has an escape hatch. Each of them has chains and hooks to latch onto the larger rocket ships. As the first iteration of this work was 20 years ago, I wondered what a rocket ship would look like now? I decided it would be symbolic of my kids and family. In the original rocket ship I had my Certificate Degree of Indian Blood (CDIB) number inscribed on the exterior of the rocket. I'm an enrolled citizen of the Navajo Nation and my CDIB number shows that I'm from a federally recognized tribe and entitled to certain rights as a Native person. The other numbers on these new rocket ships are my children's numbers. Each rocket corresponds generally to their personalities. My nine-year-old, Coco, is super loungey, which is why her rocket is the most comfortable one. There are a lot of furry blankets and pillows inside. The exteriors are all covered with symbols of colonization, such as the CDIB numbers and an American flag, which would burn up as they

> left Earth. This is about protest, but also renewal, because that's what fire does in the end.

Tsouhlarakis attended the opening and public programs of *Lux et Veritas*.[1] She made the following observation at the time:

> Several of us artists were talking at the opening about the idea of interiors and exteriors and how some of the artworks on view allow people to come into them, but how some of my pieces you can't enter. That has always been something I've been very aware of within my work, how much I want to show of who I am and of my culture. When I was younger, I was a dancer at powwows. I would dance all over the country. It was always amazing to me that people felt they could come up and touch me all the time and they could take photos of me, as close as they wanted. There was this privilege, almost a sense of ownership, that people thought they had over us as dancers. What I like about artworks like this is that I'm only allowing you to look in so far, and I'm the one that's in charge of gauging what you're able to see. I enjoy making viewers be aware of what they can see and not see.

> I wouldn't call myself a Native futurist, but I am interested in exploring those facets of the possibility of the future with the rocket ships. It is not necessarily that I am going to space, but I am going to be here repairing the Earth. Everything I do is based in Native philosophies and stories because those are the values and the stories that I learned growing up. In Navajo myths of multiple worlds, there's this idea that we're either in the fourth or fifth world, and with each world, things change. And so, the question is—are we in the final world? Is there a world after this? When I began thinking about the narrative of this artwork, my question is—once everybody leaves and the Earth is dying, are we able to repair it and regrow things to heal it? Does that become the new, the next world? For me, this way of thinking and artmaking is exactly in line with all those traditional of stories. It's about renewal, rebirth, and responsibility.

[1] The artists in attendance at the opening of *Lux et Veritas* on April 1, 2022, were: Mike Cloud, william cordova, Abigail DeVille, Torkwase Dyson, Rashawn Griffin, Loren Hudson, Mamiko Otsubo, Anna Tsouhlarakis, and Shoshanna Weinberger. The public programs were held the following day.

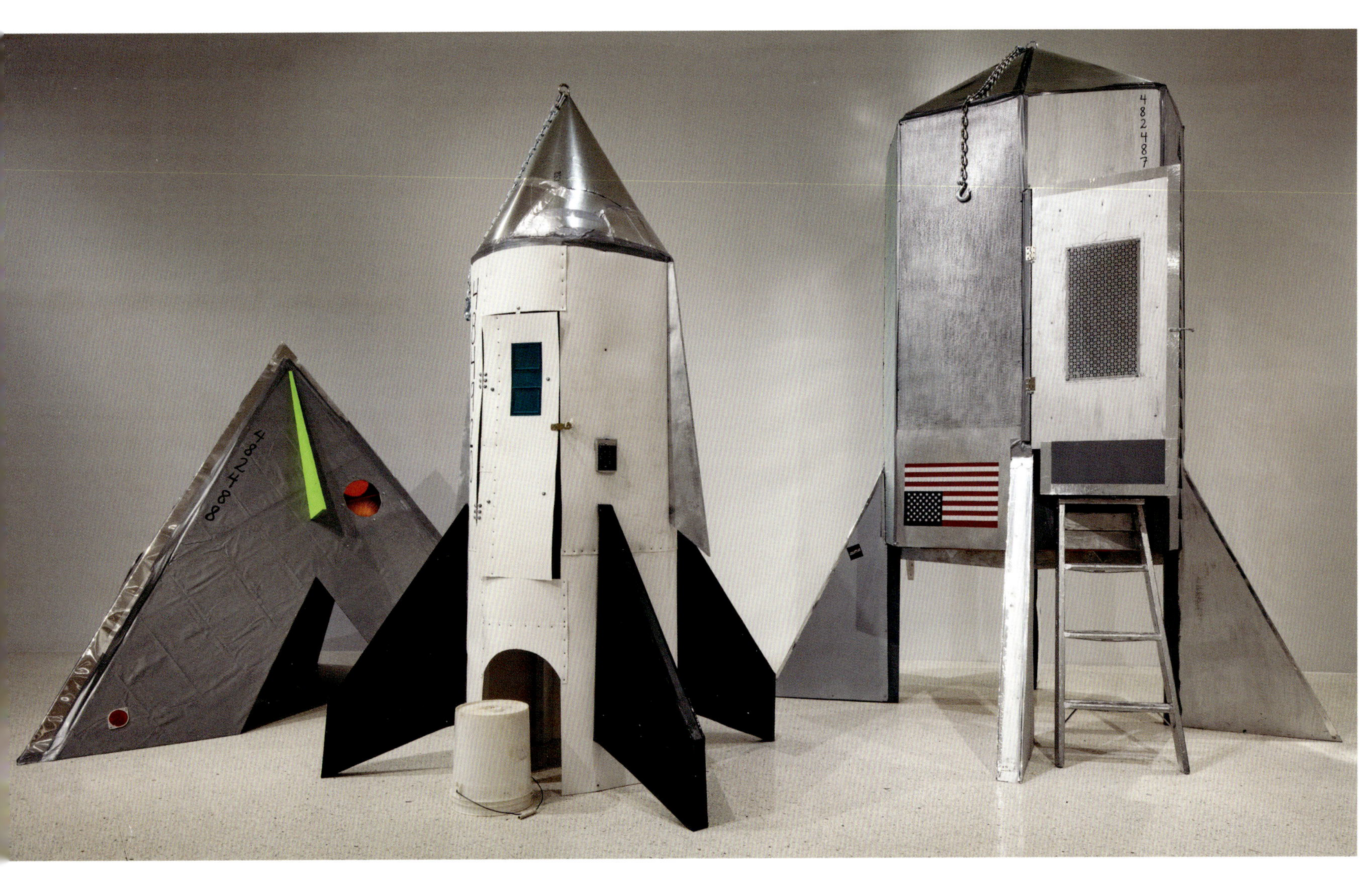

Rocketship 3/4
2002–2022
Wood, aluminum, steel, fabric, turf, paint,
duct tape, foamboard, aluminum tape,
plexi, plastic, IKEA remnants, paint,
plastic bucket, tarp, fleece, step ladder,
and nylon cord
Dimensions variable
Courtesy of the artist
© Anna Tsouhlarakis
Photo by Steven Brooke

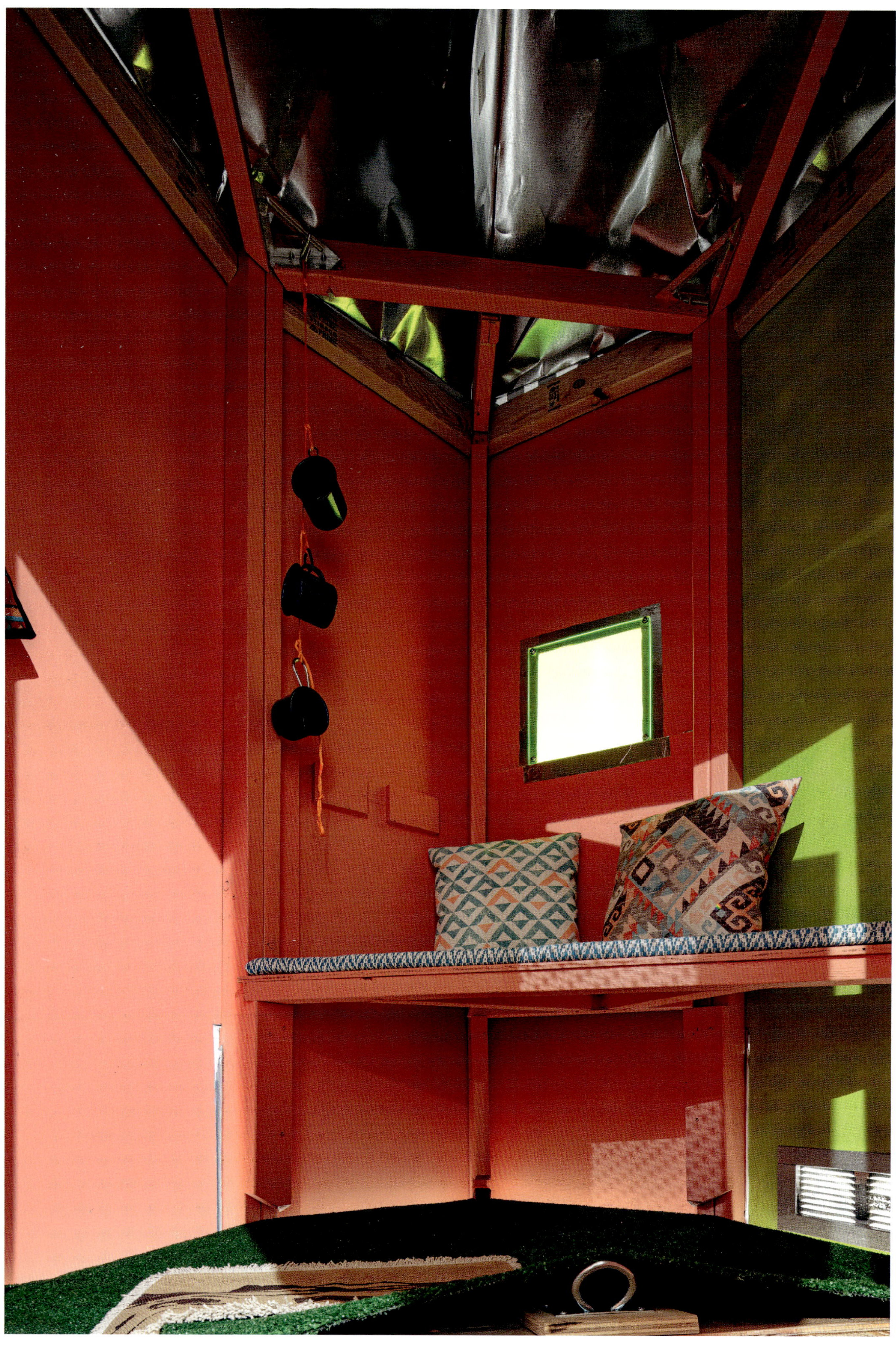

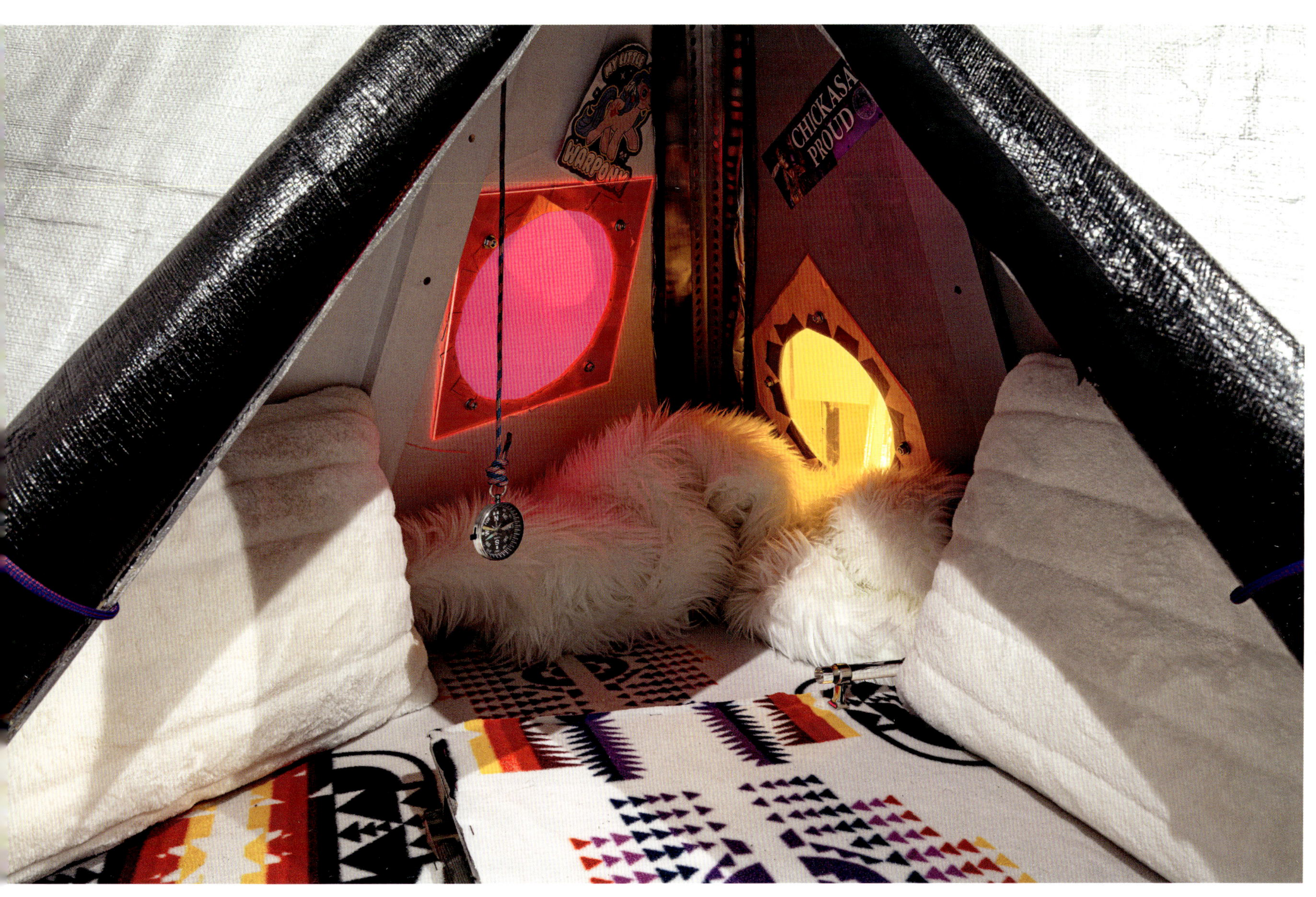

Interior views: *Rocketship 3/4*
2002–2022
Wood, aluminum, steel, fabric, turf, paint,
duct tape, foamboard, aluminum tape,
plexi, plastic, IKEA remnants, paint,
plastic bucket, tarp, fleece, step ladder,
and nylon cord
Courtesy of the artist
© Anna Tsouhlarakis
Photos by Steven Brooke

Mike Cloud
MFA 2003

Mike Cloud (b. 1974, Chicago, IL; lives and works in Chicago, IL)

Artist and educator Mike Cloud has noted that "the role of art education in the practices of prominent minority artists has never been extensively studied." When he was a graduate at Yale, he realized that the Painting department's faculty had no special preparation or philosophy for teaching artists who belonged to marginalized social groups. The predominantly white male faculty presented modern formal painting ideas to students, who generally created work that challenged this approach, which in turn reinvigorated the relevance of this medium. Although Cloud did not feel understood by his professors, he sought other students who shared his interests. He bonded with fellow painting student Dyson and first-year students cordova and Hewitt who entered Yale during his second year there. Cloud was encouraged to apply to Yale by painter Kerry James Marshall, who told him that if he wanted to paint really well, he should go to Yale where the various media disciplines were separated. Studying in the Department of Painting and Printmaking meant that Cloud, who had not painted much as an undergraduate, would focus almost exclusively on honing this medium. After graduation, Cloud realized that the mainstream "New York School" formal language he had learned to use at Yale generated a fundamental misreading of his work. He consequently rethought his approach to achieve clarity.

The network of artists he formed at Yale helped him to formulate his work and perspective and he credits the success that Yale alumni Wiley and Mickalene Thomas achieved for helping to open doors for him. His paintings probe the convention of the shaped canvas and the contrivances of abstract painting. As he noted in an interview in *The New York Times*, the way he was "taught abstraction was that it was a safe place for painters, it was a retreat from meaning… But when I went into that space and picked up those tools, it was obvious they had a history as weapons."[1] Rather than a purely formal device that creates irregular contours for the painting, Cloud's shaped canvases—the Star of David, triangle, diamond, and so forth—are based on a personal cosmology. The wooden stretcher bars are an integral part of these paintings, framing and supporting the heavily painted and collaged canvas that is stretched like a skin. The painting's negative space consists of the literal empty space between canvas and the wooden stretcher. Although abstract, his paintings incorporate objects, such as toy blocks and wooden kitchen utensils, that are in proportion to the human body. For Cloud, the critical consensus that painting had gone as far as it could go, that in fact "Painting is dead," became the medium's fundamental aesthetic message as well as its social currency. He equated the "death of painting" with the subject of his paintings by scrawling text on each painting, identifying it as a reaction to, or portrait of online searches for various catastrophic and deadly subjects on the internet. The URL incorporated into his paintings leads the viewer to the online site. While Cloud's incorporation of text into his paintings can be traced to modern and contemporary art antecedents from Picasso to Ed Ruscha, Yale painting professor Mel Bockner, and Glenn Ligon, his expressive script suggests the ecstatic energy of automatic writing associated with surrealism and outsider artists.

Mike Cloud:

I assume that my work can render a kind of sympathetic aid to my audience because I know that it does that for me and being a sensible object, not just in my head, what it does for me it can do for others. My art represents or expresses my own subjective reconciliation to the object of the painting. Death is generally the object of my paintings. There are many types of death, some are more social and others are more personal. When I address the unjust deaths of Black people in my work, as I occasionally do, I symbolically wrestle with social questions like: why do these deadly injustices happen to people like me? What should I do to prevent them from happening to other people like my children, friends, and loved ones? How do other people like me feel about these injustices? How can we use the tragic effects of these deadly injustices to improve the lives of people like me and people in general? When I address more personal categories of death like suicide, the questions are more personal. When I address other social deaths like 9/11 or the Holocaust the questions raised will differ in relation to my various intersectional social statuses and identities. It is all very complex, and I understand that other people (my audience) are also working towards their own reconciliation with these questions. Because of the positive response my work has received from my audience, I am led to believe that it has provided them with some of the reconciliation it provides me with.

[1] Will Heinrich, "Mike Cloud: Painting Outside the Safe Place," *New York Times*, May 6, 2020.

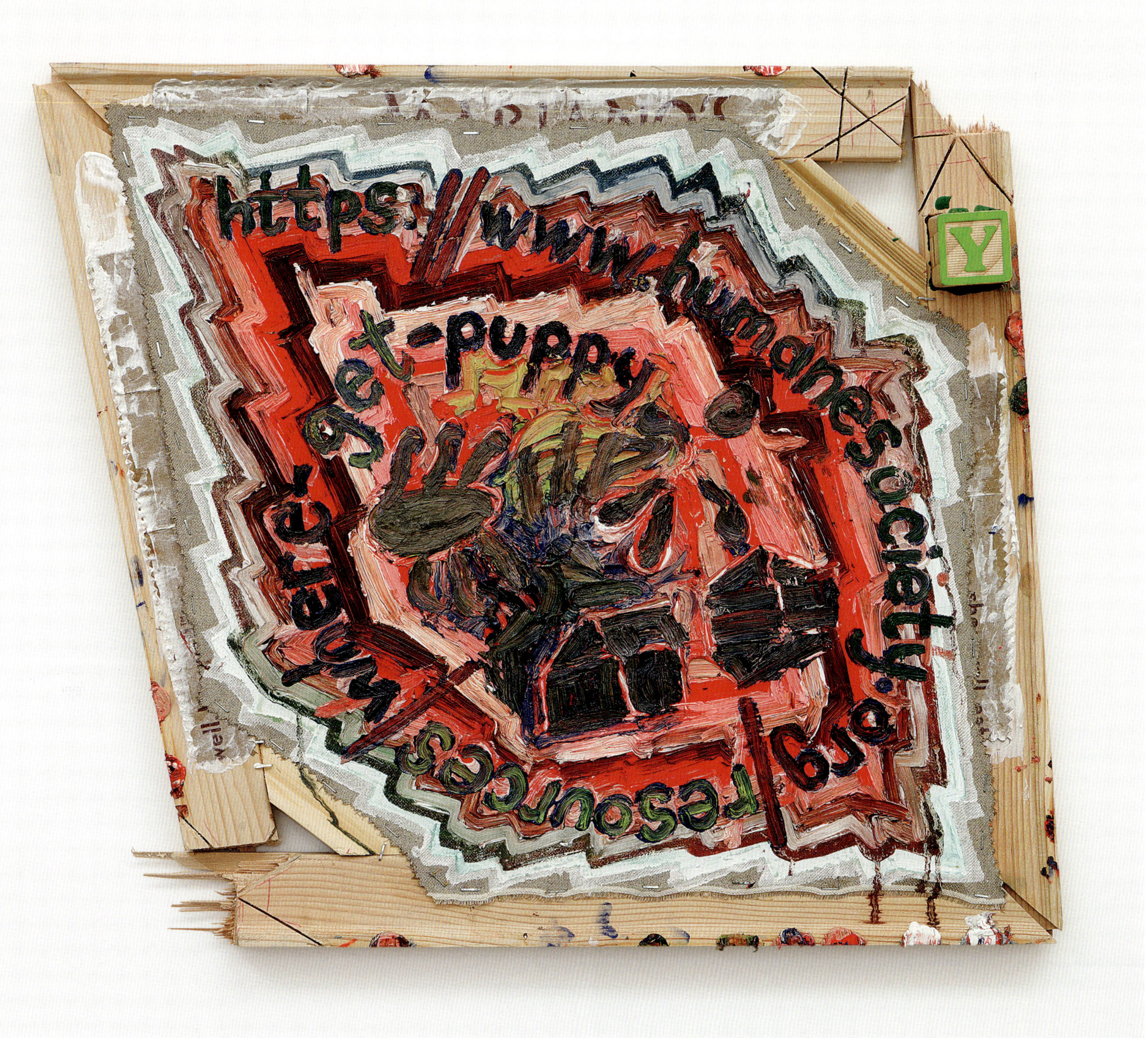

Advice Getting Puppy
2020
Oil on canvas and mixed media
27 × 33 × 3 in / 68.6 × 83.8 × 7.6 cm
Courtesy of the Landing Gallery
© Mike Cloud, 2020
Photo by Joshua White

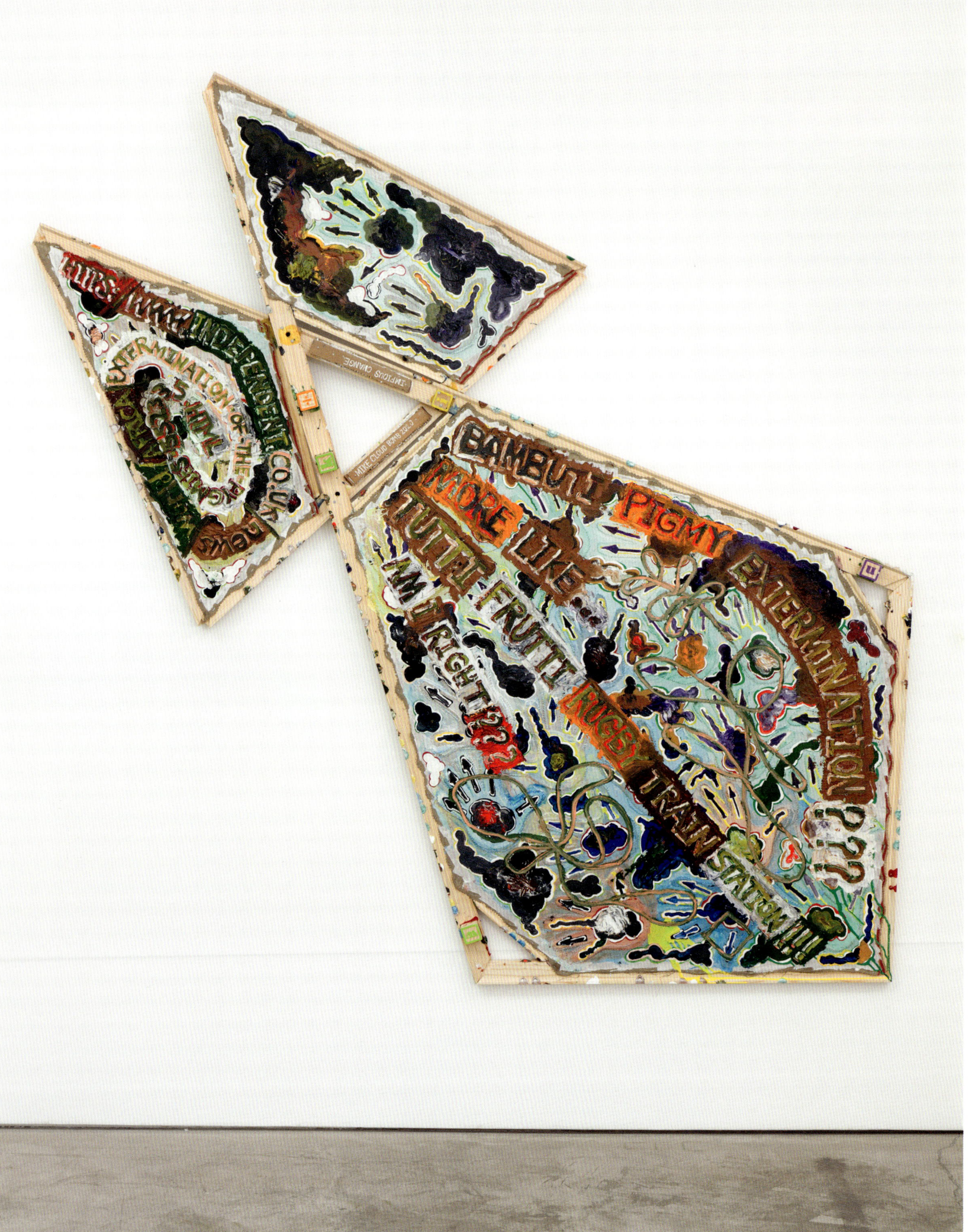

INDEPENDENT COUNT
EXTERMINATION OF THE
PIGMY
NEWS
BAMBUTI PIGMY EXTERMINATION???
MORE LIKE...
TUTTI FRUTTI
AM I RIGHT??
RUGBY TRAIN STATION!!!
IMPIOUS CHANGE
MIKE CLOUD BOMB

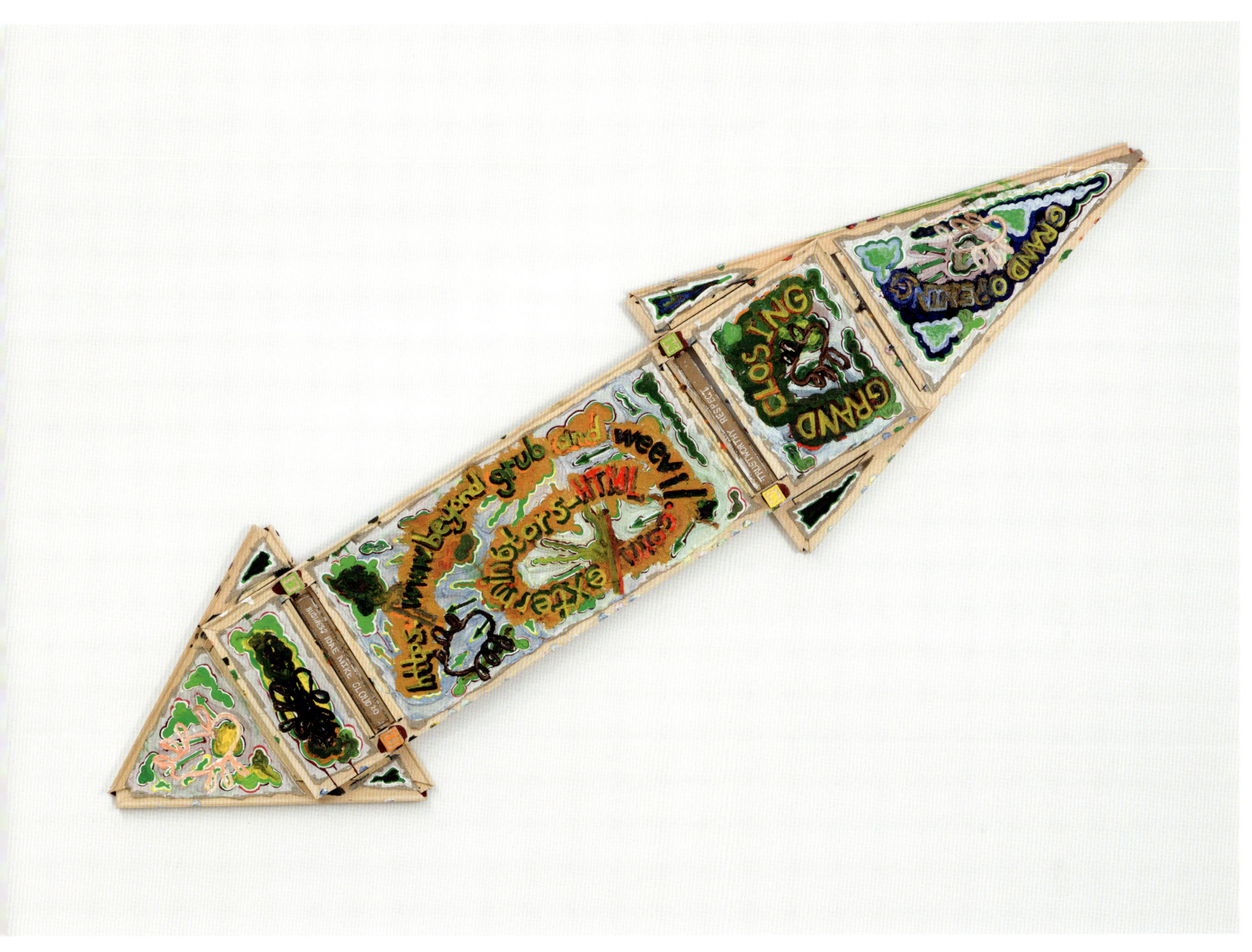

Bomb Bambuti Pigmy
2020
Oil on canvas and mixed media
109 × 59 × 3 ½ in /
276.9 × 149.9 × 8.9 cm
Courtesy of the Landing Gallery
© Mike Cloud, 2020
Photo by Joshua White

Business Idea Beyond Grub and Weevil
2020
118 × 33 × 2 ½ in / 299.7 × 83.8 × 6.3 cm
Oil on canvas and mixed media
Courtesy of the Landing Gallery
© Mike Cloud, 2020
Photo by Joshua White

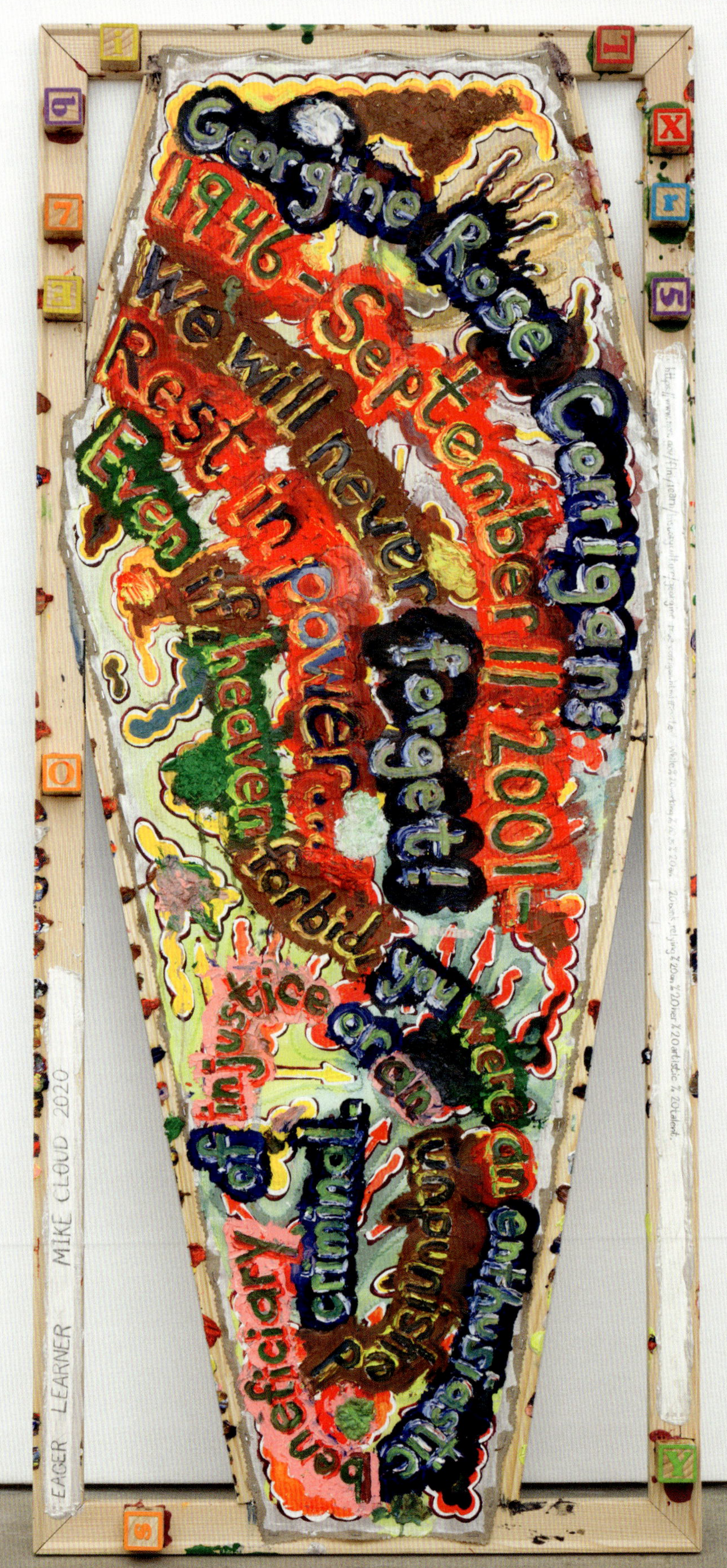
Georgine Rose Corrigan!
1946 - September 11 2001!
We will never forget!
Rest in power...
Even if heaven forbid you were an unpunished
beneficiary of injustice & criminal
EAGER LEARNER   MIKE CLOUD 2020

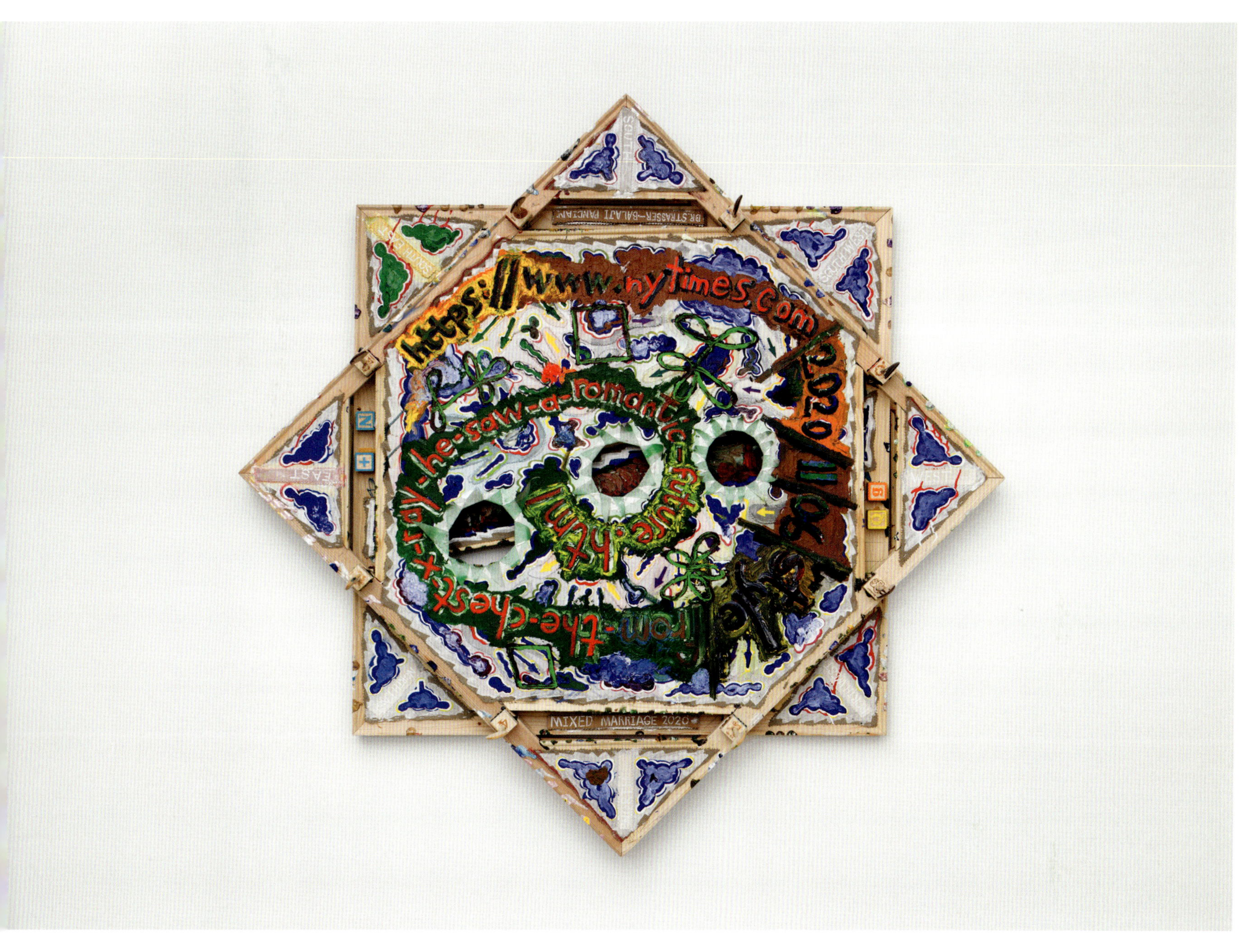

Hero Portrait Georgine Carrigan
2020
Oil on canvas and mixed media
30 × 70 × 1 ½ in / 76.2 × 177.8 × 3.8 cm
Courtesy of the Landing Gallery
© Mike Cloud, 2020
Photo by Joshua White

*Mixed Marriage Dr. Strasser
and Balaji Pandian*
2020
Oil on canvas and mixed media
71 × 71 × 7 in / 180.3 × 180.3 × 17.8 cm
Courtesy of the Landing Gallery
© Mike Cloud, 2020
Photo by Joshua White

Torkwase Dyson
MFA 2003

Torkwase Dyson (b. 1973, Chicago, IL; lives and works in Beacon, NY)

One of the unifying subjects explored by the artists in this exhibition is their focus on the body, whether depicted in representational painting and sculpture, or implied in abstract forms and structures as in the work of Torkwase Dyson. Both approaches are steeped in a reconsideration of the canon of art history from the perspective of race, ethnicity, gender, and politics. Dyson acknowledges Yale painting faculty members Mel Bochner and Sam Messer for contributing to her conceptual thinking about the body and space. Dyson's work investigates how our built and natural environment defines our conditions of movement. She notes that "for Black people, moving through a given environment comes with questions of belonging and a self-determination of visibility and autonomy." She terms her theoretical and artistic framework as "Black compositional thought," and is particularly drawn to narratives about how people use architectural, infrastructure, and environmental structures to liberate themselves.[1]

Dyson refers to the geometric shapes she uses as "Hypershapes," which, as she notes, "collectively speak to the distance, magnitude and force of Black movement toward freedom." The Hypershapes constitute a symbolic shape language that is connected to these narratives rather than exist as pure autonomous form. These symbols include the curve, which references the small compartment of the ship in which the famous fugitive slave Anthony Burns escaped to Boston from Virginia in 1854, a space so cramped that he was stuck in the same position, without room for movement, for over three weeks. The square references the enslaved Henry "Box" Brown, who escaped to freedom by mailing himself in a wooden crate in 1849 from Virginia to abolitionists in Philadelphia; and the triangle recalls the tiny garret where Harriet Jacobs hid for seven years to escape her enslaver's sexual advances; a space so low she could not stand up in it. As Dyson notes, she landed on the trapezoid (conjoining the box and the triangle) and has combined hard-edged abstraction and gesture by way of art history to think of modernism through the lens of nomadicity, liberating movement, and most of all consciousness and perception of space.

NSU Art Museum commissioned Dyson to create a new installation for this exhibition. The work is part of her ongoing series of sculptural installations, "I Belong to the Distance," composed of geometric and biomorphic shapes.

The monument is dedicated to Henry "Box" Brown, whose ingenuity is referenced in the giant box-like trapezoids. Dyson selected the site of the Museum's soaring atrium with its sloping white terrazzo floor for her installation. The atrium, designed by Modernist architect Edward Larrabee Barnes, echoes the curved shape of a ship, thereby incorporating another one of Dyson's hyperspaces into the work. The atrium's curved walls and spiraling staircase provide viewers with multiple perspectives and experiences of the installation, which combines hard-edged geometry of the structure with the intimate surface marks that visibly record the artist's hand in relation to drawing, movement, and scale. The initial approach to this monumental work is from the top of the slope where the geometrical shapes seem to align to produce the illusion of extreme pictorial perspective that projects the viewers' gaze forward into the distance, and thereby, the future. The sloped floor adds to the disorienting effect of a rising and falling horizon line, and, like the spiral staircase, conditions the viewer's movement, elevation, and descent in relation to the structure.

[1] *Torkwase Dyson* (Derneberg, Germany: Hall Art Foundation|Schloss Derneberg Museum, 2021), p. 21.

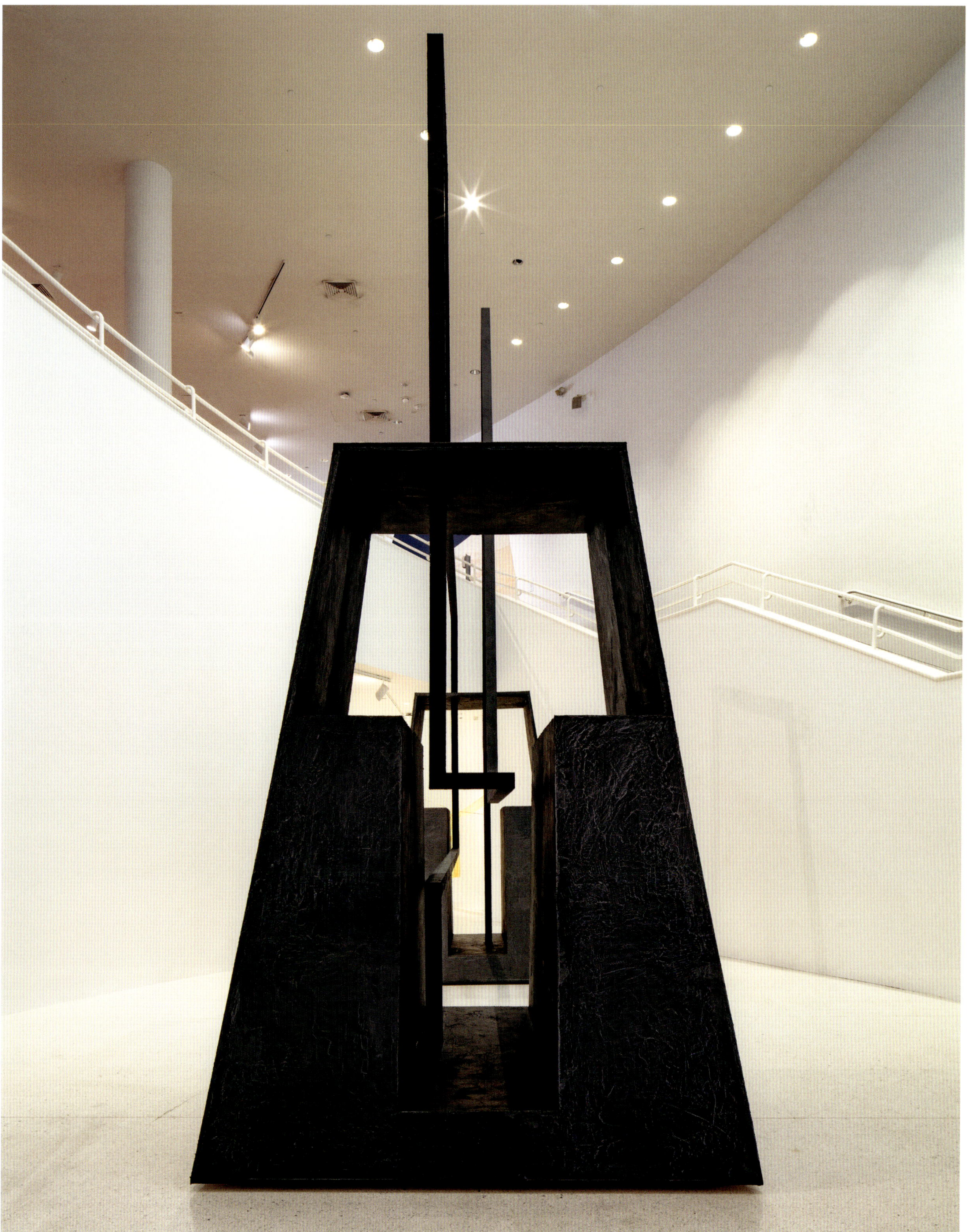

Shoshanna Weinberger
MFA 2003

Shoshanna Weinberger (b. 1973, Kingston, Jamaica; lives and works in Newark, NJ)

Shoshanna Weinberger came to America as a young child; her work explores a history navigating the standards, consequential implications, and experiences of racial identity and external perception. She connects this experience with that of W. E. B. Du Bois' concept of Double Consciousness. "Whether I was aware of it or not, 'otherness' has been at the center of my consciousness," notes Weinberger. "My early ideals of beauty were shaped through art history and advertisements in fashion magazines. These images were presented as the heroic bodies." But they did not look like her, which ultimately influenced the way she viewed herself.

Weinberger's first year at the Yale School of Art was especially difficult, as she wanted to explore her identity in her work, but was discouraged from doing so by some of her instructors, with whom it was difficult to converse. As a result, she connected and sought out dialogue among her peers. After graduating, she embarked on creating work that speaks to the "complexities of heritage, mutation, myth, and hybridity, as a Caribbean-American." Her studio practice explores this cultural history of female exposé, presentation, invisible blackness, and excessive notions of beauty. In the "Strangefruit" series included in the *Lux et Veritas* exhibition, Weinberger references "how marginalized bodies, and that of her own body, have historically been invented, categorized, controlled, excluded, exploited, and surveilled in the spaces they inhabit."

Shoshanna Weinberger:
The work in Lux et Veritas *comes from a series entitled* Strangefruit. *The title of this series comes from the famous jazz song that Billie Holiday sung. I didn't realize that a Jewish schoolteacher, Abel Meeropol wrote the poem, "Strange Fruit," after seeing a photograph of a lynching in a newspaper. When you're doing research, you connect things. You connect yourself to history and how you fit into it. I connected the song's creators with that of my own: my father is a Jewish man from Clifton, New Jersey. He seeded the poem, "Strange Fruit," into my mother, an Afro-Caribbean woman, who birthed the song "me" into existence. I connect the two words in the song's title to make it one "Strangefruit"… I am a Strangefruit. It's about a marginalization that comes with being ambiguous and peripheral and categorized.*

Potbelly Porn Star and the Rise of Bacon
2012–2013
Gouache on paper
60 × 74 ¼ in / 152.4 × 188.6 cm
Courtesy of the artist
© Shoshanna Weinberger

Following pages

Ménage à Trois
2013
Gouache on paper
60 × 72 ¼ in / 152.4 × 183.5 cm
Courtesy of the artist
© Shoshanna Weinberger

Muffin Top Banana Bottom
2014
Gouache on paper
60 × 74 in / 152.4 × 188 cm
Courtesy of Carol Jazzar Contemporary, Miami
© Shoshanna Weinberger

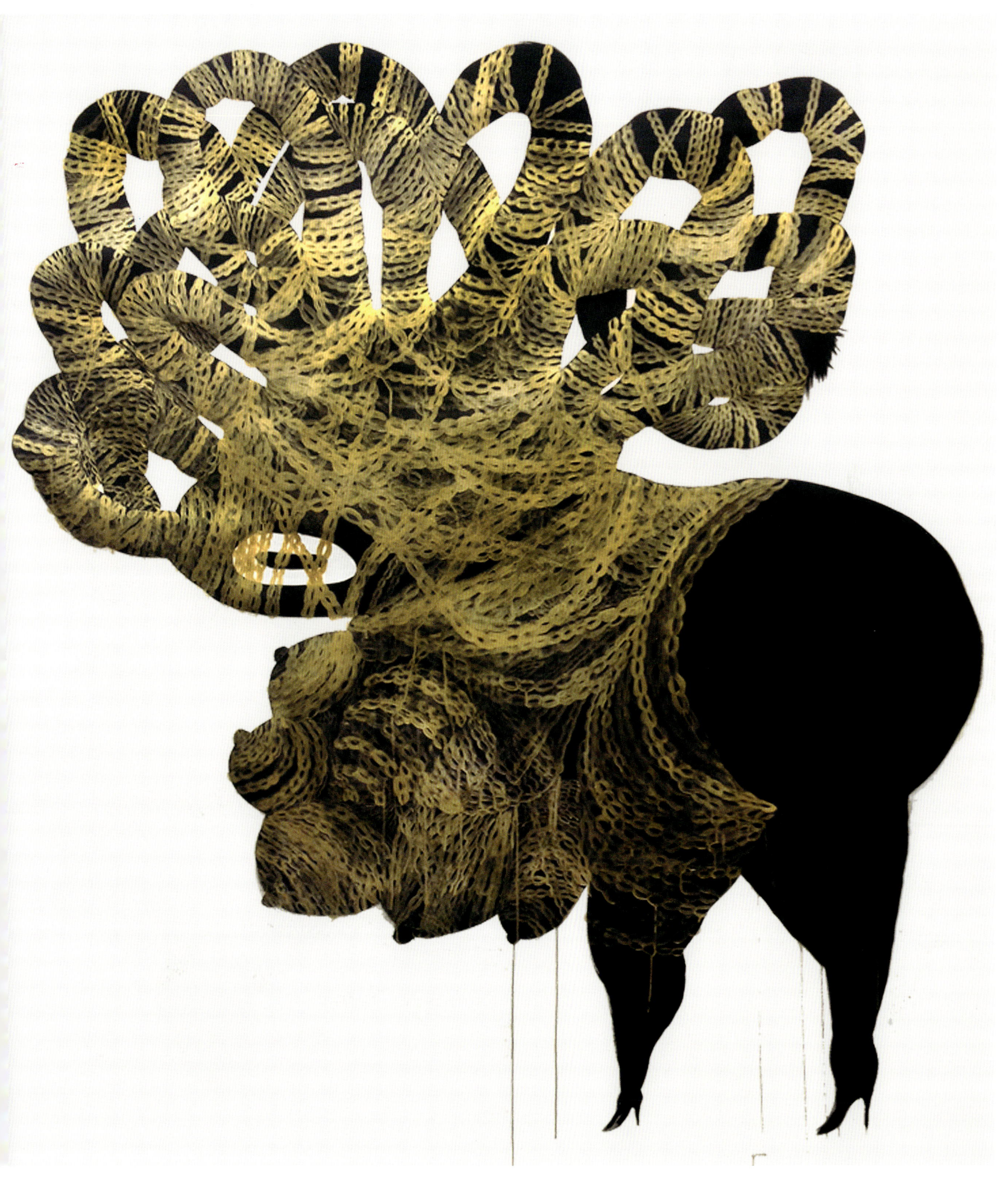

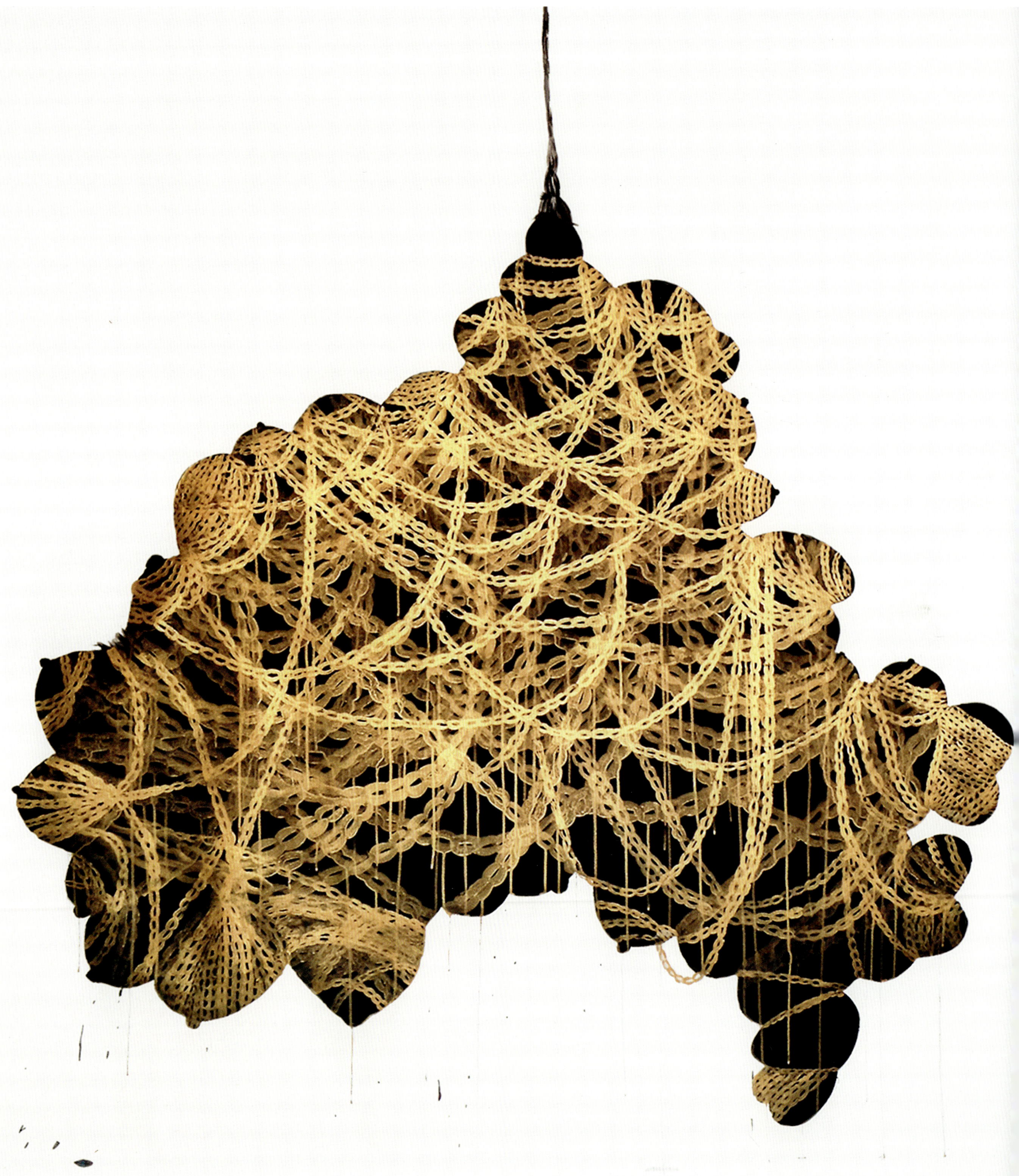

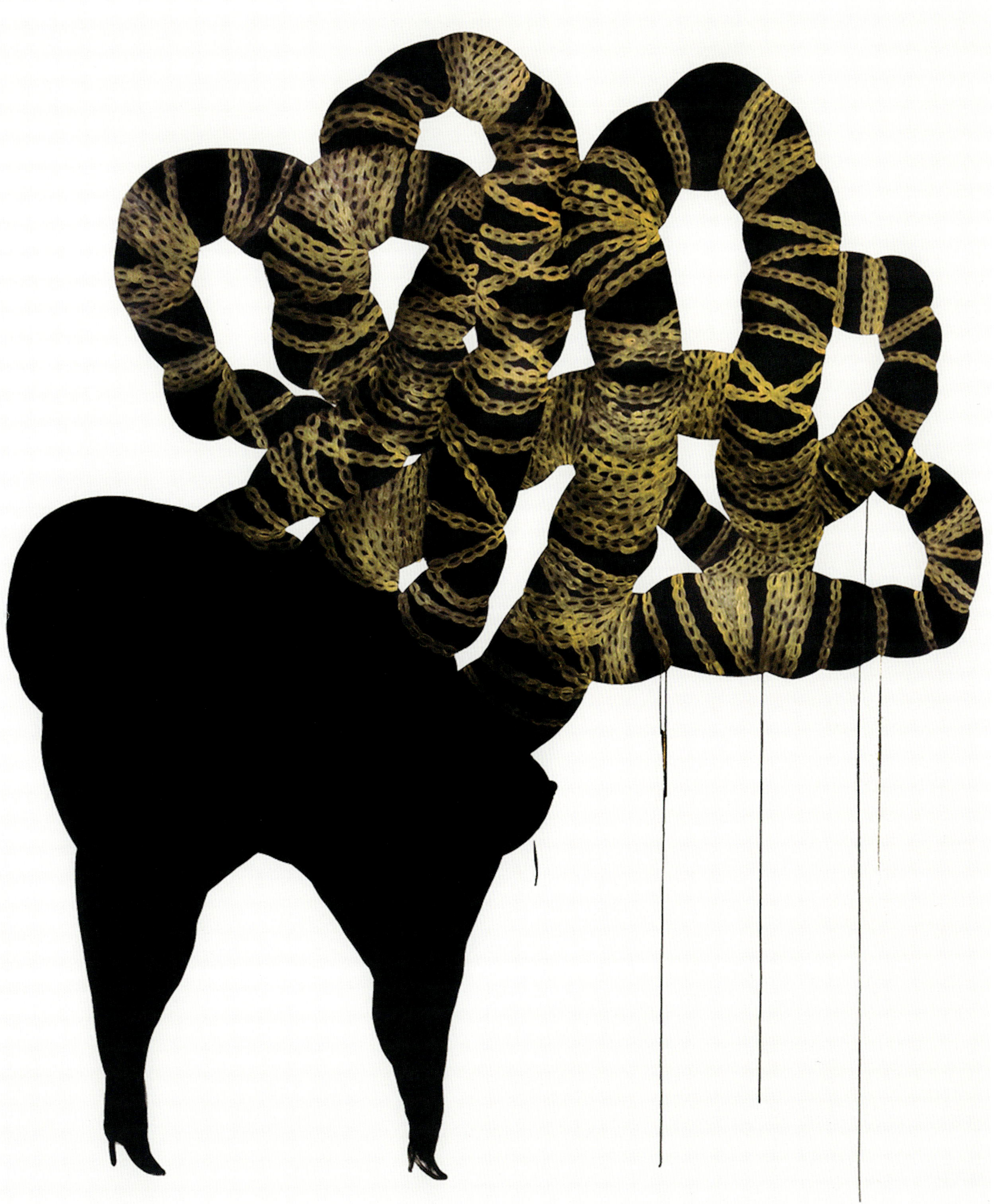

william cordova
MFA 2004

william cordova (b. 1971, Lima, Peru; lives and works in Miami, FL, New York, NY, and Lima, Peru)[1]

william cordova's practice has been motivated by a creative engagement in architecture, geometry, and history, that has also shaped his world view. He is an interdisciplinary cultural practitioner interested in the roots of abstraction, history of textile encoding, and non-linear narratives. He illuminates the synthesis of memory, ritual, and mythology to disrupt, challenge, and reassess definitions of our collective landscape. Although he was a Painting student at Yale, he brought the perspective of a documentary filmmaker to his practice, recording everything in his path, including documenting the student experience at the Yale during the first decade of the millennium and through today.

cordova describes his large work on paper *quotidian palimpsest*, as a convergence of numerous signifiers, "The harmonic fluidity of improvisational sounds (suggested by the pile of speakers), geometric principles of ancient symmetry and spirituality all of which intersect within the landscape of the piece." As suggested by the title it is a palimpsest with layers of images from different times and cultures. A rendering of the "Maison Dom-Ino," an open-floor structure designed by the Modern architect and urban planner Le Corbusier (1914–1915) dominates the composition. Le Corbusier's design was a revolutionary and utopian blueprint for a prefabricated domain that was intended to solve the housing crisis in Europe after the First World War. Like a domino, the modular structures could be joined end to end. The traces of graffiti marking the gilded surface of the work acknowledge the habitual clandestine scrawls seen throughout urban public spaces, which cordova makes his own by using custom-designed alphabets and acronyms. It also makes an ethnographic reference to

Andean Inca architecture, culture, gold, silver, geometry, spiritual and religious ideologies.

It was through Barkley Hendricks, whom he met at Yale, that he reimagined the use of gold leaf in his work to elevate the quotidian. cordova's gold field brings to mind this precious material's use in architecture, religious icons, and medieval manuscripts, as well as its presence in the modern period from the late nineteenth-century paintings by Gustav Klimt to Andy Warhol's *Gold Marilyn Monroe* (1962) and Hendricks' *Lawdy Mama* (1969).

The Inca riches lured the Spanish conquistador Francisco Pizarro to Peru, which he and Spanish soldiers invaded in 1532. Gold as an alchemical, malleable, and symbolic element, both monetarily and spiritually valuable, is also a significant reference in this and other works by cordova that incorporate gold leaf.

cordova's early work from the late 1990s (created prior to attending Yale), primarily consisted of intimate drawings of reclaimed objects, boom boxes, and other music references, toys, architectural structures, airplanes, and contrasting aerial and ground-level views. These drawings suggested an ongoing autobiographical journal of his youth in Miami—his arrival by airplane, the influence of music and hip-hop, and toys rescued from the garbage heap. By 2000 he began to realize these two-dimensional drawings in sculptural form. The sculpture *machu picchu after dark* originated in cordova's 2003 solo exhibition, *No More Lonely Nights*, at the Museum of Contemporary Art North Miami (organized by the museum's Director and Chief Curator Bonnie Clearwater). The second iteration was included in cordova's thesis exhibition at Yale in 2004, which also included work by Sculpture students Hewitt and Otsubo. This version of the sculpture dates to 2014 with some additional modifications.

machu picchu after dark refers to the sacred Inca citadel high atop the Andes Mountains. cordova's monument is built entirely with stacked found speakers using Andean masonry

technology. His sculptural interpretation alludes to the "temporal complexities inherent in architecture; race, identity, history, and nationalism" as suggested by the dedication of this work to Victoria Santa Cruz (a Peruvian choreographer, composer, and activist, credited for preserving, articulating, and reintroducing Afro-Peruvian contributions in the 1960s), Macario Sakay (a late nineteenth-century Filipino revolutionary who fought against the USA annexation of the Philippines), and Damion Thurston (aka McMadness, who along with DJ Laze was instrumental as the *Vicious Bass* duo, in developing early Miami Freestyle Rap). A small devotional altar at the base of the sculpture assembles sacred items that include stacks of vinyl LP jackets representing various genres of music from different decades, all alluding to the use of music as a tool to express subversive topics. Those include Peter Tosh's *Wanted Dread & Alive* (1981) and *Geto Boys* (1990) with its self-titled mugshot LP cover, The Richard Davis Trio, *Songs for Wounded Knee* (1973), and salsa musician Willie Colon, *La Gran Fuga* (1971) that represents the musician's face on an FBI wanted poster. The car rear view mirror incorporated into this tableau, suggests the theme of the "infinite past" and self-reflection that novelist Toni Morrison frequently addressed as a constructive means to meditate on the pursuit of a better present and future. This is a recurring theme in cordova's work.[2]

---

[1] william cordova: *Now's the Time: Narratives of Southern Alchemy*, by Maria Elena Ortiz et al. (London: Perez Art Museum Miami and Del Monico Books - prestel, 2018)

[2] Toni Morrison, *Conversations,* ed. Carolyn C. Denard (Jackson, Mississippi: University Press of Mississippi, 2008), p. 27. cordova made a direct reference to Toni Morrison's "Infinite Past" as the title for a group exhibition he organized—*The Past is More Infinite than the Future*, at the alternative space Under the Bridge Art Space, North Miami in 2018. (This alternative space was founded by artist Lou Anne Colodny.)

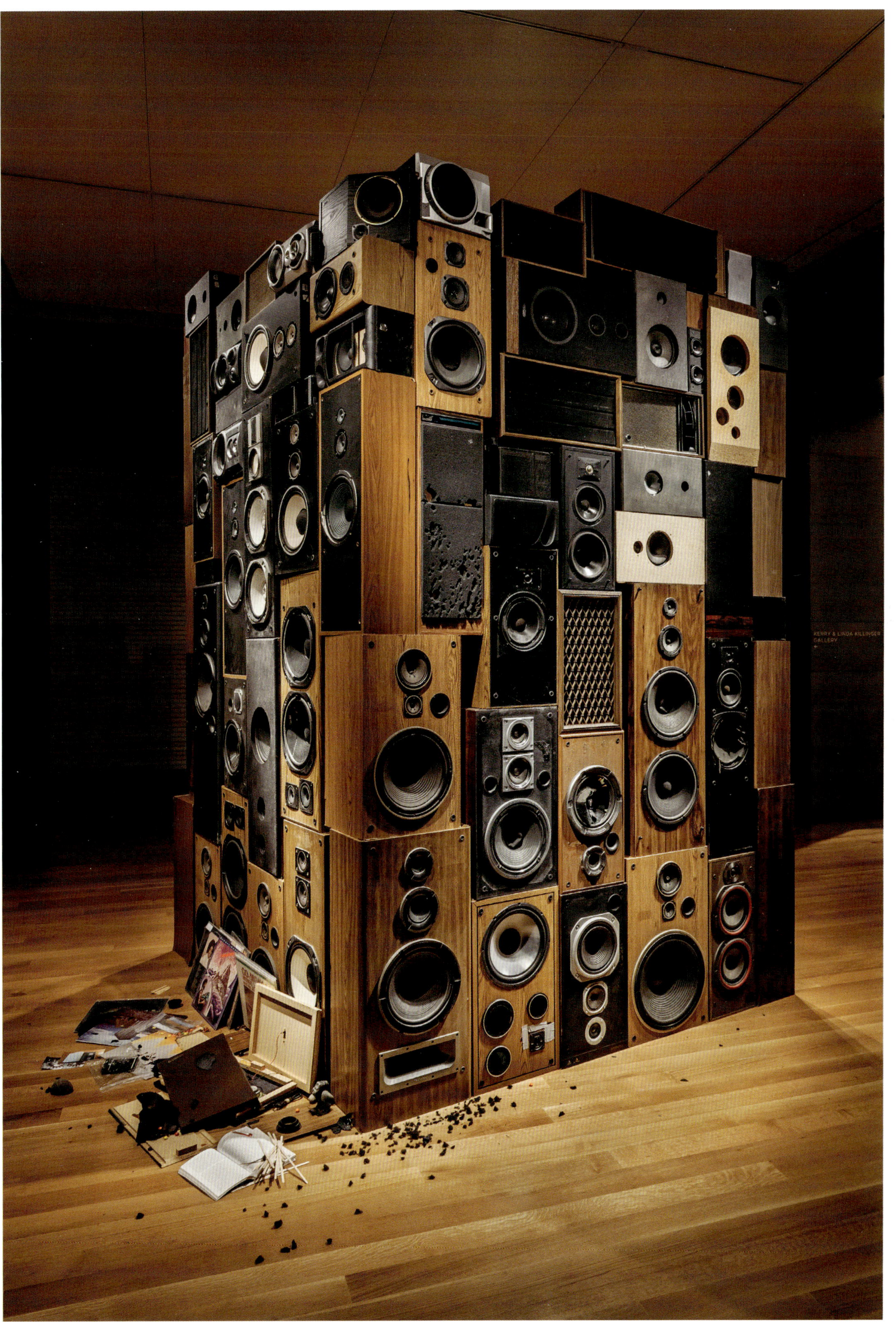

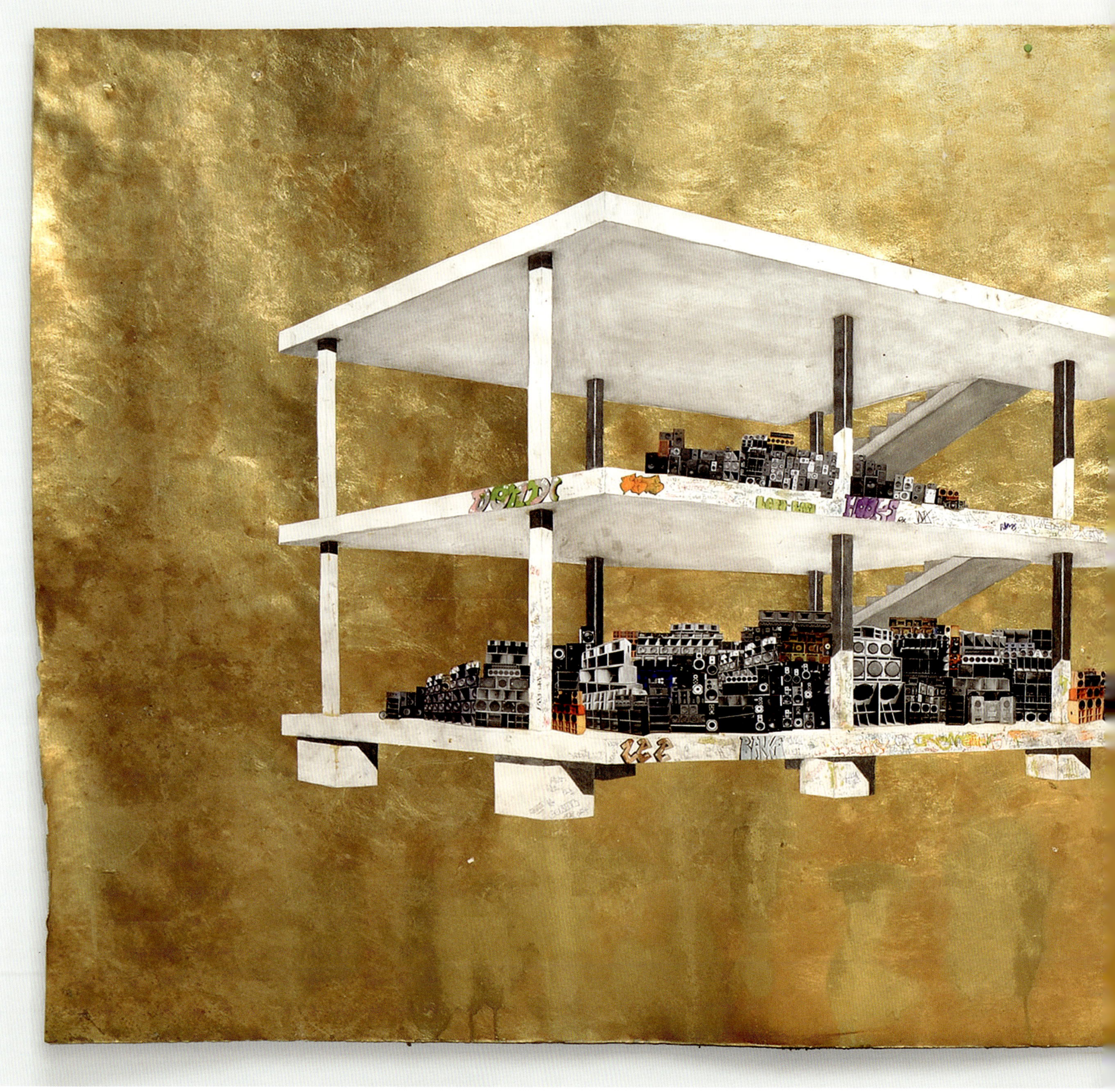

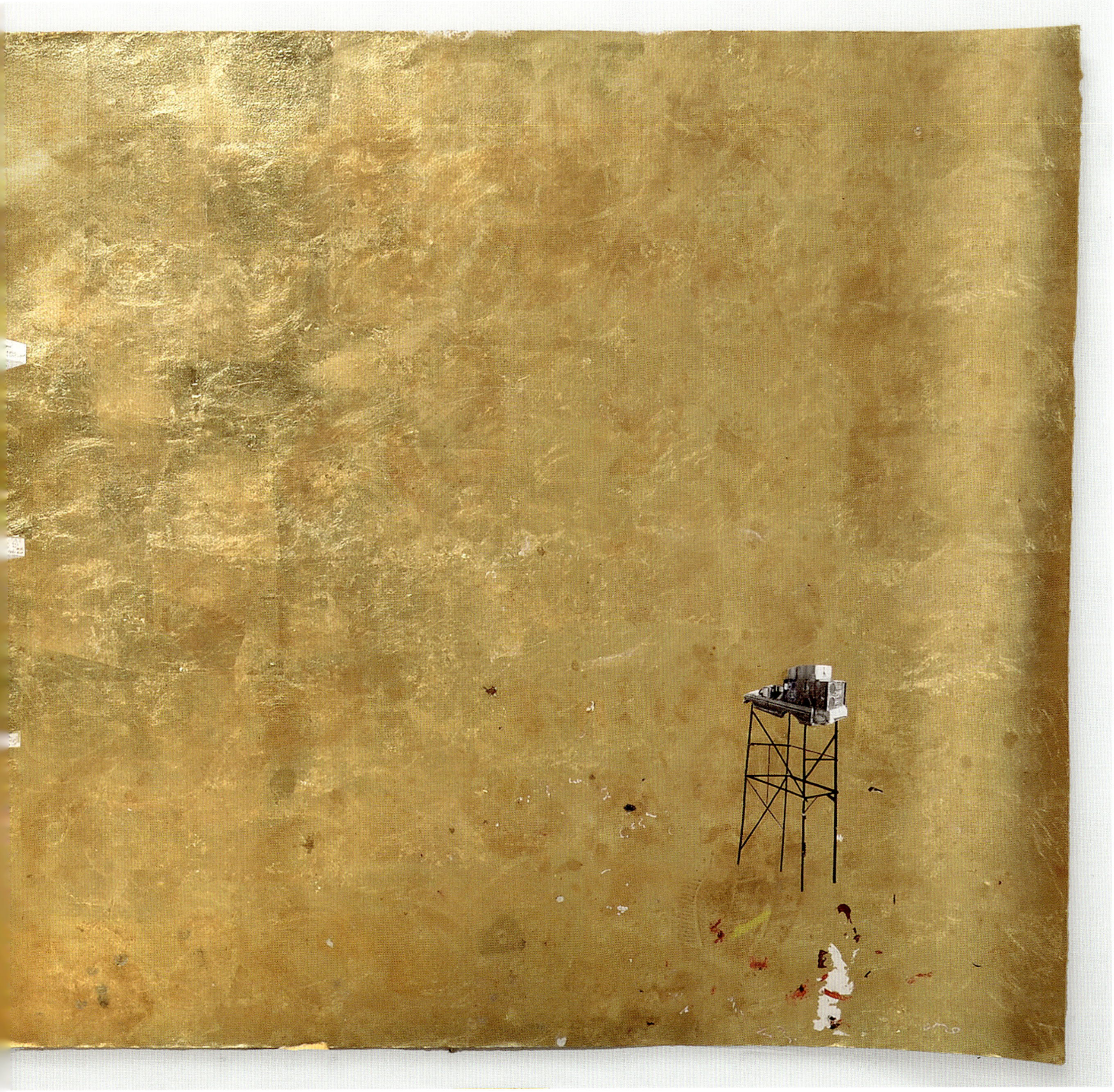

Leslie Hewitt
MFA 2004

Leslie Hewitt (b. 1977, Saint Albans, Queens, NY; lives and works in New York, NY)

After completing her BFA at Cooper Union and attending New York University as a Clark Fellow in Africana Studies and Cultural Studies, Leslie Hewitt was accepted to the Yale School of Art for her Master's in the Department of Sculpture, led by artist Jessica Stockholder.

Today, Hewitt considers her work an amalgam of all her interests. Although she works in a variety of mediums, the unifying characteristics are construction and space and time (elements formally associated with sculpture.) Her photographs are of still lifes which she constructs in her studio. She creates meaning through the juxtaposition and framing of the various components in these compositions, and her choice of images reference time. For example, her photographs of flowers suggest the transience of life and are reminiscent of the seventeenth-century Dutch tradition of still life painting, with flowers being a visual trope of the genre.

For Hewitt, the desire to allow for multiple historiographic moments to converge is essential. For example, her interest in the seventeenth century includes the entanglements of the Atlantic slave trade and that of post-colonial texts of the twentieth century. In her photograph *Topologies (Fanon mildly out of focus)* (2017), Hewitt brings Frantz Fanon's book *The Wretched of the Earth: The Handbook for the Black Revolution*—first published in English from French in 1963—into the viewer's present. Her minimal sculptures are physical constructions that reveal themselves over time from various perspectives, providing a formal counterpoint to the socio-political and art historical references that inhabit her work. The materials Hewitt uses for her sculptures and still life arrangements appeal to the viewer's sense of touch and curiosity. As she notes, the objects raise such questions as "What is this? What does it feel like? How does the photograph describe surface? Time? Even if it's closed, a book has a material history."[1]

Leslie Hewitt, *RAM*, 2011:
Walking into the Yale Art Gallery in 2004, while studying Art History with Kellie Jones, who opened my mind to learning about the intricacies of early American decorative arts, I was drawn to the uncanny craftsmanship of this seventeenth-century pine-and-maple bible box as part of the collection. In addition to the details of size, date, and material, the object label included geographical location, this was intriguing as it was only part of a longer conversation about place.

[1] *Leslie Hewitt*, ed. Cay Sophie Rabinowitz; Nana Adusei-Poku, Lisa Lee, and Eva Respini (New York: Osmos, 2018), p. 125

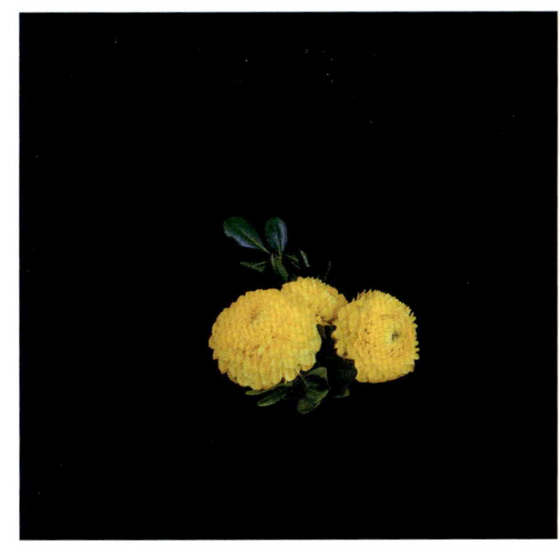

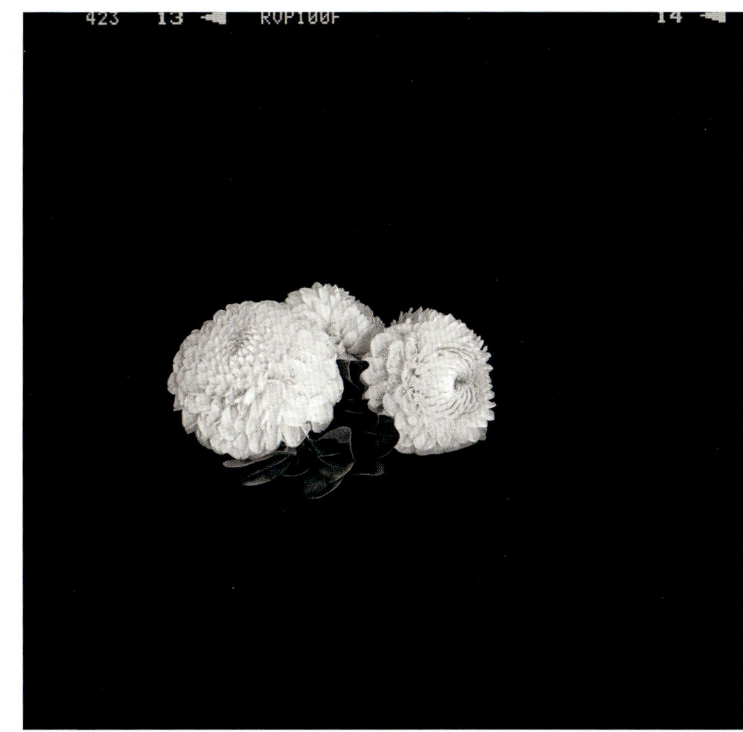

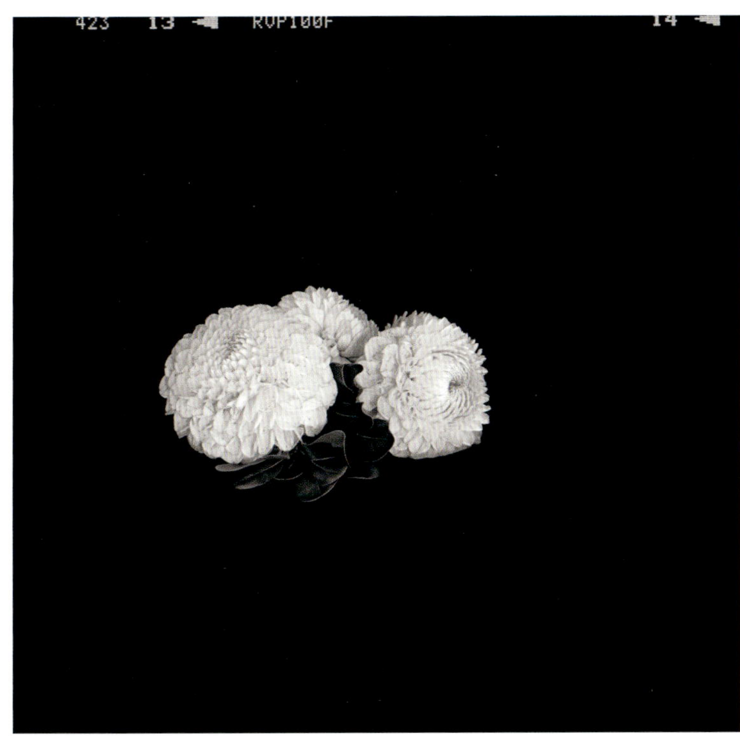

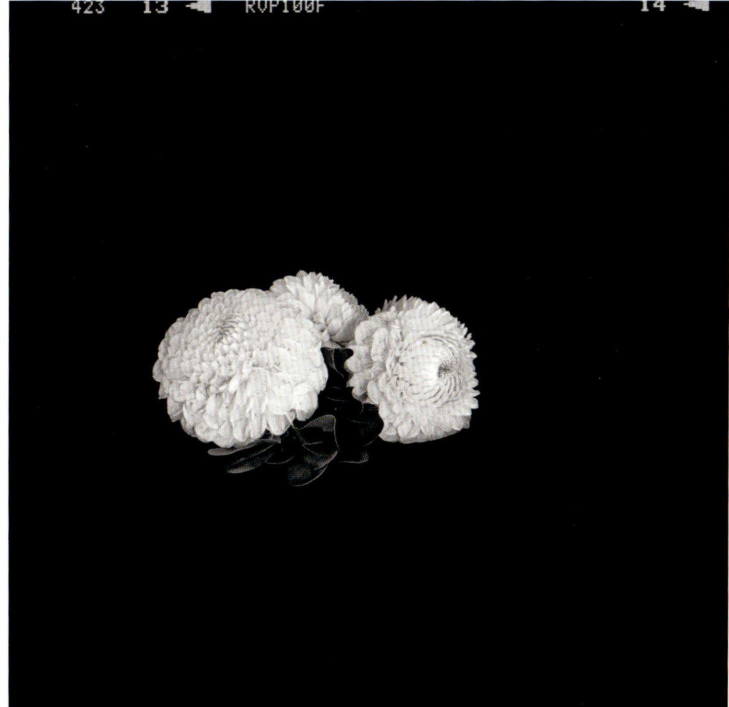

Color Study_01
2016
Digital chromogenic print
15 × 15 in / 38.1 × 38.1 cm
Courtesy of the artist and Perrotin
© Leslie Hewitt
Photo by Guillaume Ziccarelli

Aura
2016
Digital chromogenic print
30 × 30 in / 76.2 × 76.2 cm
Courtesy of the artist and Perrotin
© Leslie Hewitt
Photo by Guillaume Ziccarelli

Screen
2016
Digital chromogenic print
30 × 30 in / 76.2 × 76.2 cm
Courtesy of the artist and Perrotin
© Leslie Hewitt
Photo by Guillaume Ziccarelli

Object
2016
Digital chromogenic print
30 × 30 in / 76.2 × 76.2 cm
Courtesy of the artist and Perrotin
© Leslie Hewitt
Photo by Guillaume Ziccarelli

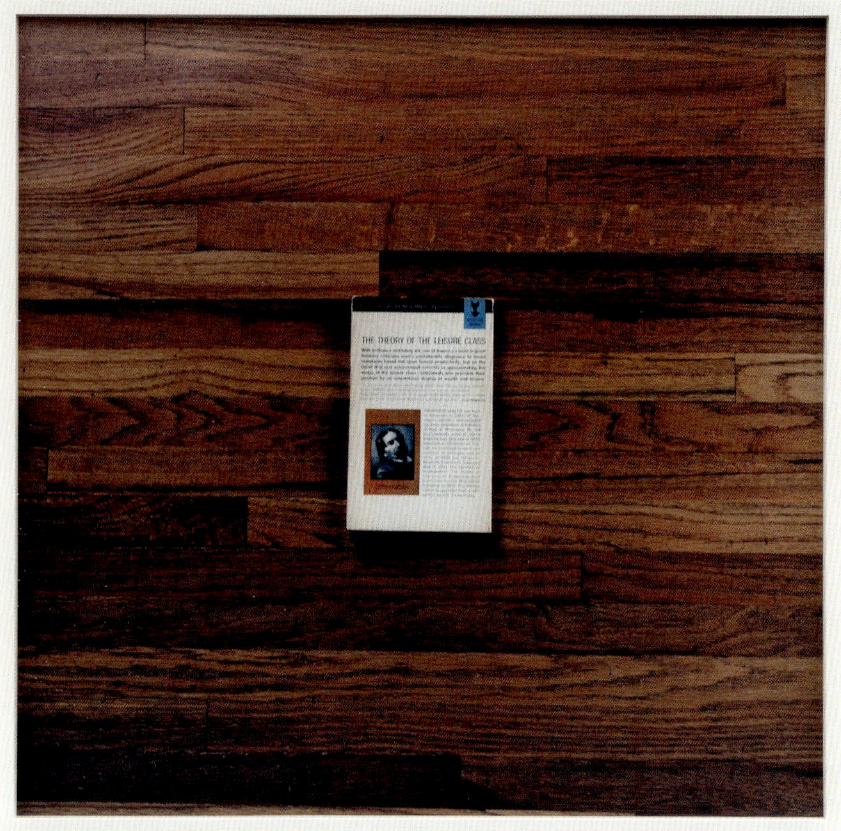

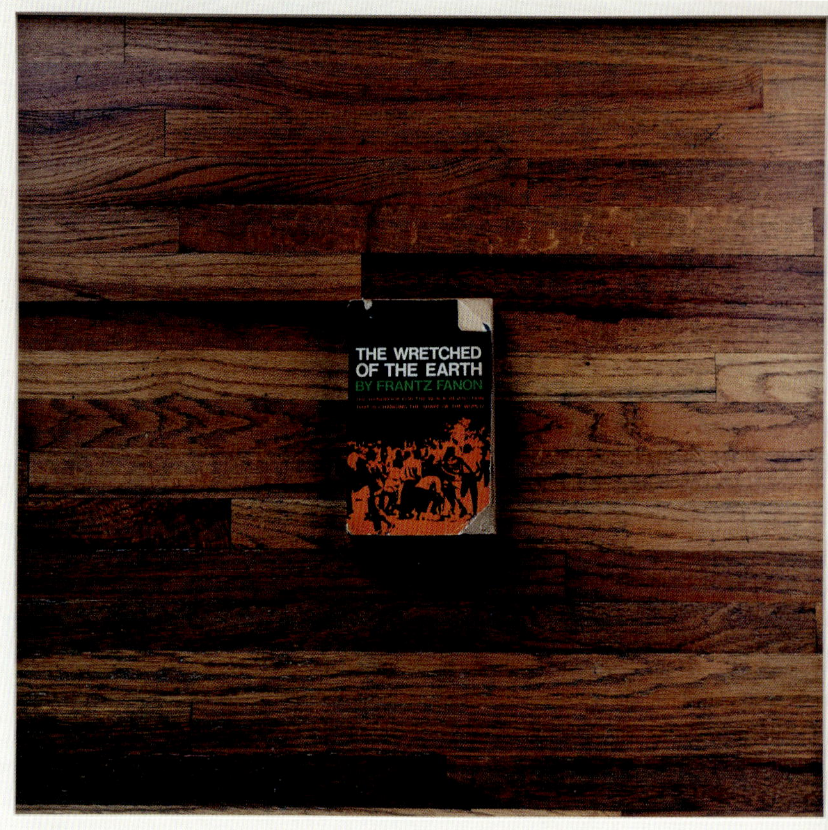

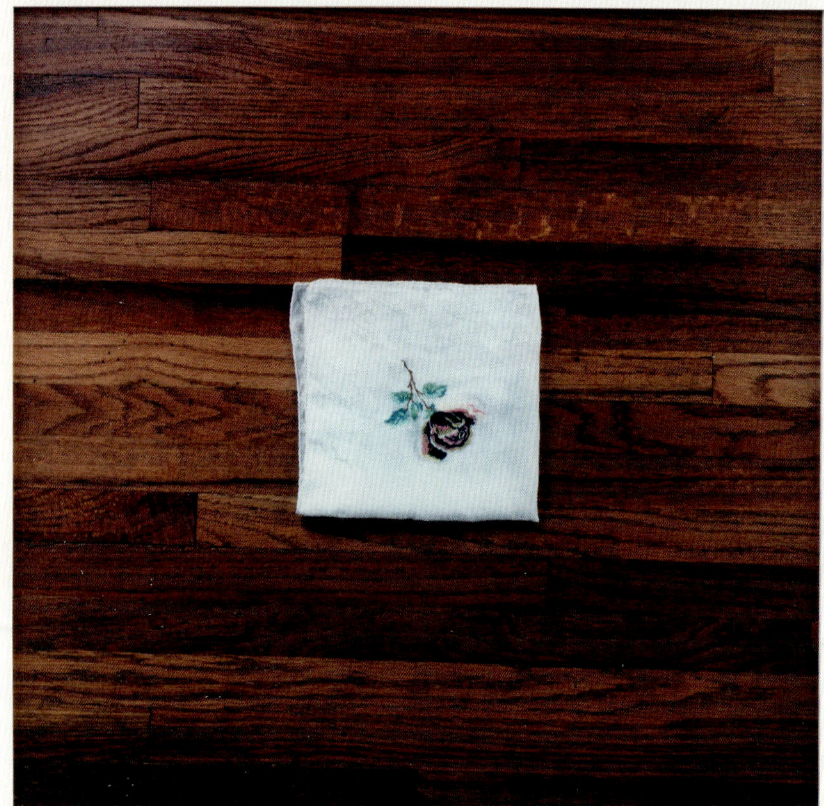

Above

Topologies (Veblen with camera shake)
2017
Traditional chromogenic print
30 × 30 in / 76.2 × 76.2 cm
Courtesy of the artist and Perrotin
© Leslie Hewitt
Photo by Guillaume Ziccarelli

Topologies (Fanon mildly out of focus)
2017
Traditional chromogenic print
30 × 30 in / 76.2 × 76.2 cm
Courtesy of the artist and Perrotin
© Leslie Hewitt
Photo by Guillaume Ziccarelli

Bottom

Topologies (folded memory object)
2017
Traditional chromogenic print
30 × 30 in / 76.2 × 76.2 cm
Courtesy of the artist and Perrotin
© Leslie Hewitt
Photo by Claire Dorn

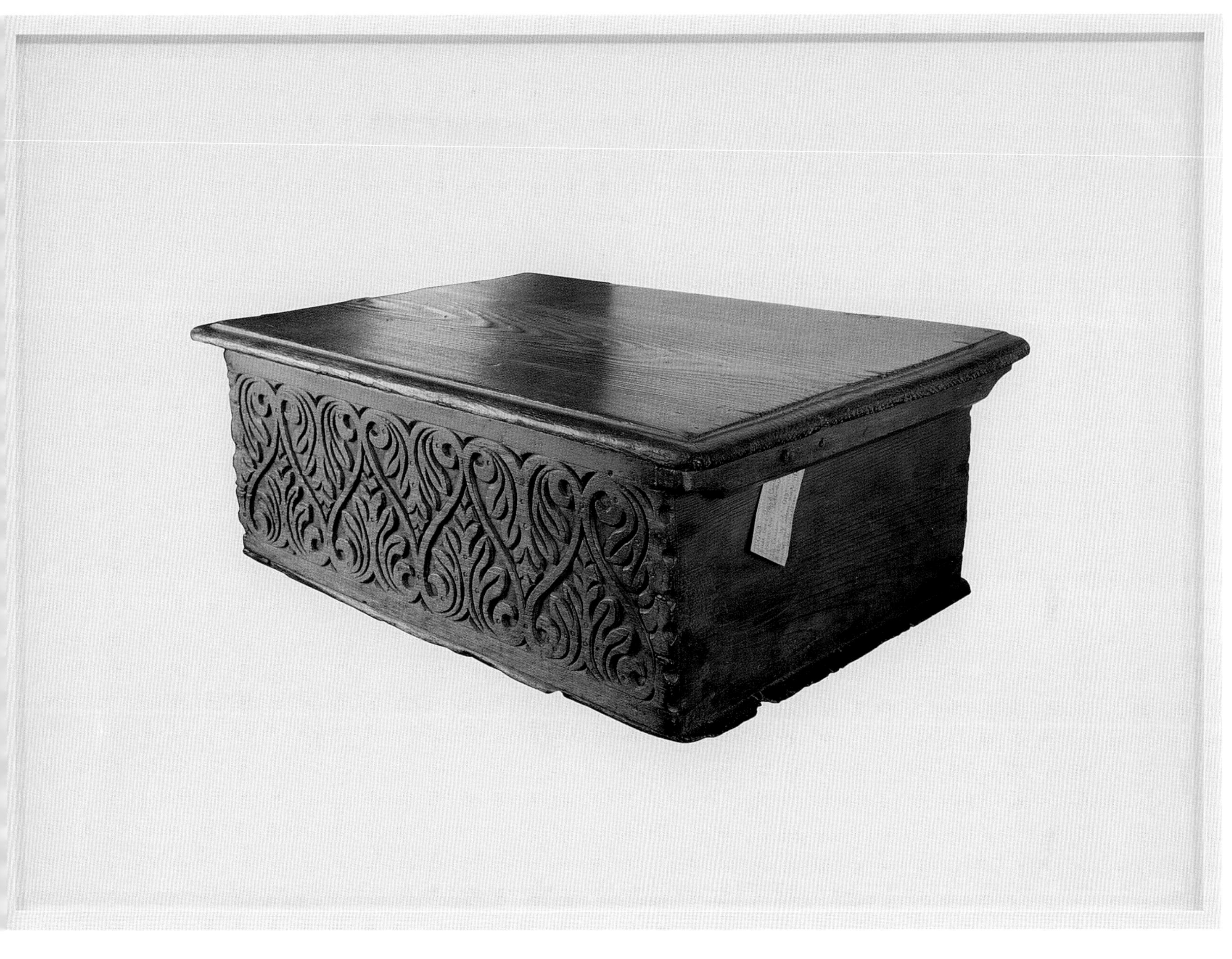

RAM
2017
Digital chromogenic print
30 × 40 in / 76.2 × 101.6 cm
Courtesy of the artist and Perrotin
© Leslie Hewitt
Photo by Guillaume Ziccarelli

111

Wardell Milan
MFA 2004

Wardell Milan (b. 1977, Knoxville, TN; lives in New York City, NY)[1]

Wardell Milan was the first Black artist to enter the Yale School of Art's Department of Photography since Dawoud Bey (MFA Photography 1993). Milan received early encouragement as a child in his artistic pursuits from his parents and teachers. After completing his BFA at the University of Tennessee in 2001, he immersed himself further into his practice as an artist-in-residence at the Skowhegan School of Painting and Sculpture. With his extensive art education, he entered Yale with the goal of "discovering" his inner self. As was the case with other artists in this exhibition, he reached out to fellow students, particularly Sculpture major Hewitt and Painting major cordova, for the guidance and perspective he sought and expected from his academic advisors. He recalls that the critiques at Yale could be brutal and at the time he lacked the words to defend his work. In retrospect, these confrontations forced him to hone his skills at standing up for his work.

Literature, cinema, and art history are important sources for Milan's work. At Yale, he transformed the cardboard models he had been making since childhood into elaborate dioramas, dense with surreal narratives, which he dramatically lighted and photographed as in *I'm trying to keep my faith. But, I'm searching for more. Somewhere I can be safe*. In this cinematic photomontage, Milan uses mostly personal images to build his narrative, with the exception of the rainbow-colored Skittles candy in the foreground, which has become a public symbol of the innocence of the unarmed Black teenager Trayvon Martin, whose pocket contents consisted only of a bag of candy and some personal items when he was fatally shot ten years ago in Sanford, Florida.

Milan's collage series *Battle Royale*, takes its title from the opening chapter in Ralph Ellison's 1952 novel *Invisible Man*, in which the story's Black male protagonist narrates the surreal and violent turn of events that occurred when he arrives to give a speech to town leaders accepting the college scholarship they have awarded him, only to be forced to compete in a bloody boxing match with other young Black males. In this series, Milan cinematically cuts and fragments the photographs of the boxers, suggesting the sequential movement and time lapses within these dramatic scenes.

[1] *Wardell Milan:Between Late Summer and Early Fall*, ed. Cay Sophie Rabinowitz; Alvin Hall, Carter Foster, and Leslie Hewitt (New York: Osmos, 2015).

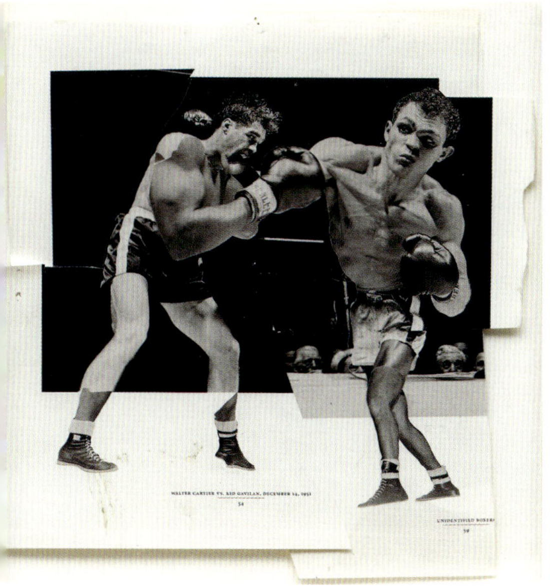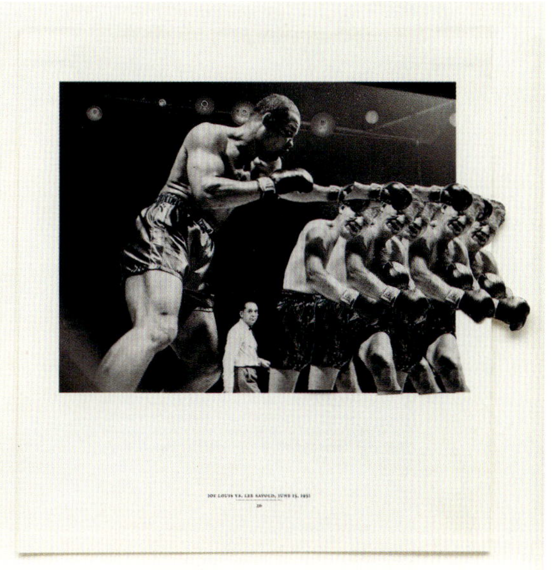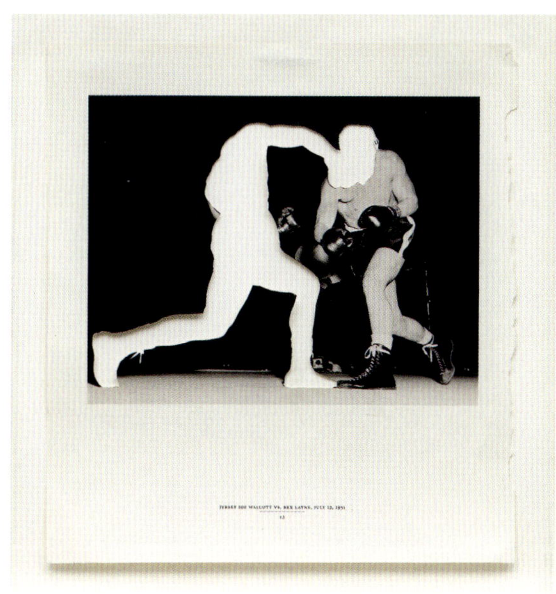

Battle Royale
2007
20 individual mixed media paper collages
8 ¾ × 10 in / 22.2 × 25.4 cm
Courtesy of the artist and David Nolan
Gallery
© Wardell Milan

113

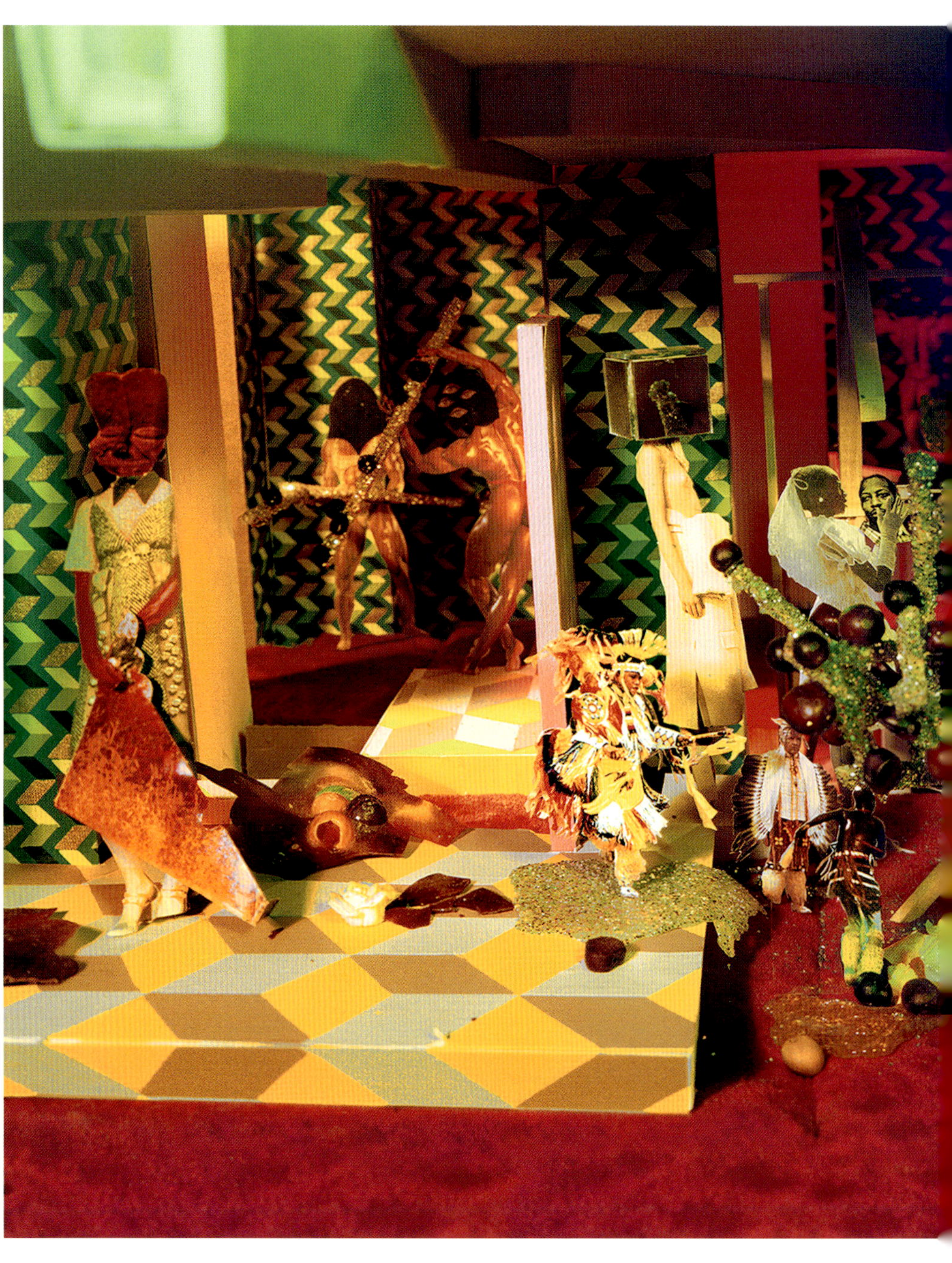

*I'm trying to keep my faith. But, I'm searching
for more. Somewhere I can be safe*
2017–2018
Digital C-print, mounted on Dibond
44 × 98 in / 111.8 × 248.9 cm
Courtesy of the artist and David Nolan
Gallery
© Wardell Milan

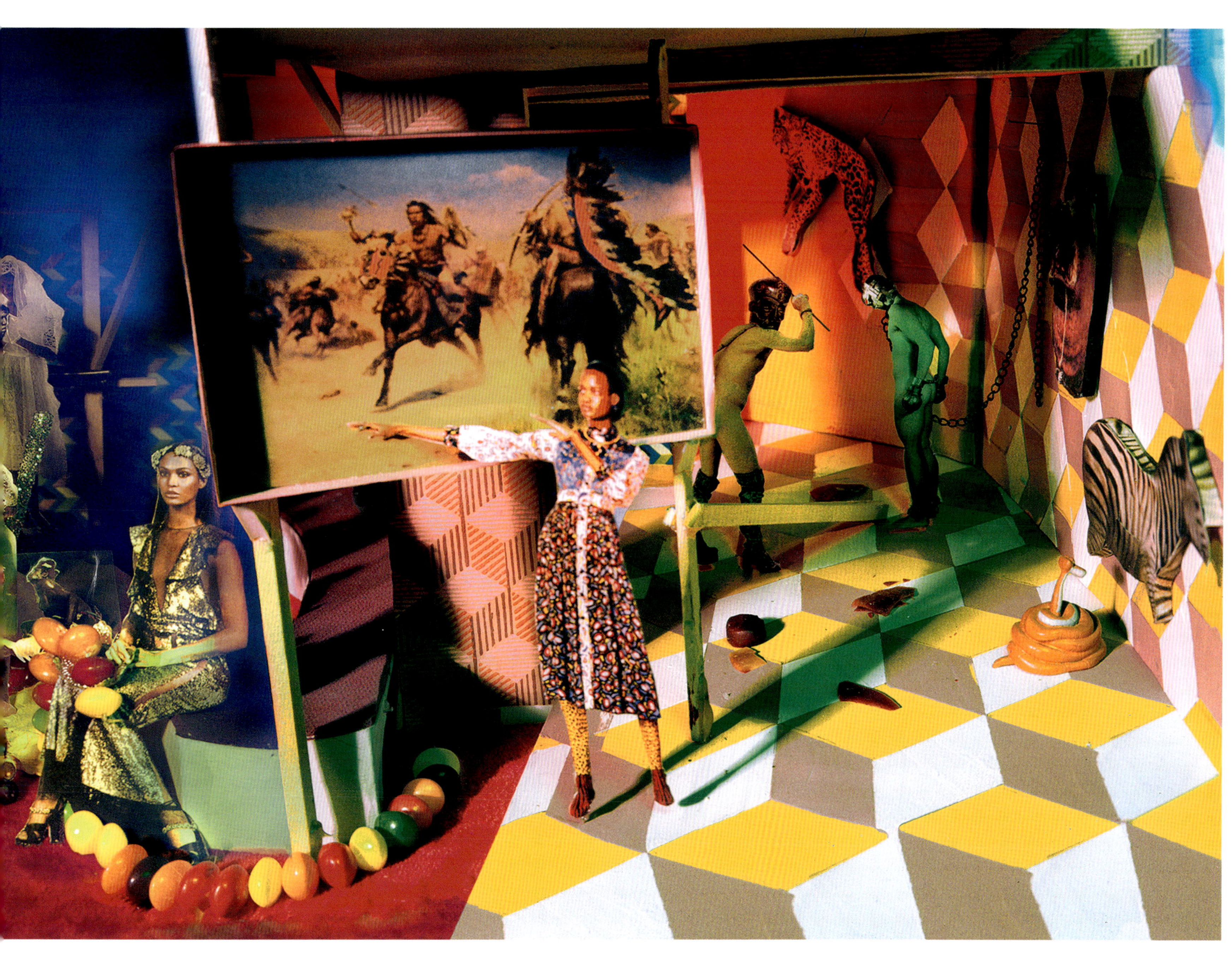

Mamiko Otsubo
MFA 2004

Mamiko Otsubo (b. 1974, Nishinomiya, Japan; lives and works in Los Angeles, CA)

Although the trend among art schools in the United States in the latter half of the twentieth century was to combine the various art disciplines, the Yale School of Art not only upheld these distinct disciplines but housed the Department of Painting and Printmaking and Department of Sculpture in separate buildings. Students were also cognizant of a clear hierarchy among the various mediums at Yale, with painting at its pinnacle. As a Sculpture student, Mamiko Otsubo found it difficult to gain access to the Painting faculty, which had the largest enrollment of students. However, under the leadership of Director Jessica Stockholder, the Sculpture department was the spot where artists with multiple interests in other disciplines—including performance—had freedom to explore. Otsubo and Hewitt ran the Visiting Artist program for the Sculpture department. In addition to visiting artists who were specifically requested by the students, Stockholder also invited artists whom she thought would interest the Sculpture students. As evidenced in the *Lux et Veritas* exhibition, some of the Sculpture students share similar pursuits that took root during their time at Yale. Although distinct in appearance, both Otsubo and fellow Sculpture student Rashawn Griffin's address the way viewers navigate the space of their work and how to frame the whole structure so as to define what constitutes its inside and its outside.

Inspired by the designs of traditional Japanese tea rooms, Otsubo's sculptural structure created for the *Lux et Veritas* exhibition was conceived as a priming device to hone and quiet the viewer's attention. As the viewer walks through the structure, they are greeted by a series of sculptural works that invite them to pay attention and look further inward. Individual works contained within its interior include *Keeping Your Ear to the Ground*, a pair of bronze ears suspended from the ceiling on a steel rod, *On the Edge of the Western World*,

a mixed-media work consisting of a ceramic swimming pool attached on the surface of a mirror polished stainless panel, and *Time Traveler*, a wooden cabinet constructed in conversation with Tadashi Kimura, an Edo Sashimono master woodworker in Tokyo, Japan. The ornate natural pattern of the 200-year-old Japanese Ash is a record of the tree's specific life lived under extreme weather conditions. The bronze casts of Otsubo's fingertips embedded into the sliding doors, similarly exhibit ridges that are unique to the artist. This dense layering of information and time stands in stark contrast to its minimal Modernist proportions. As a sculpture, *Time Traveler* has an odd presence, not fully located within the present or past time. Stylistically independent, it is neither Bauhaus, nor is it quite traditionally Japanese. Rather, it appears to be containing and negotiating its several histories in real time.

Mamiko Otsubo:

I set out to make Time Traveler *after I made a very large piece that was designed to expand infinitely outward. The primary question occupying my mind was, "Does ambition always have to be expressed through 'largeness' and take up more and more territory? Can something be ambitious and expansive, but expansive inward?" I didn't originally intend to make this piece in Japan. I just had this idea of making a cabinet with sliding doors that would be unlocked by my fingerprints. I liked this funny sci-fi and/or iphone reference. I made some drawings and took them to a number of different fabricators in Los Angeles. It was hard to say why exactly, but they were all just wrong for the piece. Around the same time, my grandmother passed away, and my mother brought me a very small chest of drawers that belonged to my grandmother. It was elegant, lightweight, and surprisingly modern. She told me that this chest represented a specific type of woodworking they used to do in Japan. Each city was known for having their own specific style. This chest was made in the Edo (Tokyo) style, because that's where my grandmother was from. Although humble and meant for daily use, they were also meant to be*

beautiful everyday objects. When I saw the cabinet, I began to really understand my project. I researched and looked for an Edo Sashimono woodworker who could help me make my piece. How I ended up finding Mr. Kimura is a funny story. One day, my mother called me and said, "I found your guy. He's on TV." She saw him featured on a Japanese television show as a master woodworker. I wrote Mr. Kimura a letter describing my project. He wrote me back and we agreed to meet in his studio on my next trip to Japan.

Over the course of our nine-month collaboration, I made several visits to his studio. The experience of making this piece was a highly unusual one for me as an artist. Although Mr. Kimura and I are technically both Japanese, we speak different languages. By "languages" I am referring not to words, but to the visual and cultural language. Upon seeing the drawing of my Bauhaus-inspired cabinet, he immediately commented on the strangeness of its proportions. When selecting the wood to be used for the cabinet, he suggested and ultimately made the choice, an ornately patterned piece of 200-year-old Japanese Ash. Mr. Kimura had been saving it for over 30 years hoping to use it on a project worthy of its individuality. He was right to save it, as this was no ordinary piece of wood. Grown on an island off the coast of Japan, often caught in the path of severe typhoons, the tree faithfully recorded its turbulent life in its dramatic grain. His choice to use this prized material for my project was generous, but I think also playful. It seemed to me an expression of faith in chance and serendipity. When the cabinet was finally finished, I was struck by its deeply complicated presence and uncommon glow. It was an intense forcefield expanding infinitely inward. Throughout the course of our collaboration, we had a number of discussions about the cabinet design. In reality though, these discussions weren't really about the cabinet at all. They were about something more subtle and fundamental. From Mr. Kimura's perspective, the discussions were really about what it means to make something that is Japanese. To me, I was getting an education about my own history, of what it actually means to be Japanese.

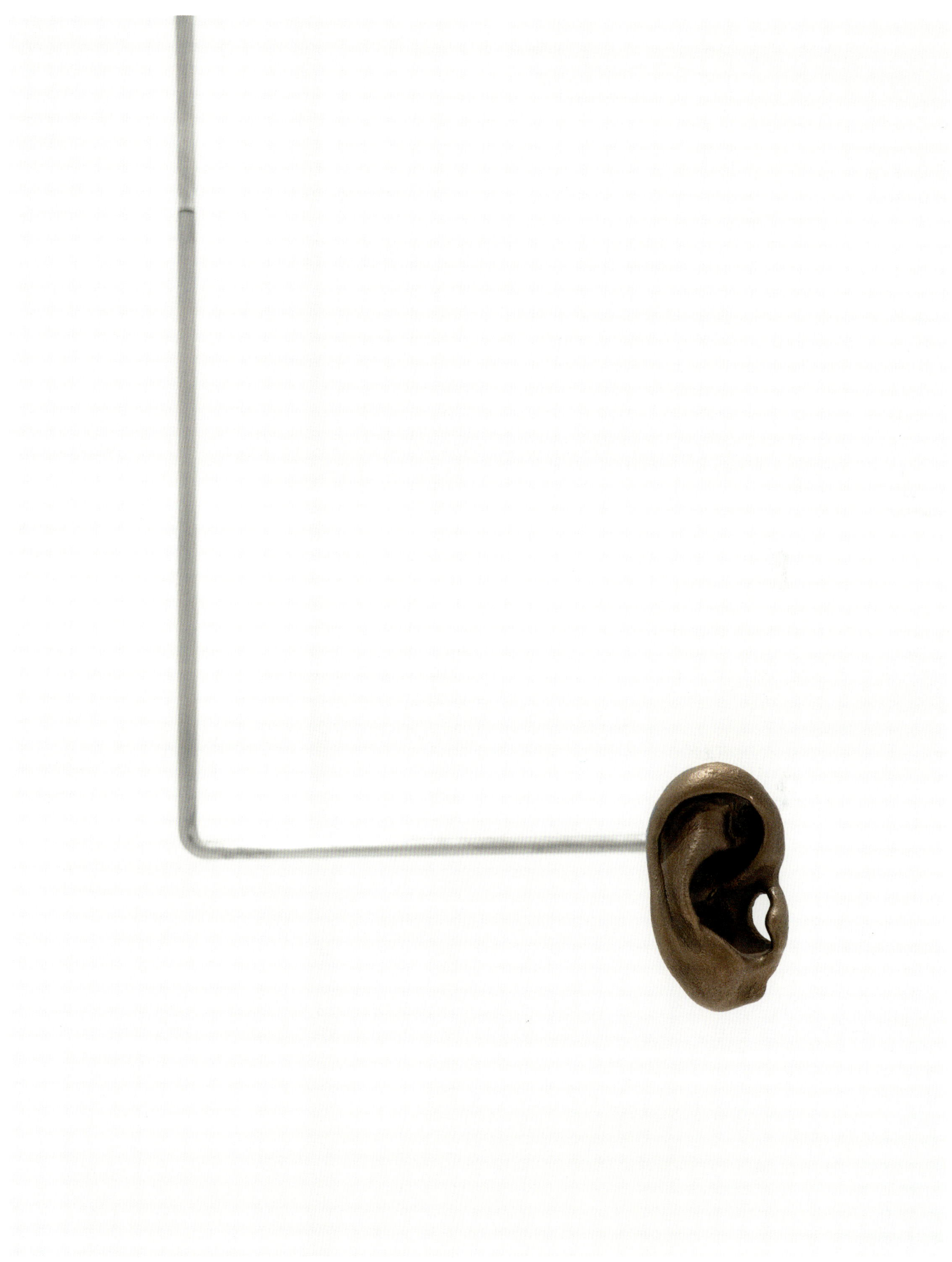

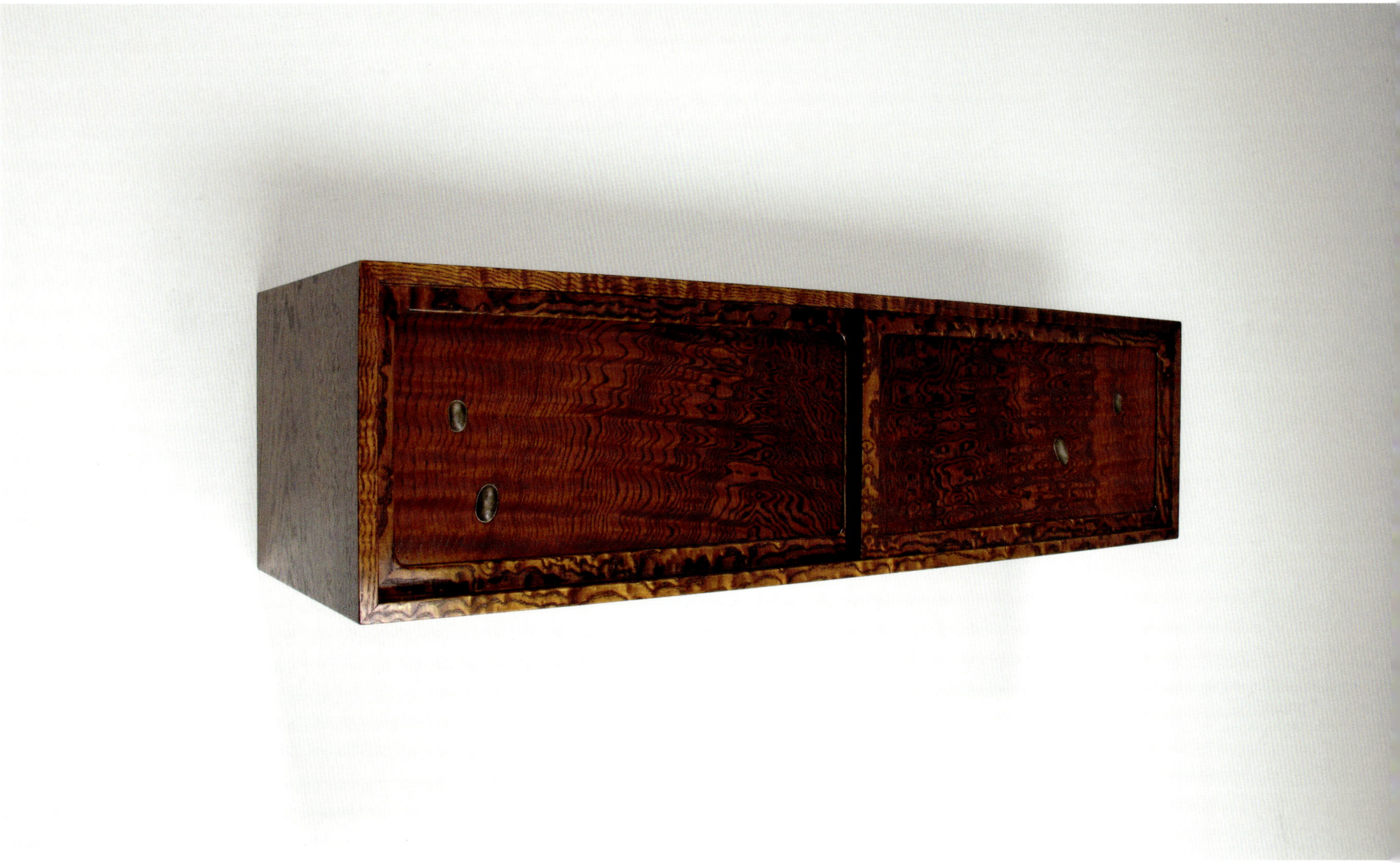

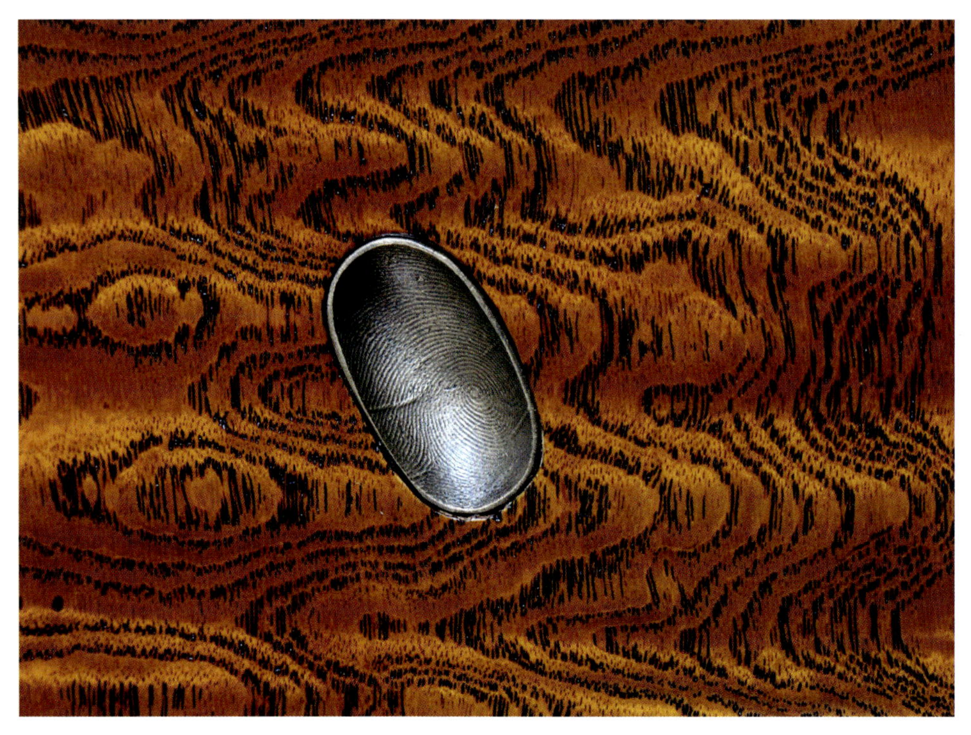

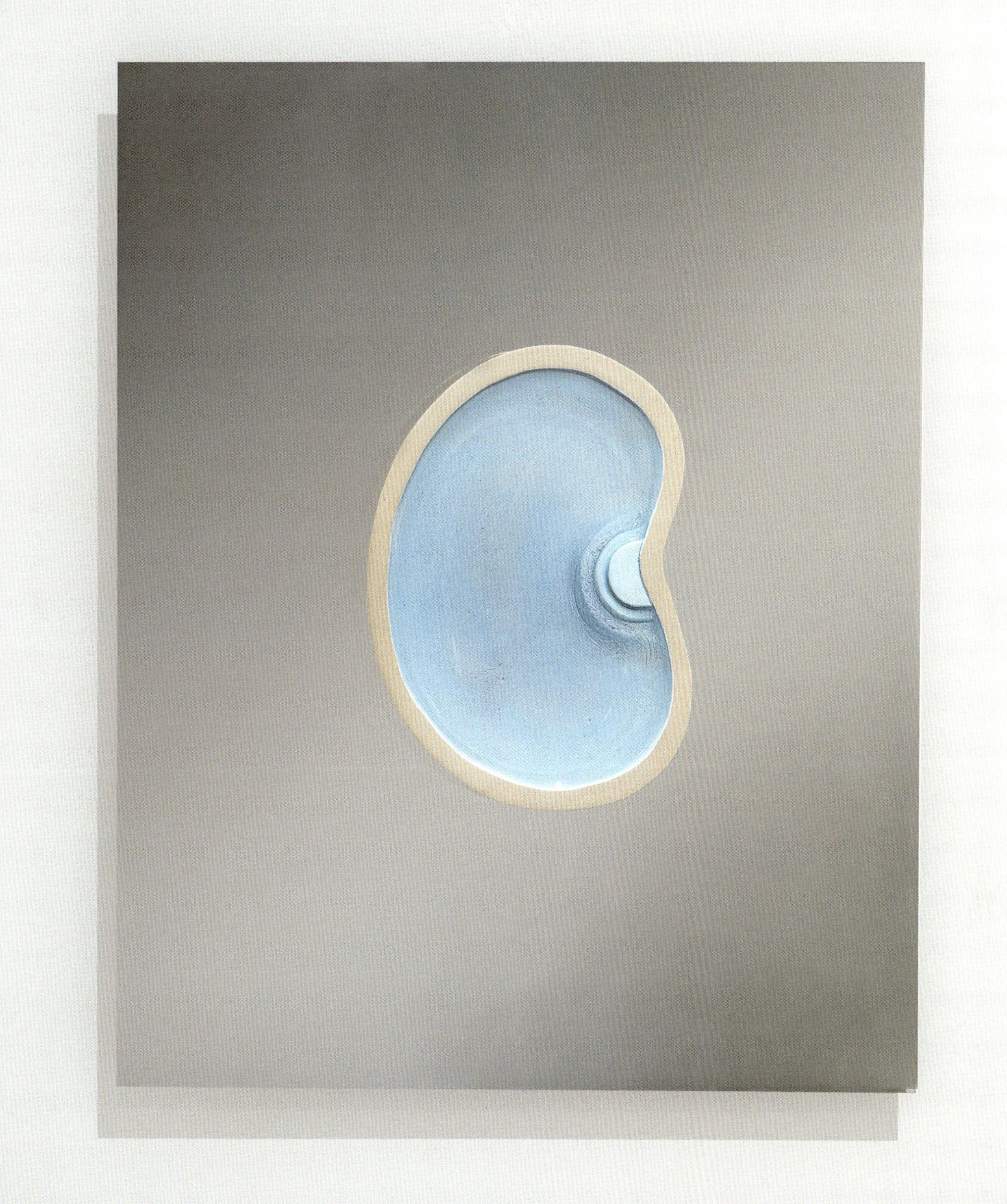

Time Traveler
2016
Whole and detail
200-year-old Japanese Ash, hand rubbed
lacquer, and cast bronze
11 ¼ × 53 ½ × 9 ½ in /
28.6 × 135.9 × 24.1 cm
Courtesy of the artist
© Mamiko Otsubo

On the Edge of the Western World
2022
Ceramic, urethane casting resin, mirror
polished stainless steel, aluminum,
and epoxy adhesive
20 × 16 × 2 ⅜ in / 50.8 × 40.6 × 6 cm
Courtesy of the artist
© Mamiko Otsubo
Photo by Steven Brooke

Rashawn Griffin
MFA 2005

Rashawn Griffin (b. 1980, Los Angeles, CA; lives and works in Olathe, KS)

Rashawn Griffin credits his time studying abroad in France as an undergraduate at the Maryland Institute College of Art (MICA) in 2001, for providing him with the foundation for his work. At MICA, working with Ken Tisa, a Yale alumnus, Griffin began using clothing, food, and non-traditional materials, and experimenting with both two- and three-dimensional forms of art making. Tisa, and later Nari Ward, during a residency at Skowhegan in 2004, introduced him to Robert Farris Thompson's work on the Afro-Atlantic world. Griffin would subsequently encounter Thompson at Yale. With MICA's strong focus on painting, Griffin explored the continued relevance of abstraction and its potential, researched artists of color and studied poetry.

Griffin met cordova and Wardell Milan at Skowhegan during his residency there. Directly after, he studied in the Department of Sculpture at Yale, along with Hewitt, Otsubo, and Tavares Strachan. Kellie Jones' class on the aesthetic traditions of African American artists who migrated west, from the American South to California made a deep impression on him.

During his time at Yale, Griffin continued the investigation into the potential of abstract painting he began at MICA, questioning the very nature of the medium and exploring how it could encompass things as diverse as clothing, narrative, and poetry. He later began conceiving his paintings as rooms that physically enveloped the viewer, allowing them to be aware of abstraction as the artist's hermetic language. His structure *The Changing Room*, was created for the exhibition *Lux et Veritas*. Based on the concept of a dressing room, the work embodies his experimentation with three-dimensional painting, his investigation into the nature of painting, and the creation of a disorientating space that changes the viewer's perspective.

Rashawn Griffin:
The Changing Room is a sculpture I made like a painting. That is, it's made from many separately stretched [pieces of] felt. Similarly, a lot of shifting comparisons run through it: fabric like painting, painting like windows, windows in walls like outfits, and so on. It's a proposal for a room one could change clothes in, but things have also settled. It has become a little stagnant, like a storage closet. It has an inside and an outside, a public face and a private one. It wears an outfit of itself.

I broke my leg before I finished this piece. I would say it's strange doing work with a useless and fractured limb, but I don't remember much of putting it together; the deep and garish palette, the arrangement of elements, the secret moments—its meaning changed as I lost access to my body. I have vitiligo, so my body is often in flux. It can change at a rapid pace, as the pigment comes and goes. A lot of pigment left my body when I broke my leg while I was making this. The broken leg went white first, then my biceps, some of my thighs, a few spots on my torso, which was untouched before. It's almost settled for now, but it changed. I'm not sure anyone else would notice but me. It's a private conversation with myself.

With the mirrors on the inside, viewers are never not seeing themselves inside this work. Everyone is changing, but maybe not as fast as I. But I like that you can see yourself as I fade away. Perhaps I'll come back as I was, but I don't know. I'm not in control of that. Maybe you can see yourself as you see me, or what I can't remember now.

The Changing Room
2022
Pool top felt, fabric, glass, wood, mirrored plexiglass, ceramics, acrylic, oil, gouache, and mixed media
84 × 107 ½ × 87 ½ in /
213.3 × 273 × 222.2 cm
Courtesy of the artist
© Rashawn Griffin
Photo by Steven Brooke

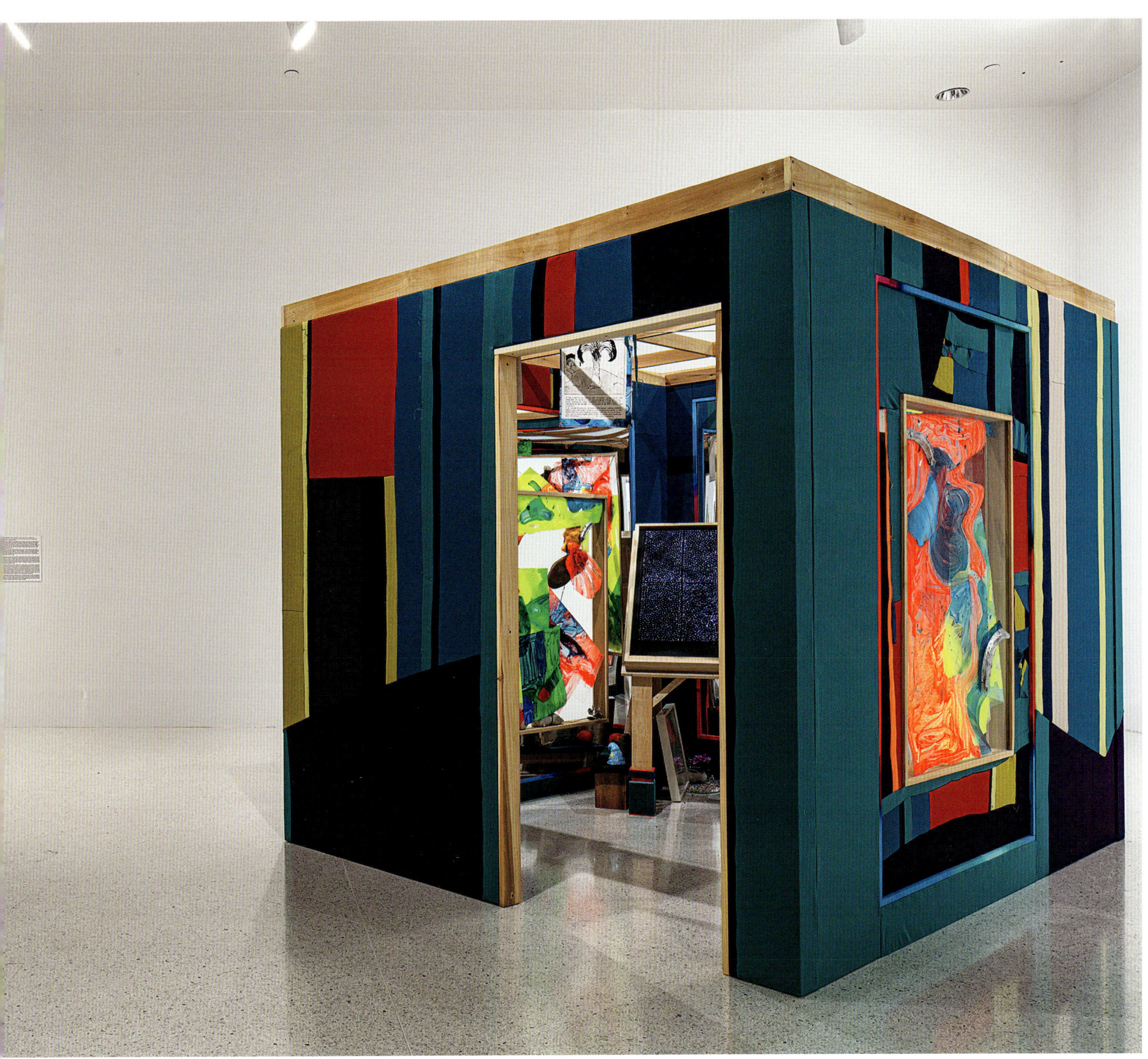

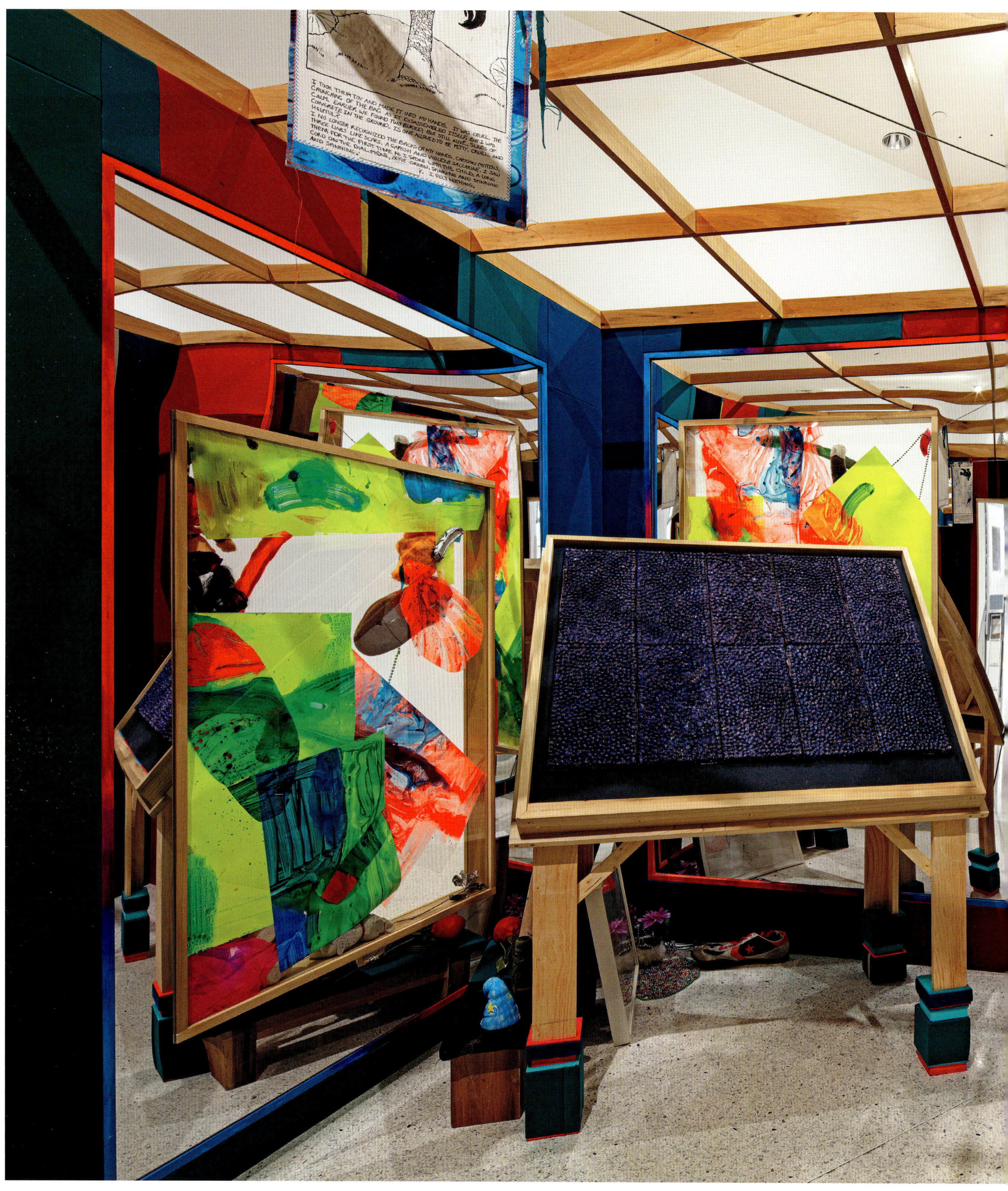
I TOOK THEIR TOY AND MADE IT INTO MY HANDS. IT WAS CRUEL, THE
CRUNCHING OF THE BAG AS IT DISASSEMBLED ITSELF, BUT I WAS
CALM. EARLIER WE FOUND TWO BURIED, BUT STILL ALIVE. SLABS OF
CONCRETE IN THE GROUND. IS ONE ALLOWED TO BE PETTY, CRUEL, AND
HELPFUL?
I NO LONGER RECOGNIZED THE BACKS OF MY HANDS. CARTOON MITTENS,
THREE LINES LIKE SCARS. A GARISH AND VIOLENT SACCARINE. I SAW
THEM FOR THE FIRST TIME AS I SPOKE WITH THE CHILD. A LONG
CORD ON THE DIAL PHONE, OLIVE GREEN, SPINNING AND SPINNING
AND SPINNING. Y. I FELT NOTHING.

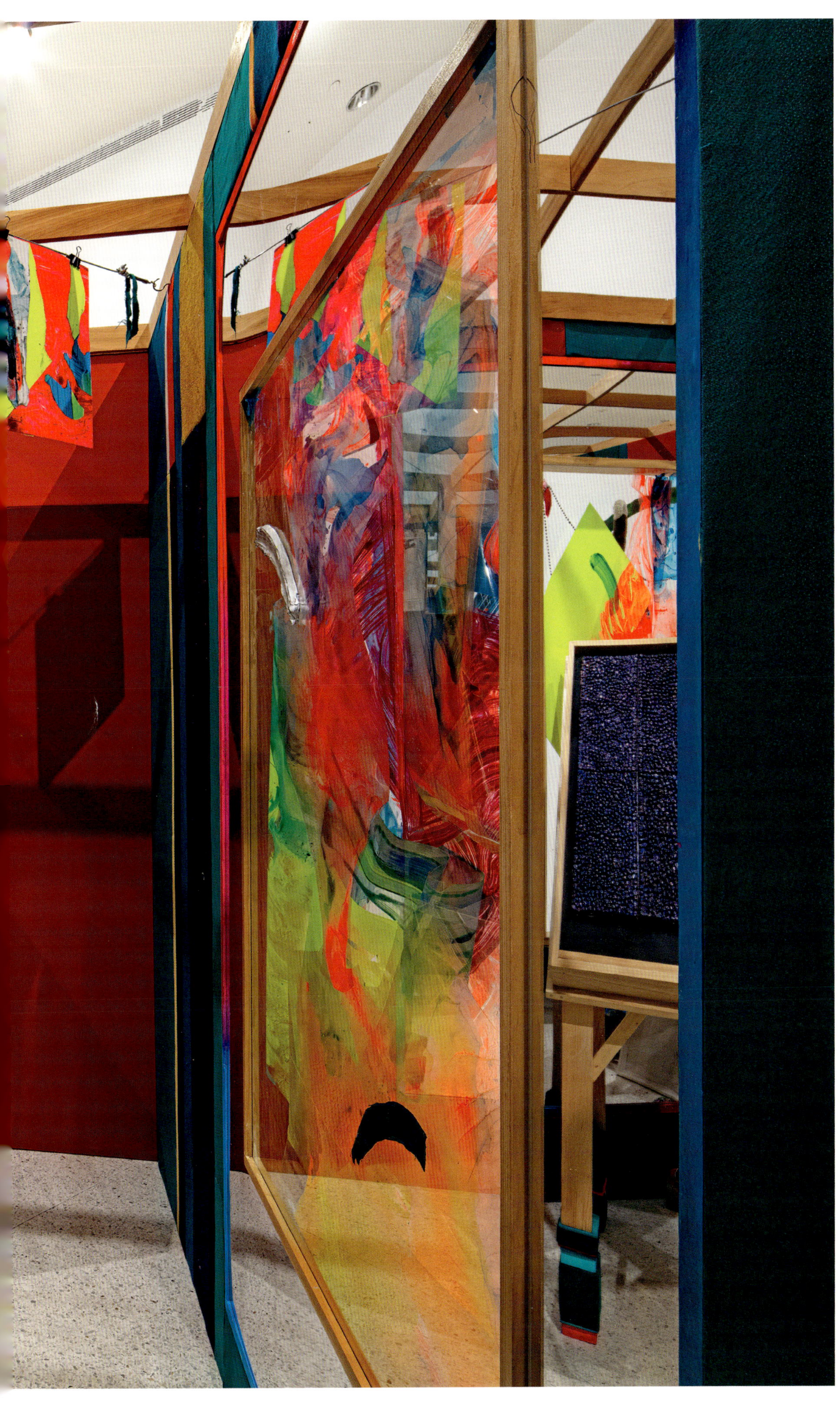

The Changing Room
2022
Interior view
Pool top felt, fabric, glass, wood, mirrored
plexiglass, ceramics, acrylic, oil, gouache,
and mixed media
84 × 107 ½ × 87 ½ in /
213.3 × 273 × 222.2 cm
Courtesy of the artist
© Rashawn Griffin
Photo by Steven Brooke

Jamerry Kim
MFA 2005

Jamerry Kim (b. Germany;
lives and works in New York, NY)

Born in Germany, and raised in South Korea, Jamerry Kim grew up in Flushing, Queens. Although she was a Graphic Design student at the Yale School of Art, she engaged with other students across disciplines: cordova, Hewitt, Cloud, and Milan, among others. She also attended lectures by cultural critics and scholars at Yale, including Paul Gilroy. Kim found a shared alignment in her peers and in the work and pedagogical approach to the Design program's Director and Professor, Sheila Levrant de Bretteville. These opportunities contributed to Kim's formulation of a post-graduate career as a multi-disciplinary artist focused on social practice, and as an educator whose interest is the themes of diaspora, language, and history. Currently, she is the Director of The Cooper Union Saturday Program, which was founded in 1968 based on Peter Cooper's vision of a tuition-free education for all. Every Saturday during the academic year, the program provides free art classes and mentorship to over 200 New York City public high school students who are taught by The Cooper Union undergraduate students.

Kim's project *To Translate Is to Cross a Bridge: Flushing Remonstrance, A Protest*, is drawn from her experience as a Korean émigré in the multicultural community of Flushing, Queens. Vestiges of Flushing's history as a seventeenth-century Dutch settlement of New Netherlands that was cohabited by Quakers (English religious dissidents), are still evident today in such sites as the John Browne House and The Quaker Friends Meeting House. Kim notes that both sites are historical references for the religious freedom and tolerance stated in the Flushing Remonstrance of 1657, a document that was written and signed by members of the Dutch Vlissengen (Flushing) community in support of the English Quaker's right to practice their religion without persecution. This text proclaims:

"For we are bound by the laws of God and man to do good unto all man and evil to no man."

As the modern-day signage for these historic sites are only in English, this valuable history is unavailable to most of Flushing's current foreign-born residents. This paradox inspired Kim's project as a means to cultivate an understanding of local history within a larger historical narrative that would lead to "an act of inclusion into the fabric of American history."

The video component of this work features current-day residents reading aloud translations of the Flushing Remonstrance in their own language. The multiple translations are printed on a stack of paper for visitors to take away. For Kim, translation as a bridge is a metaphor that is evocative of the journey one takes on multiple levels: from one's mother country to a new country, from one language to another, from one culture to another, from history to the present, from the personal to the collective.

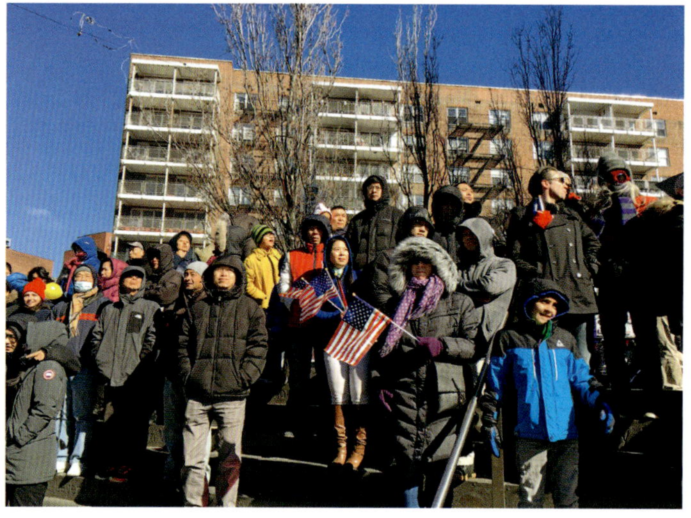

*To Translate is to Cross a Bridge: Flushing
Remonstrance, A Protest*
2019–2021
32 mins
Digital video
Image courtesy of the artist
© Jamerry Kim

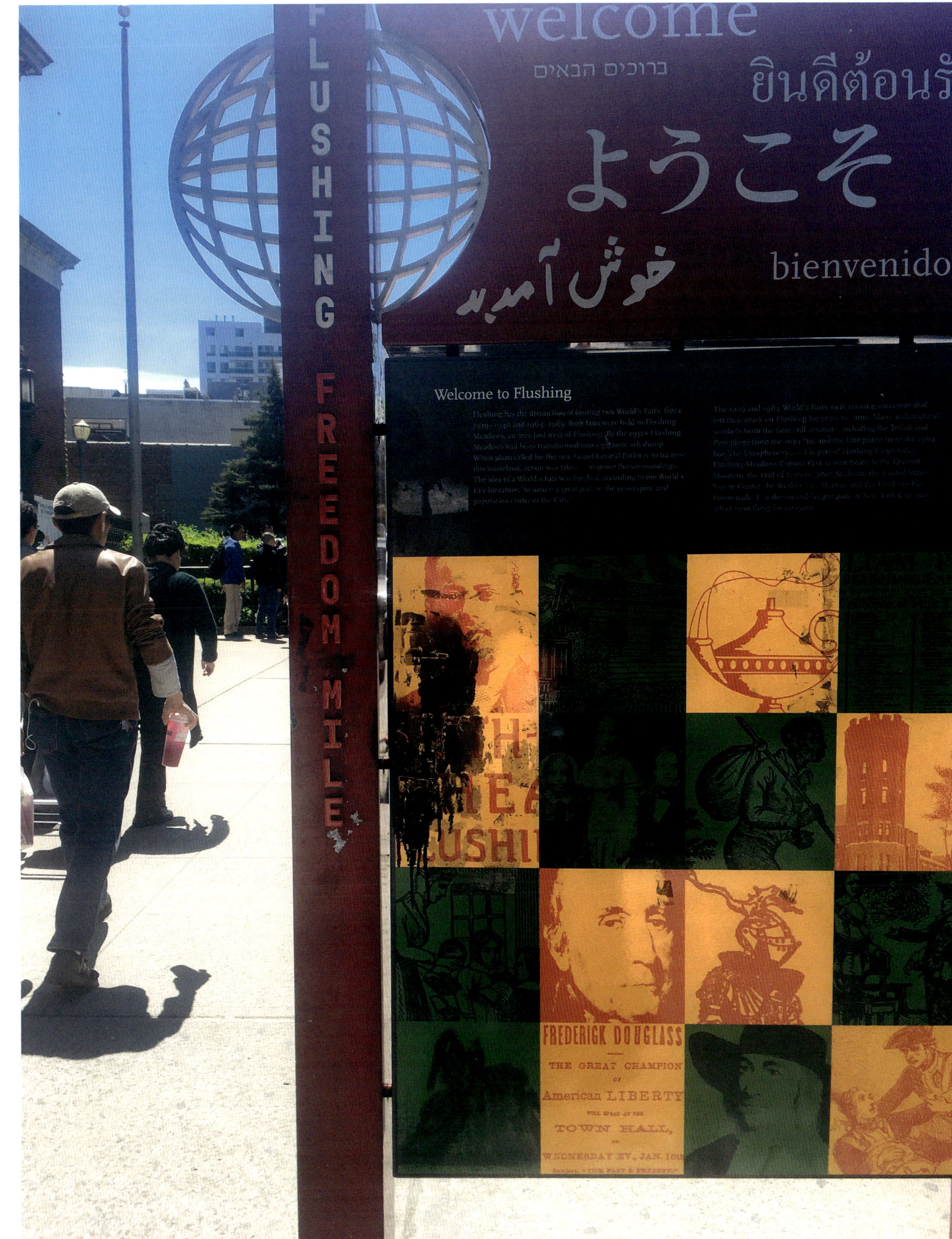
FLUSHING FREEDOM MILE
welcome
ברוכים הבאים
ยินดีต้อนรั
ようこそ
خوش آمدید
bienvenidos
Welcome to Flushing
FREDERICK DOUGLASS
THE GREAT CHAMPION
OF
American LIBERTY
TOWN HALL,
WEDNESDAY EV., JAN. 18

Loren Holland
MFA 2006

Loren Holland (b. Los Angeles, CA; lives and works in Los Angeles, CA)

Beginning in childhood, Loren Holland developed a broad appreciation of music which she shared with her father. His extensive collection of jazz and funk albums was an especially rich resource, as she was drawn as much to the cover art as the music itself.

With interest in both the medical field and visual arts, she chose Brown University in Providence, Rhode Island, for her undergraduate studies, as it was known for cross-disciplinary studies and a prestigious visual arts program. As a Brown University student, she was also able to attend classes at the nearby Rhode Island School of Design (RISD). She credits RISD graduate Kara Walker for inspiring her dedication to art. Holland notes that Walker's work, which uses vernacular art forms to address the history of American slavery and racism was a revelation—she never knew art could look the way Walker's did, and found it especially relatable.

Looking to follow in the path of the artists of color who attended the Yale School of Art, Holland was surprised to discover that she was the only Black first-year Painting student in her cohort. Her personal iconography was influenced by her interest in art history, literature, and mythology. Determined to make art that would be broadly accessible, she drew inspiration from the funk record covers she admired as a child. These images were familiar and relatable to her peers as they were appropriated and popularized by contemporary musicians such as Sean "Diddy" Combs, Snoop Dogg and Dr. Dre as part of their hip-hop aesthetic. This interest ran counter to that of most of her instructors, who considered her appropriation of funk and Afropop album cover graphics as kitsch and low brow. Although figurative painters Wiley and Mickalene Thomas—whose image references frequently aligned with Holland's—had completed their Yale MFAs the same year she entered the program, their work had not yet achieved the widespread recognition that would ultimately contribute to the resurgence in figurative painting, and specifically the representation of Black figures, which significantly increased towards the end of the decade. She realized that if she had followed the Yale instruction template, many of her friends at home in Los Angeles would have difficulties understanding her work, which was important to her. She now feels she has the "status, credentials, and knowledge" to say what she needs to say in her work.

Loren Holland:

I frequently analyze the effect of beauty and how we perceive beauty. Beauty is often associated with classical traits that are not normally associated with Black or brown bodies, yet I deliberately associate my protagonists with them. They are even dressed in Grecian and Roman-style clothing or they will have proportions that mimic classical beauty standards. I enjoy playing with these different visual and contextual layers. Kara Walker was another early influential artist who tackled some of the same subject matter as me—subtle (and sometimes not-so-subtle) hinting at that deviant side of things.

The Bathers is loosely based on the myth of Diana, Roman Goddess of the Moon, and her nymphs being disturbed while bathing. This poor fellow Actaeon, the hunter, happened to spy on her during her bath, which had dreadful results. In my version, they are women of a particular appearance being spied upon, being intruded upon, like they do not really have control of their bodies. I scattered the placement of various things: little binoculars in the background (implying surveillance) or a literal barrel of toxic waste floating in the background, while the amphora is a direct classical reference. Details will force people to slow down.

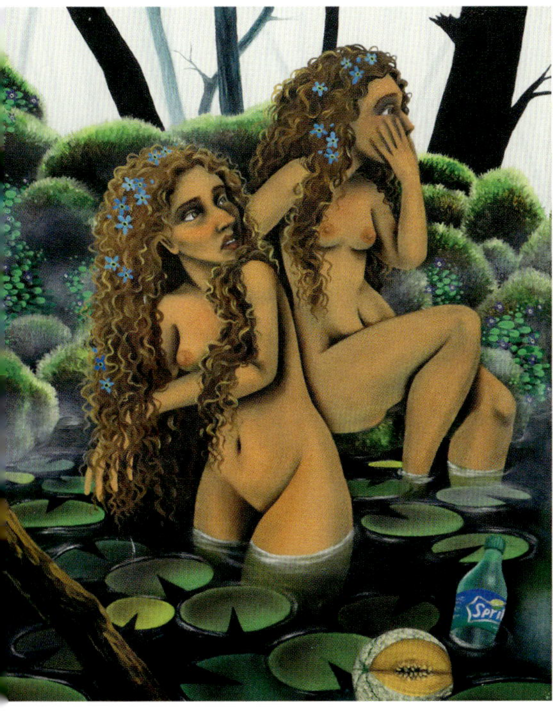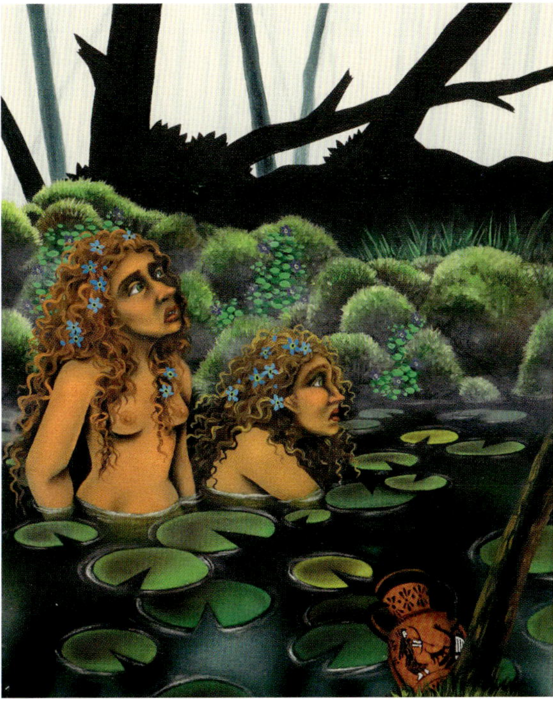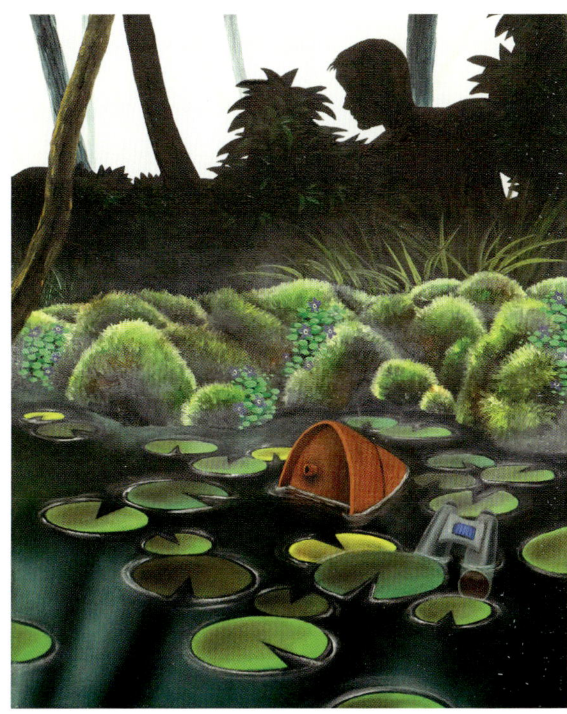

The Bathers
2018
Oil on canvas
35 × 14 in / 88.9 × 35.6 cm
Courtesy of the artist
© Loren Holland
Photo by David Guidi

Following pages

The Shadown Queen
2018
Oil on canvas
30 × 24 in / 76.2 × 61 cm
Courtesy of the artist
© Loren Holland
Photo by David Guidi

Bait and Switch
2018
Oil on canvas
30 × 24 in / 76.2 × 61 cm
Courtesy of the artist
© Loren Holland
Photo by David Guidi

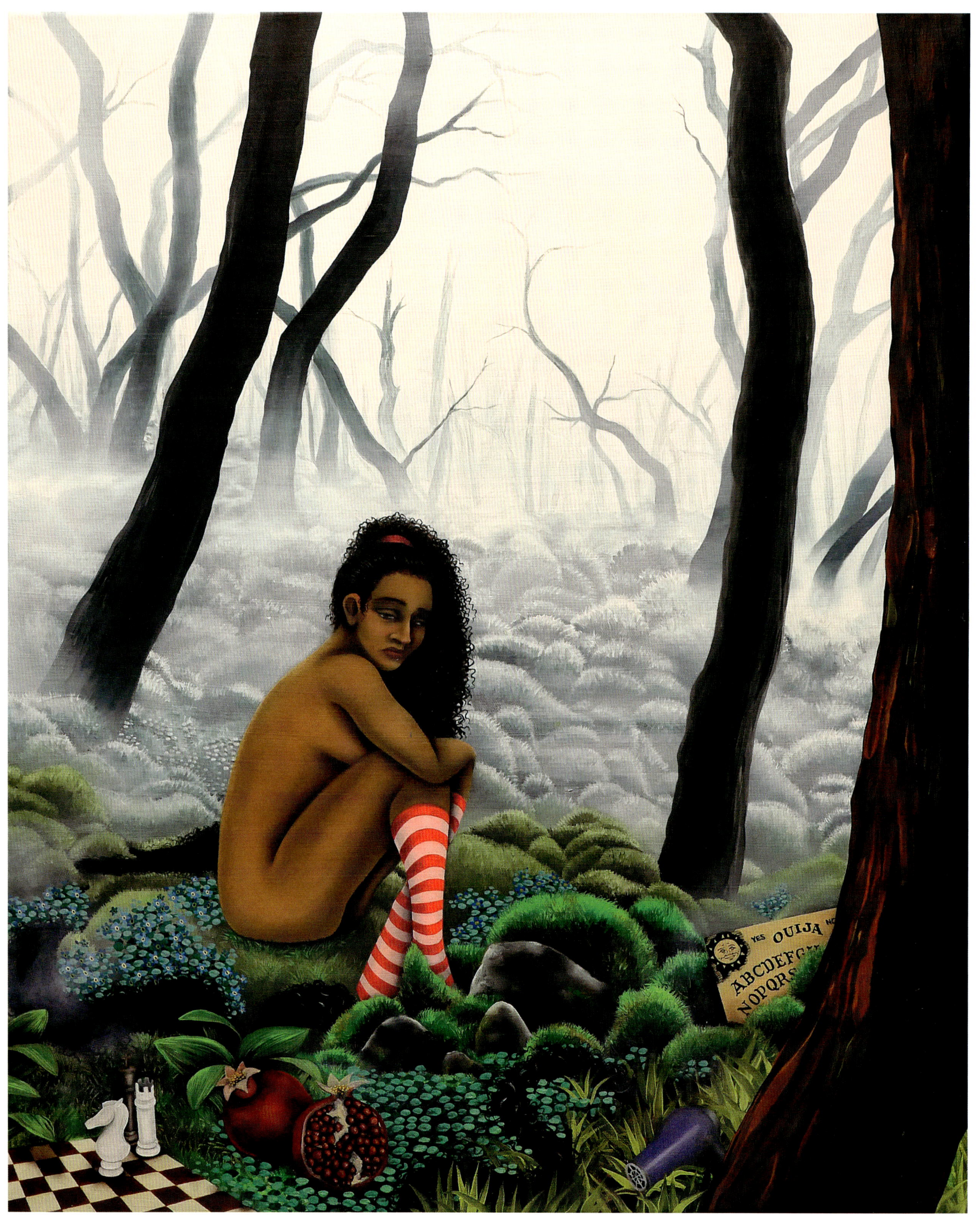

YES OUIJA NO
ABCDEFG
NOPQRS

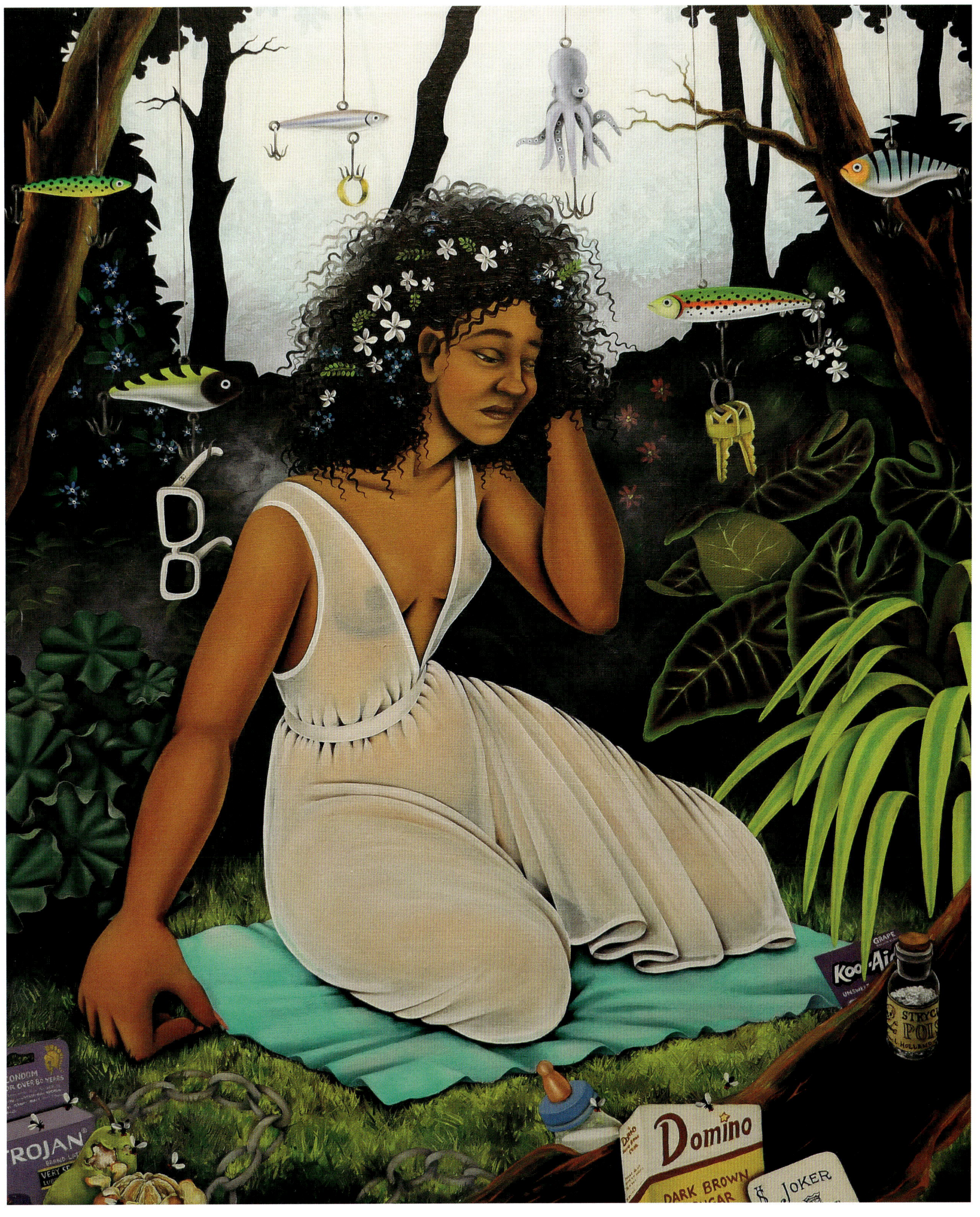

Titus Kaphar
MFA 2006

Titus Kaphar (b. 1976, Kalamazoo, MI; lives and works in New Haven, CT)

Titus Kaphar was inspired to paint after taking an art history class at a junior college when he was 27 years old. His work—like that of Yale alumni Wiley and Mickalene Thomas—examines the history of representation, particularly the representation of Black subjects, in order to unearth its contemporary relevance. His selection of materials and techniques contribute to the meaning of the work. The painting *Another Fight for Remembrance (Study)*, 2014, belongs to a cycle of paintings depicting Black men with their hands raised in the air; their body and most of their face painted over with white paint and a hint of a gold-leaf halo hovering above their heads. *Time* magazine published one of these paintings to accompany an article on the protests in Ferguson, Missouri, which began on August 10, 2014, the day after the fatal shooting of Michael Brown by a white police officer. The protest sparked a nationwide reckoning between law enforcement officers and Black Americans. Rather than focus on the death of Michael Brown or the ensuing protests

directly, Kaphar's painting is a personal response that speaks to how society erases the presence of Black men. Two weeks after the tragic murder of George Floyd, *Time* magazine once again turned to Kaphar to communicate the pain of the Black experience with a painting for its cover of a Black mother clutching a baby to her chest. The infant, however, is cut out of the scene so that it appears as a silhouetted absence, the very essence of loss and sorrow.

While Kaphar appreciated the time he was able to devote to concentrating on his work during his graduate studies at Yale, he realized the cost of attending traditional MFA programs was prohibitive for most students. His social engagement has led to the establishment (with Jason Price) of the nonprofit arts organization NXTHVN, in the predominantly Black Dixwell neighborhood of New Haven, Connecticut, close to Yale's campus. Launched in 2019, NXTHVN is a national arts model that empowers high school students, emerging artists, and curators of color by providing intergenerational mentorship, professional development and cross-sector collaboration to accelerate professional careers in the arts.

Another Fight for Remembrance (Study)
2014
Oil and gold leaf on canvas
59 × 40 ⅜ in / 149.9 × 102.5 cm
Private collection
Courtesy of the artist and Gagosian
© Titus Kaphar

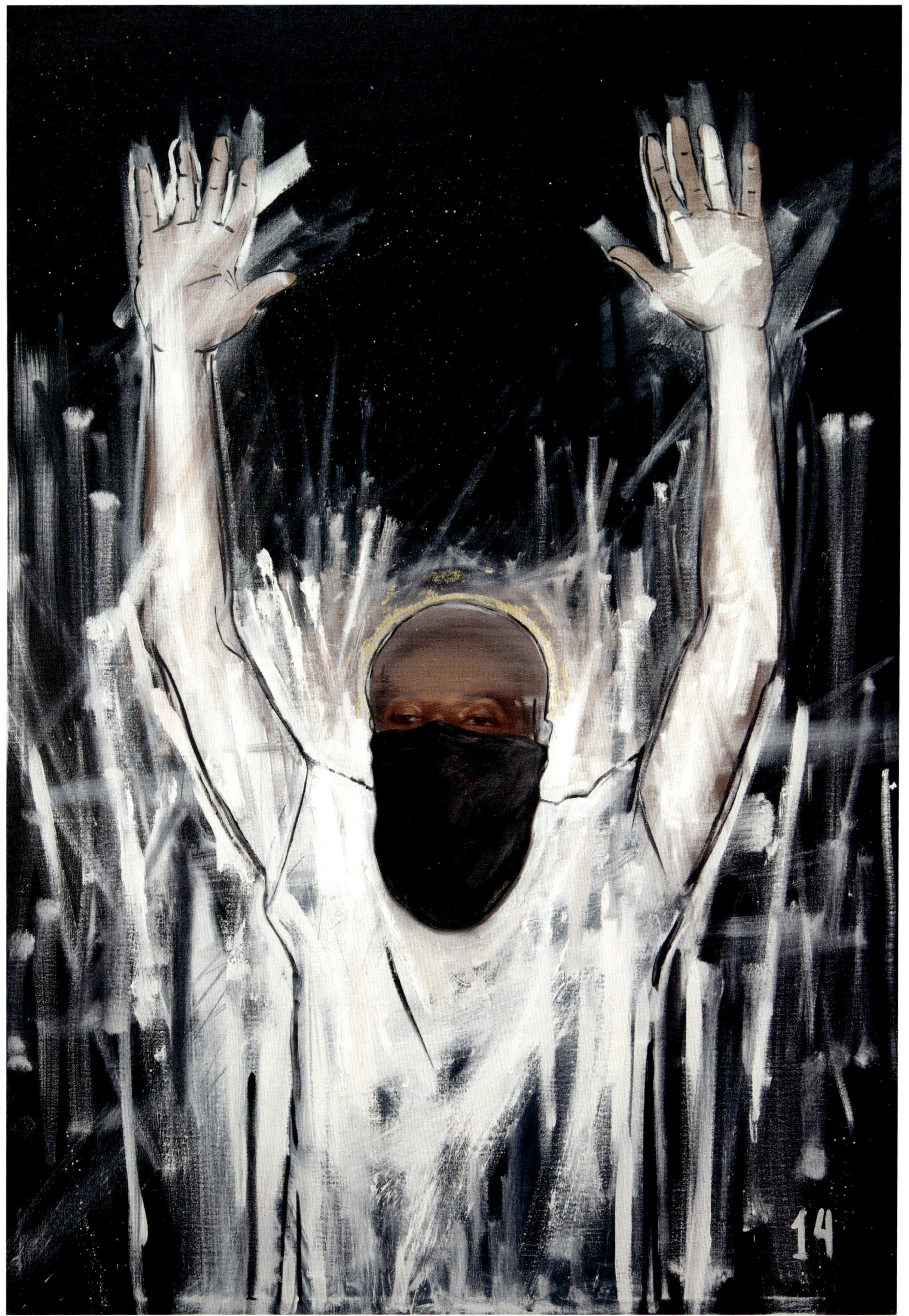
14

Njideka Akunyili Crosby
MFA 2011

Njideka Akunyili Crosby (b. 1983, Enugu, Nigeria; lives and works in Los Angeles, California)

Growing up in eastern Nigeria, Njideka Akunyili Crosby had little access to Western art historical sources and contemporary art discourse but remembers copying pictures from her father's subscriptions of *Time* and *Newsweek* magazines.[1] She moved with her sister to Philadelphia when she was 16. After graduating with a BA from Swarthmore College in 2004, she returned to Nigeria where the country was experiencing a renaissance of art, music, and film. Inspired by how her generation was standing up and telling their own stories, Crosby committed herself to art. She returned to Philadelphia to study at the Pennsylvania Academy of Fine Arts before entering the Yale School of Art for her graduate studies. During her first year at Yale, the most consistent critique given by her peers and professors was that her figurative paintings did not look "contemporary." The challenge she faced was how to make paintings that looked like they existed in the present. One of her solutions was to avoid painting faces altogether by representing them turning away from the viewer's gaze. It was only after graduation, during a residency at The Studio Museum in Harlem (2011—2012), that she returned to painting faces, which she figured out by studying the portraits of seventeenth-century Spanish painter Diego Velázquez. She observed how the sitters in Velázquez's paintings looked very present, much like subjects in modern portrait photography and candid snapshots. This revelation led her to begin making portrait paintings of children from old family photos as well as photographs that she took in Nigeria. Overlaid into these portrait paintings are smaller photographs and other images culled from Nigerian family archives and Nigerian sources using a photo-transfer technique.[2]

Access to the Yale University Art Gallery was an important resource for many of the MFA students. Crosby was particularly intrigued by the collection's Kerry James Marshall painting that she saw there as a graduate student. She remarked that "His use of different visual languages resonates with my practice," adding "It's hard to find a relevant mode of figurative painting because it's been done so well for so long, so it's invigorating and to see a work like [Marshall's] *Untitled* (2009) that reinvents the form while simultaneously participating in the history, and critiquing its exclusion of women and people of color."[3]

Crosby's painting *Nyado: The Thing Around Her Neck*, is an important early transitional work painted during the year she graduated from Yale. The faces of the embracing couple are concealed as they merge into one figure, while photographic family mementos, news clippings, DVD and album covers transferred to the painting's surface radiate throughout the composition. Encountering this couple from behind contributes to the immediacy of the viewer's experience of encroaching on such an intimate moment. The title references *The Thing Around your Neck*, a short story by Nigerian author Chimamanda Ngozi Adichie, written from the perspective of an immigrant Nigerian woman in America. Crosby does not expect viewers to recognize the Nigerian sources or her references to art historical sources. These paintings are about what it means to be someone who exists between two worlds, and carries these influences within. As Crosby notes, she is trying to use her work and her life story "to explore this idea of a liminal space, or a third space, where multiple things come together to yield a new thing."[4]

[1] Deborah Vankin, "Njideka Akunyili Crosby: The painter in her MacArthur Moment," *Los Angeles Times*, November 2, 2017.

[2] "At home: Artists in Conversationl Njideka Akunyili Crosby," with Courtney J. Martin, Yale British Art, video, July 15, 2021.

[3] "The Artist: Njideka Akunyili Crosby," interview, *Luxury Defined* (by Christie's International Real Estate), January 12, 2016.

[4] Vankin, "Njideka Akunyili Crosby: The painter in her MacArthur Moment," cit.

Nyado: The Thing Around Her Neck
2011
Acrylic, photographic transfers, colored pencil, charcoal, lace, and collage on paper
81 ½ × 81 ¾ in / 207 × 207.6 cm
Collection of the artist
Courtesy of David Zwirner and Victoria Miro
© Njideka Akunyili Crosby

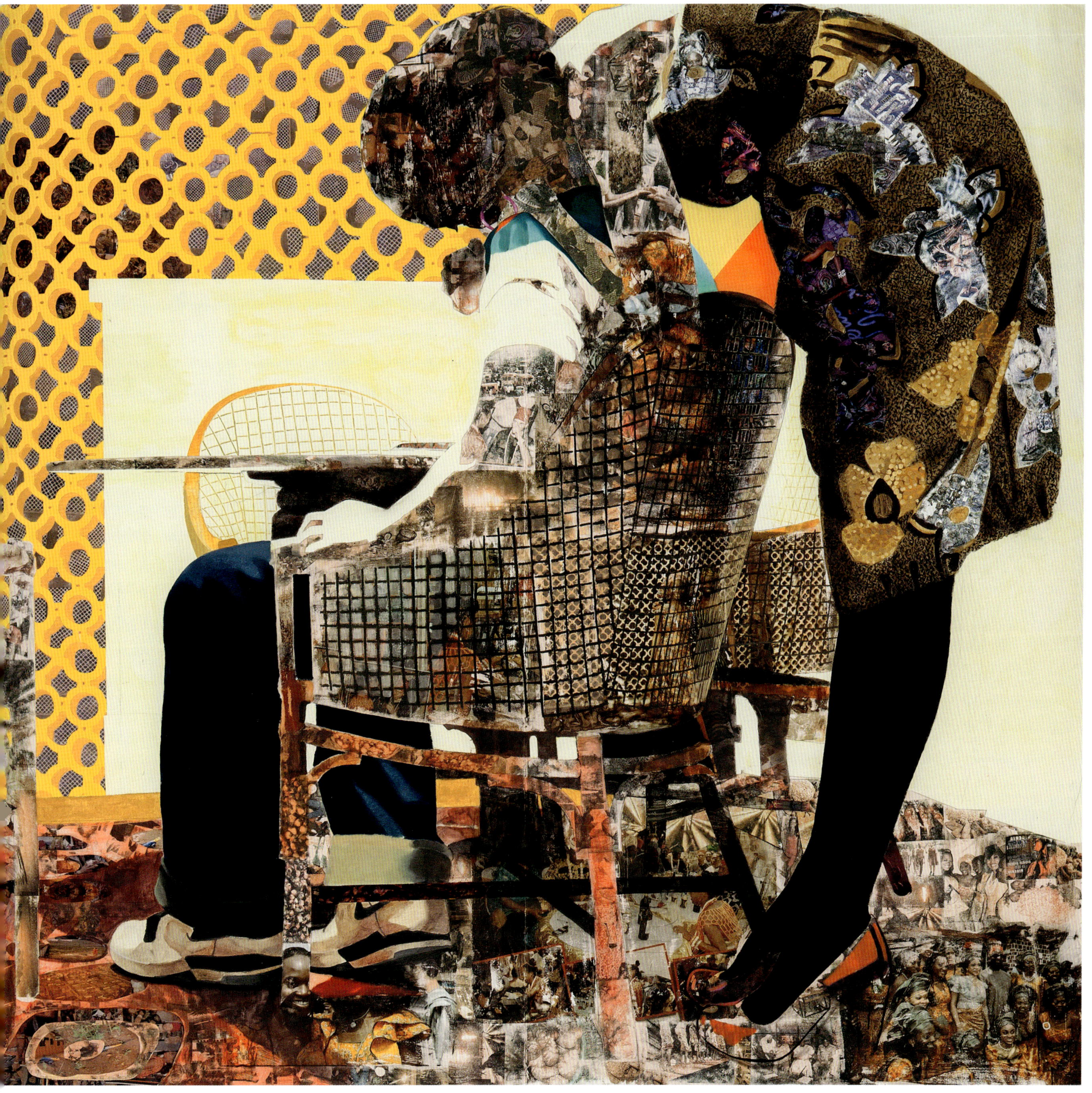

Abigail DeVille
MFA 2011

Abigail DeVille (b. 1981, New York, NY; lives and works in Bronx, NY)

Abigail DeVille attended the Yale School of Art at the close of the first decade of the new millennium, by which time the demographics had turned, with an increased enrollment of artists of color. According to Peter Halley (Director of Painting and Printmaking, 2002–2011), the number of artists of color in the Painting department had increased by 33 per cent during his tenure. The early success of alumni Gispert, Mutu, Thomas, and Wiley, the inclusion of several Yale MFAs in the 2008 Whitney Biennial, and the increased number of recent Yale graduates teaching at art schools throughout the country, were among the contributing factors to this increased enrollment. DeVille first became aware of the Yale School of Art at Kehinde Wiley's exhibition at Deitch Projects in the fall of 2005. She immediately requested the school catalog and enrolled there four years later. She described her time at the art school as an intense experience; the discussions with other students helped her shape how she thought about material. These relationships remain vital to her work and career.

James Baldwin's seminal essay, *The Creative Process* (1962), has become DeVille's mission statement. Baldwin writes, "We know, in the case of the person, that whoever cannot tell himself the truth about his past is trapped in it, is immobilized in the prison of his undiscovered self. This is also true of nations. We know how a person, in such a paralysis, is unable to assess either his weaknesses or his strengths, and how frequently indeed he mistakes the one for the other... the war of an artist with his society is a lover's war, and he does… what lovers do, which is to reveal the beloved to himself and, with that revelation, to make freedom real."[1]

From this position of the lover, DeVille has centered her practice. She asks "What is love? What is truth? These are questions that can only be answered with compassion and unyielding curiosity. In my estimation, the truth is in the bungled attempts to care for one another. Our understanding of where we stand in time and space is a collage of societal and internalized projections. Through investigating historical fragments of information and the material waste of the present, I interrogate our future past." She further states:

America has numerous black holes in which it tries unsuccessfully to bury the bodies of its many democratic operatives. I use black holes as a loose metaphor for historical erasure. Black holes eviscerate matter, but the gravity of the matter remains to be discovered, interrogated, and recognized. Specifically, I structure work on ancient models of Greco-Roman architecture. It is a kind of time travel to what the West considers the apex of human civilization. The installation work connects the birth of power architecture to the birth of the universe. Creating multiple portals in the material are further metaphors for the slipperiness of time and the holes in America's foundational myths.

The works included in the *Lux et Veritas* exhibition were based on DeVille's public art project *Light of Freedom*, which was conceived in the aftermath of the George Floyd murder and protests, and during the pandemic and a period of political turmoil in 2020.[2] (ill. p. 156) DeVille describes this work with its caged-like torch as an allusion to the Statue of Liberty:

Filling a Torch—refers to the Statue of Liberty's hand holding a torch which was on view in Madison Square Park from 1876 to 1882— with a timeworn bell, a herald of freedom, and the arms of mannequins, reaching to viewers. A golden scaffold summons the glory of labor and the hope that struggle can lead to change. Formative to Light of Freedom *are the words of the abolitionist, author, and statesman Frederick Douglass, who proclaimed in 1857: "If there is no struggle, there is no progress." In my research, I have found that the first Blacks to be brought to New York City were eleven Angolans in 1626. Unfortunately, history has erased the contributions and victories of this group. I wanted to make something that could honor their lives and question what it means to be a New Yorker, past, present, and future.* Light of Freedom *has given birth to an in-depth exploration of Libertas (the Roman goddess the Statue of Liberty is based on) and where she lives in monuments of American democracy.*

Abigail DeVille:

Thinking through this idea of Libertas, is how the sculptures [on view in *Lux et Veritas*] *were born.*

I was thinking through how many different kinds of icons and classical sculptures exist already in our public squares and facades of buildings and [in] marble, and about how these things talk to us over time; how there's always this hypocrisy embedded within that. There's always this complicated way in which we are unsure of the soft power that public art and sculpture has over us. You walk by a particular sculpture a thousand times a day, in a park, or over the course of a lifetime, and you don't realize the kind of soft power effect that it's having on you psychologically. The way that you're thinking about the legitimacy of your government is in a particular way, and that is exercised through these public monuments.

I made [these three sculptures] simultaneously in the studio, so they were all talking to each other, and I made them specifically for this exhibition. So I'm not 100 per cent on what they're actually doing in space. The one that's on the commercial garment rack is just me trying to challenge myself to think about, "How can I make a painting without actually using any paint?" and thinking about this story. [It's] called Pharaoh's March. *The chains, the rope, the wire [are used as] a drawing device but also for binding these bodies together. All materials inherently have this embedded history to them. This is why I like using found materials, because it's already a loaded thing, and then you're just making all of these different connections by putting it next to something else. I get a lot of joy out of that, of putting different, disparate things next to one another. The [wooden triangle in the other sculpture] is like a mast from a ship that I had in [an exhibition at] Socrates Sculpture Park in 2016. The mannequin has been haunting my studio for years. The [stapling on its surface came out of my] thinking about community boards or signposts where flyers are [attached]. I was also thinking about [statues of] saints that are paraded down the street in a ritualistic festival situation. And then thinking about hedging your bets on liberty, right? What is liberty, actually? Or what is freedom, actually?*

[1] James Baldwin, "The Creative Process," *Creative America*, ed. Adolph Suehsdorf (New York: Ridge Press, 1962), p. 21.
[2] Madison Park, New York, NY (2020–2021): *Momentary* at Crystal Bridges Museum of American Art, Bentonville, AR (2021); Hirshhorn, Washington, D.C. (2021–2022).

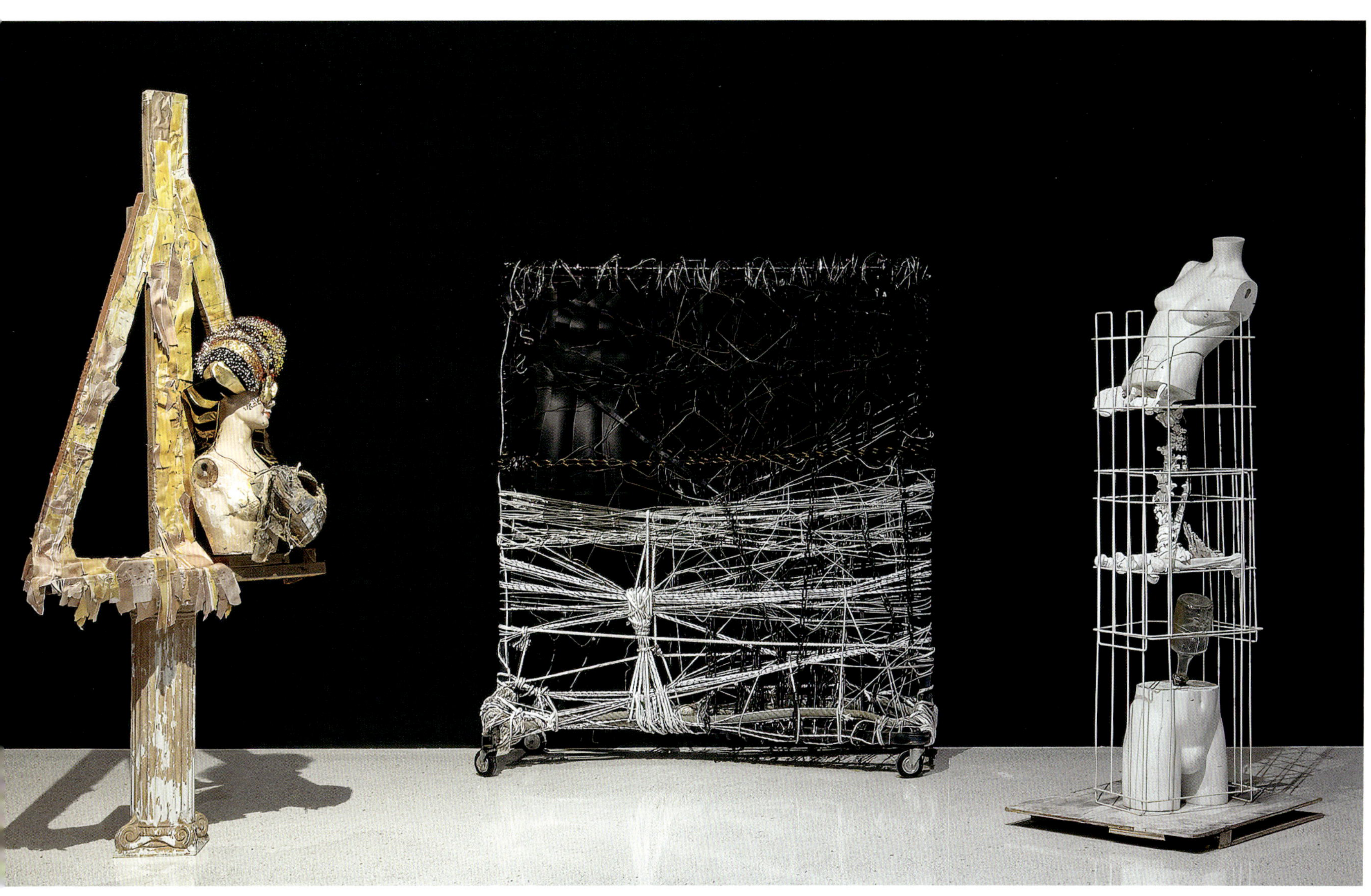

Eric N. Mack
MFA 2012

Eric N. Mack (b. 1987, Columbia, MD; lives and works in New York)[1]

By the time Eric N. Mack entered the Yale School of Art in 2010, it was associated with the figurative painting of Mickalene Thomas, Wiley, and other prominent alumni who graduated earlier in the decade. Mack, however, was committed to abstract painting. Growing up in Maryland, near Washington, D.C., he frequented its museums and attended an art magnet high school before enrolling in the Maryland Institute College of Art in Baltimore, which was known for its strong focus on abstract painting. He transferred to Cooper Union in his second year. There he studied with Yale graduate Hewitt and attended the summer residency program at The Yale Norfolk School of Art.

Mack's exploration of abstract painting coincided with new scholarship and exhibitions that focused attention anew on abstract painting by Black artists in the 1960s, '70s, and '80s. Among these influential revisionist studies was art historian Kellie Jones' exhibition *Energy and Experimentation: Black Artists and Abstraction 1964–1980* at The Studio Museum in Harlem (2006). During the 1960s abstract painting was a controversial mode for Black artists who were marginalized by the mainstream art world and the Black Arts Movement that favored figurative art to promote social and political engagement. These new studies focused on how the formal experiments by many of these abstract artists reflected or addressed social and political subjects. Concurrently, a new generation of Black abstract painters achieved prominence in

the early 2000s, including Mark Bradford, Ellen Gallagher, Rashid Johnson, Julie Mehretu, Odili Donald Odita, and Shinique Smith, among others, who used form, color, materials, and personal archetypes to address social structures and interactions, history, and aesthetics.

Although Mack experimented with dyeing fabrics prior to enrolling in Yale, he acknowledges Visiting Artist Shinique Smith's use of found and personal textiles and other materials to construct private narratives, for opening up areas of exploration. In his work, Mack considers the essential elements of abstract painting, including color, form, and gesture, through a distinct focus on non-traditional materials, such as multi-textured and hand-stained textiles. His assemblage *Tessuti Raponi* (*Ciao Milano*) features textiles he sourced at a fabric store in Milan, which he arranged and sewed together to form an abstract "painting." While the materials are unconventional and the fabric is draped rather than stretched and hung flat on the wall, the colors and forms echo the push-and-pull pictorial space of the mid-twentieth-century American Abstract Expressionist painters, in which bold color planes appear to emerge and recede from the picture plane.

The relationships the Yale MFA students formed at the school extended to the art history Ph.D. candidates. These relationships often continued beyond graduation. Such was the case with Mack and curator Ashley James (Yale Ph.D. 2021, English Literature, African American Studies, and Gender Studies, currently Associate Curator, Contemporary Art, at the Guggenheim Museum, New York), who organized the exhibition *Eric N. Mack: Lemme walk across the room*, for the Brooklyn Museum (January 11, 2019 – August 4, 2019). This exhibition was reimagined for NSU Art Museum Fort Lauderdale in 2021, and included *Tessuti Raponi* (*Ciao Milano*), which was subsequently acquired for the museum's permanent collection.

Eric N. Mack:

I'm essentially a formalist. I don't give the material over to its worldly meaning. I see [my] way to create [as] a rupture or different system, a mapping system. Even though some of the colors [in Tessuti Raponi (Ciao Milano)*] look quite close, none of the same kind fabrics are repeated. The neon green comes close pictorially and the light green is able to recede and all the colors create a kind of depth but are structured as one surface that is sewn together. But they are able to create these push-and-pull dynamics that are very much central to a lot of the principles that I have always valued in painting and abstract expressionism. I see that there is a kind of singularity. You don't count the number of lines to create a stripe. There's a compression of image and information. Thinking about the floral pattern, I wanted there to be associations that people would have that would bring some specificity to it. The references keep the work alive. Those points of reality or consecutiveness add a conceptual aspect to the work. It's not something I want to overly name. I wanted to maintain the levity and lightness of the work. It's not about the color or materiality but those are the things that immediately function in the work and are quite important.*

[1] Antwaun Sargent, ed., *Young, Gifted and Black: A New Generation of Artists* (New York: D.A.P., 2020).

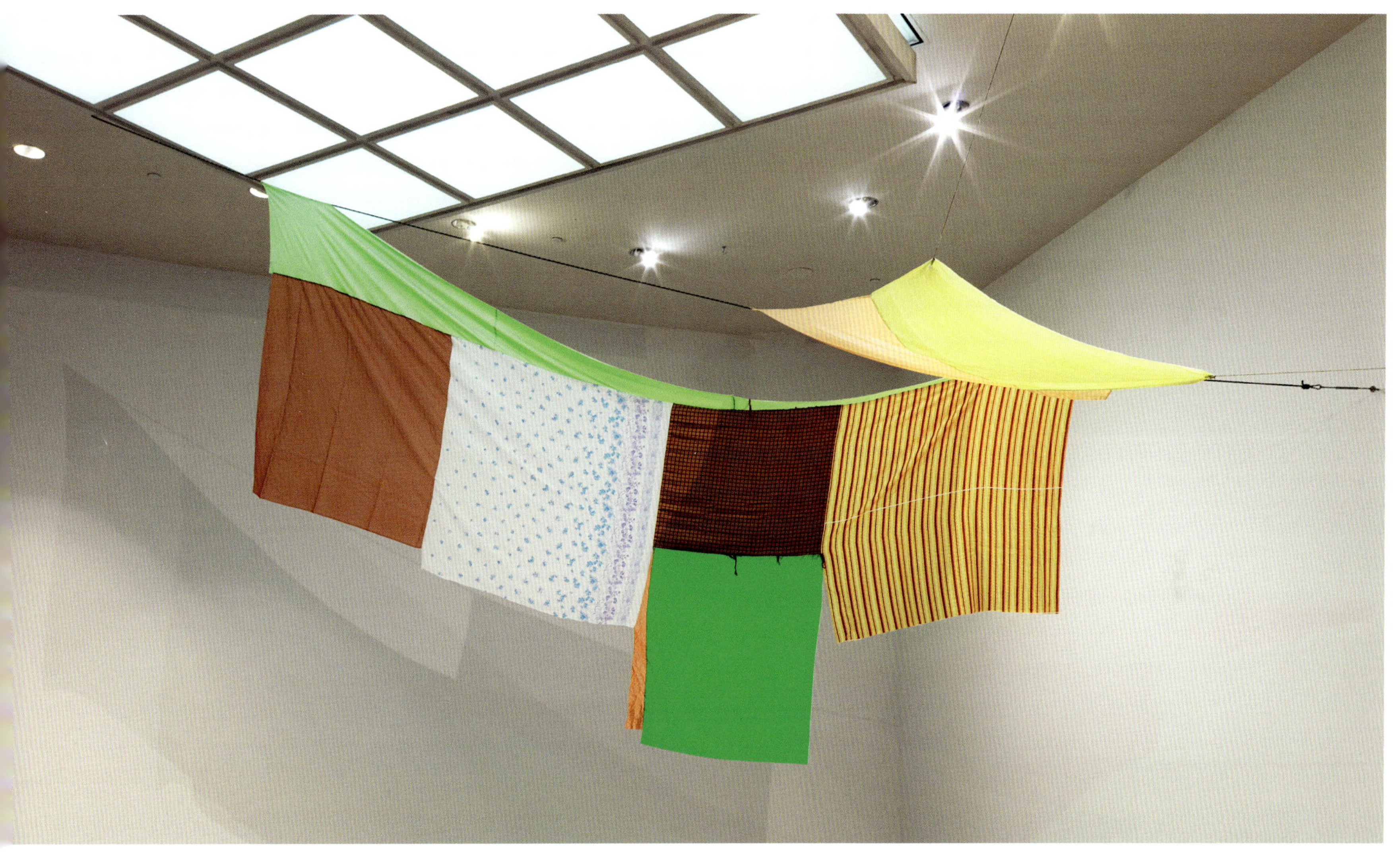

Tessuti Raponi (Ciao Milano)
2018
Installation view, Eric N. Mack:
Lemme walk across the room,
March 6, 2021 – January 2, 2022,
NSU Art Museum Fort Lauderdale
Fabric.
193 × 322 ½ × 87 in /
490.2 × 819.1 × 221 cm
NSU Art Museum Fort Lauderdale;
purchased with funds provided by Michael
and Dianne Bienes, by exchange
© Eric N. Mack
Photo by Steven Brooke

Ronny Quevedo
MFA 2012

Ronny Quevedo (b. 1981, Guayaquil, Ecuador; lives and works in the Bronx, NY)

Ronny Quevedo chose the Yale School of Art for his graduate studies because of the depth and rigor he observed in the work of its graduates. Having attended art school as an undergraduate at Cooper Union, he was drawn to the liberal arts education that was available to graduate students at Yale. He frequently audited art history classes, African American studies with Kobena Mercer, Professor of History of Art and African American Studies, and took Caribbean Studies with Yale Ph.D. student Edgar Garcia, author of *Signs of the Americas: A Poetics of Pictography, Hieroglyphs, and Khipu* (The University of Chicago Press, 2020).

Quevedo recalls that there was a hesitancy about talking about race and ethnicity during formal critiques. When these issues were brought up, "the content was generalized and from the perspective of high and low art." This situation made inviting visiting artists and critics who could provide a broader perspective crucial to their studies. Particularly memorable was a studio visit he had with painter Kerry James Marshall. At the time Quevedo was using shoe polish to create reverse prints of dance steps, and Marshall pointedly critiqued him for not taking into consideration the smell of the shoe polish as integral to these works. This critique reverberates with Quevedo to this day as he consciously considers the nuances of the various properties of his materials.

Quevedo credits his residency at Skowhegan following graduation in 2013, as the turning point in forming his personal vision, with his video *Critical Mass*, 2013. The video combines his interest in the floor as the active ground of his work and American art forms, such as tap dance. The soundtrack is a mix that he had made at Yale of two songs: "The Sound of da Police" (1995) performed by Bronx rapper KRS-One, and the 1960s ballad, "The Sound of Silence" by singing duo Simon & Garfunkel. The video focuses on the performer's feet tapping on a stage illuminated at its perimeter by colored lights that flicker on every time the dancer's foot taps the surface. The recorded music Quevedo used in the video is deliberately out of sync with the dancer's steps.

The soccer field is a consistent trope in Quevedo's work, which reinforces his focus on the ground as the locus of his work. It is at once broadly recognizable, as well as an autobiographical reference to his father, who was a professional soccer player and referee in Ecuador. The gesture also connects his work with minimal artist Carl Andre's copper floor tiles. In his installation *errantry (the benefit of being offsides)* (ill. pp. 64–65) Quevedo arranged cheap linoleum tiles gilded with luxurious gold leaf on the floor. The gold leaf and the labor-intensive gilding process draw attention to how the value of art is based on the effort devoted to its creation, and the preciousness of its materials. Each step viewers take as they walk across the floor installation erodes the gold leaf and reveals the linoleum below.

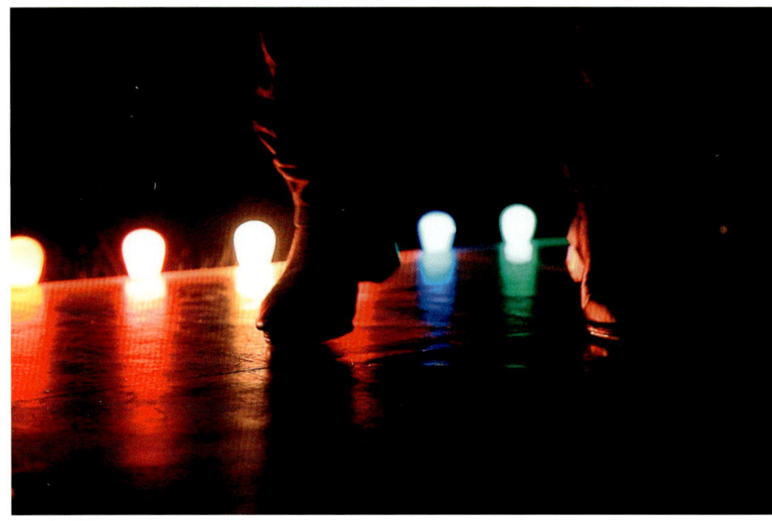

Critical Mass
2013
Video. 3 mins, 5 secs
Courtesy the artist and Alexander Gray Associates, New York
© 2022 Ronny Quevedo

migration lines
2019
Gold leaf on carbon paper
35 × 25 ½ in / 89 × 65 cm
Courtesy the artist and Alexander Gray Associates, New York
© 2022 Ronny Quevedo

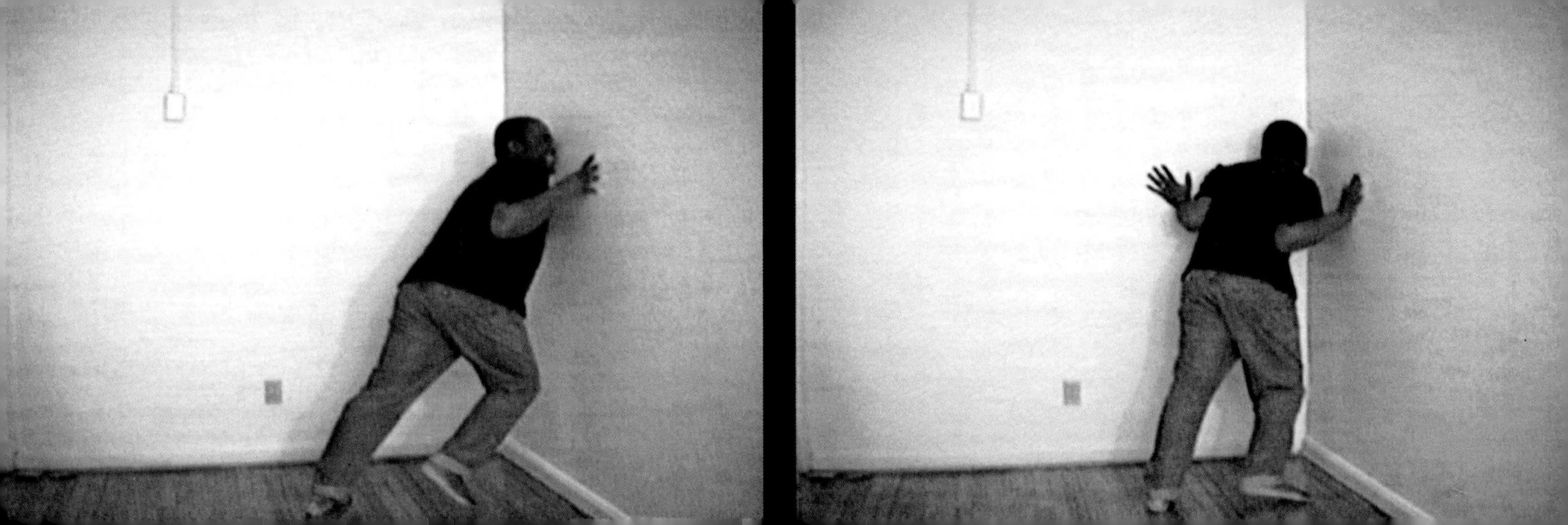

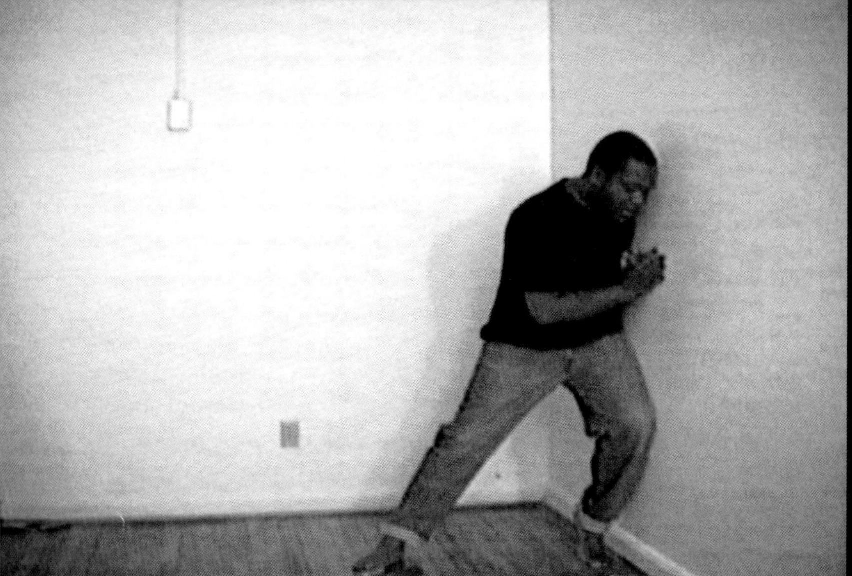

Keith Obadike, *Pushing White Walls/360 (a resistance study)*, 1998

The subtitle of the book *Pushing a white wall*, references the performance *Pushing White Walls/360 (a resistance study)*, 1998, by Keith Obadike (MFA Sound Design 2004). This performance on video documents "three minutes and sixty seconds" of the artist pushing against a solid white wall. The piece was performed in 1998 as a private action and a resistance study.

Photos courtesy of Mendi + Keith Obadike / Obadike Studio

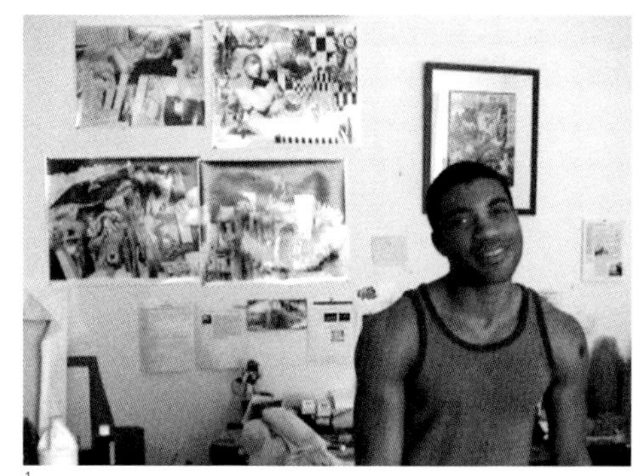
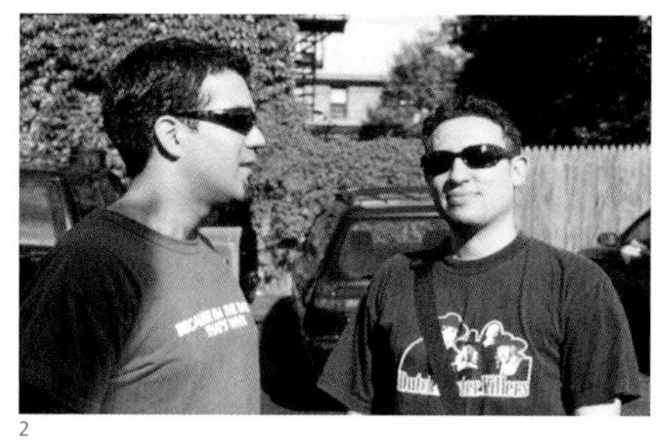
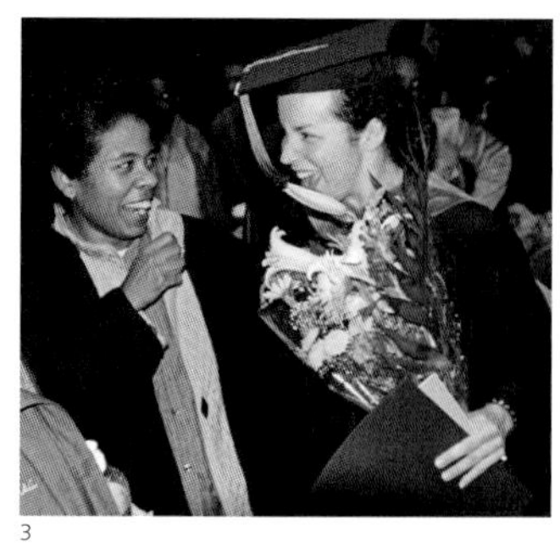
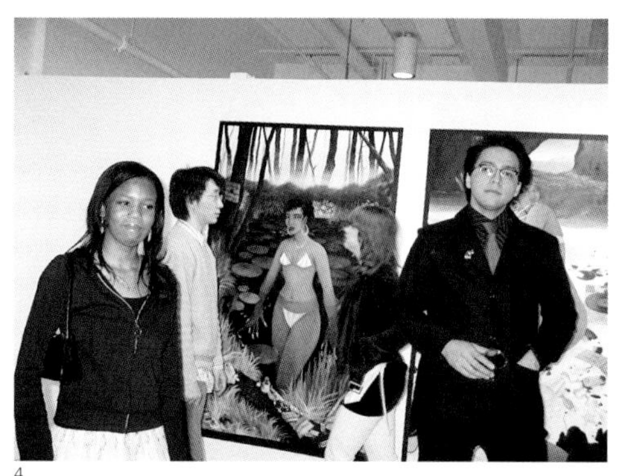
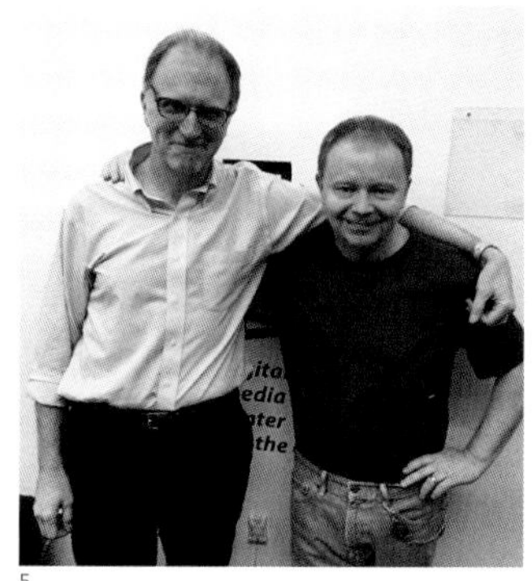
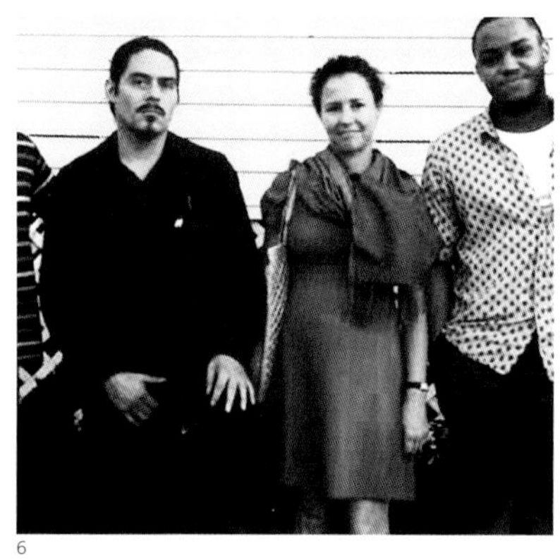
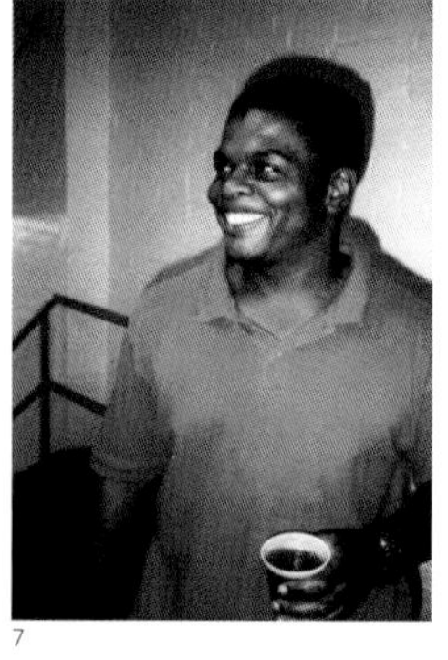
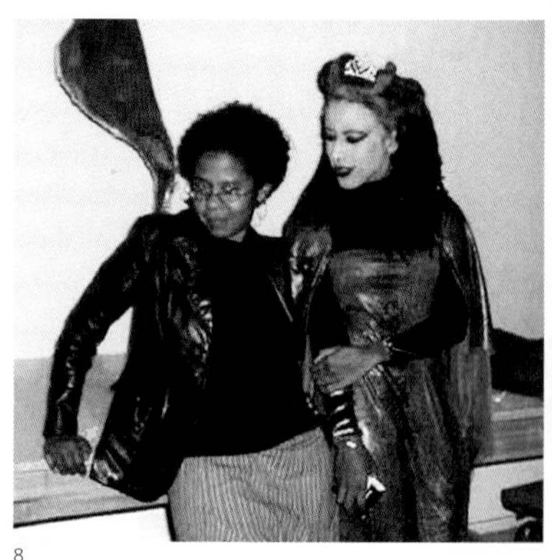
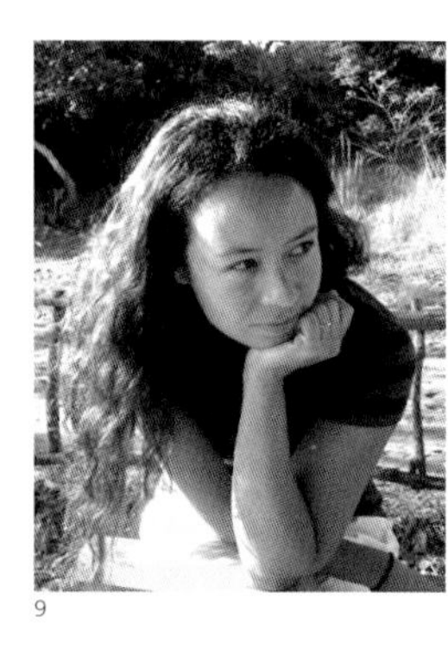
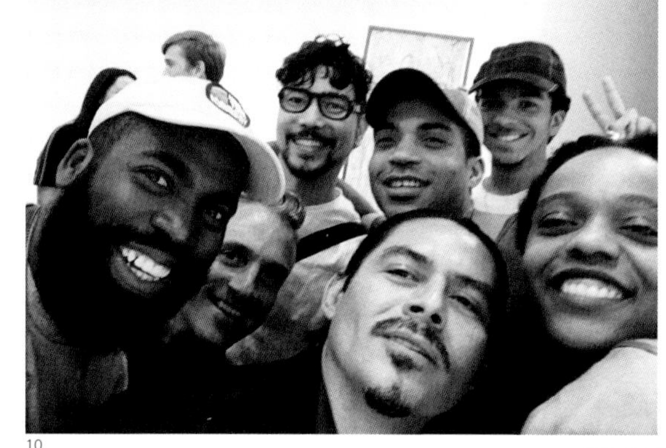
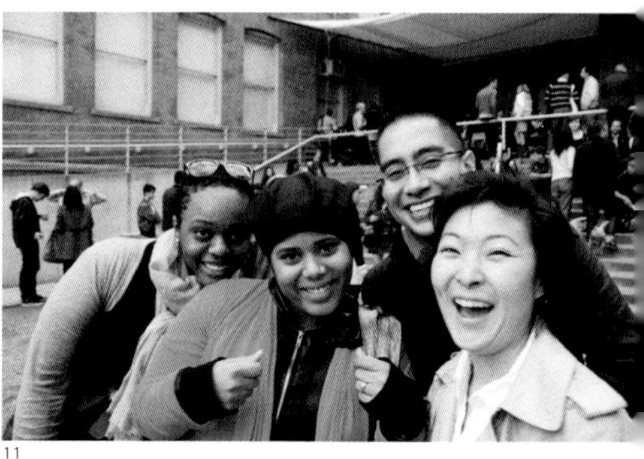
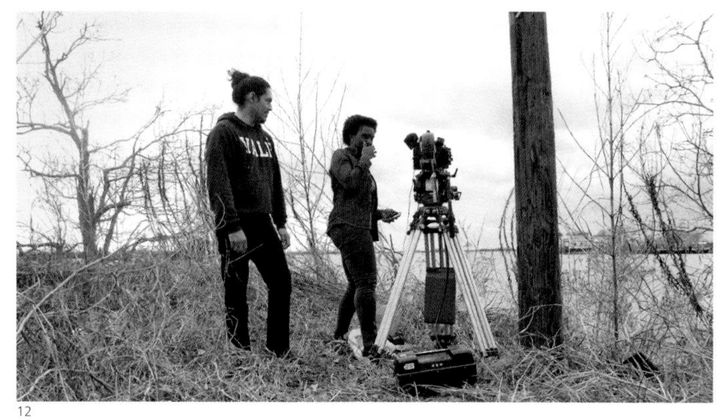
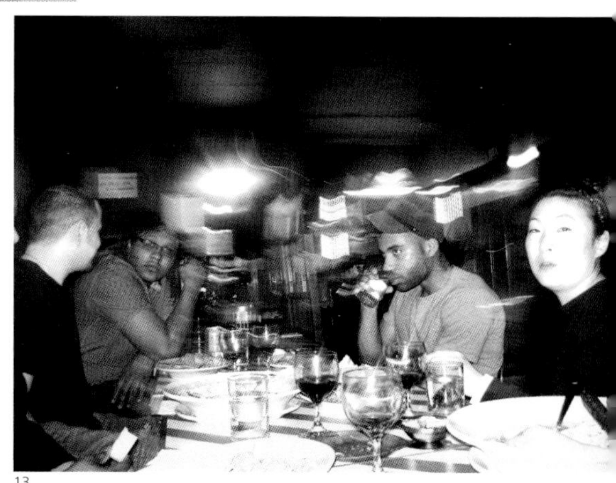

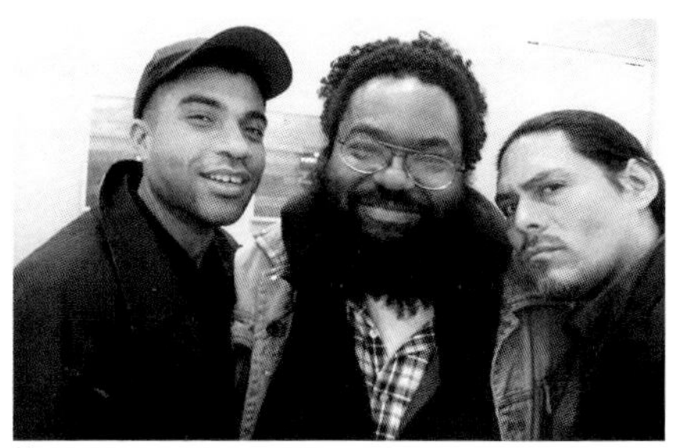
14

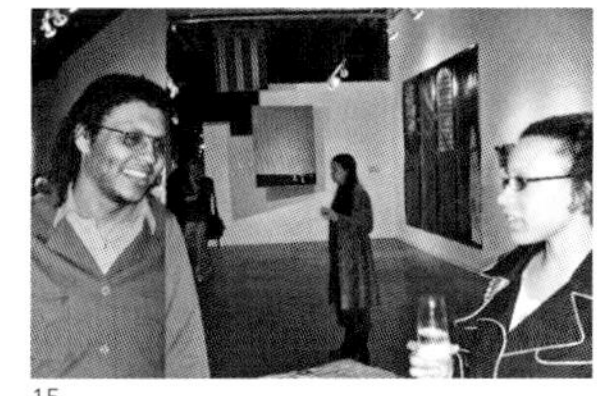
15

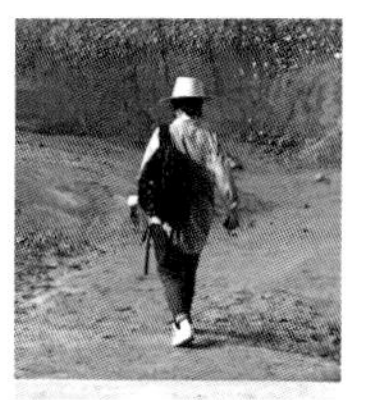
16

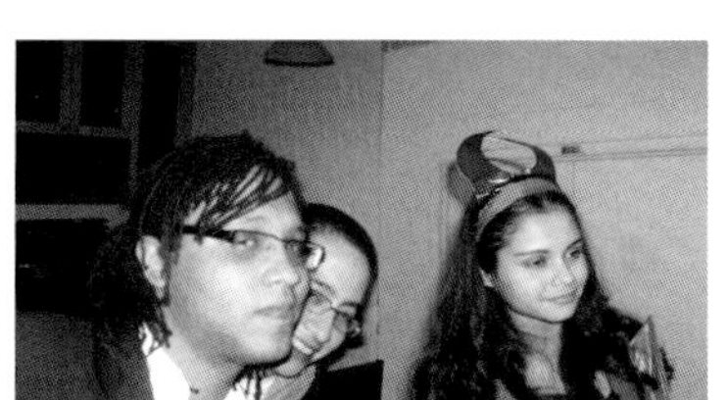
17

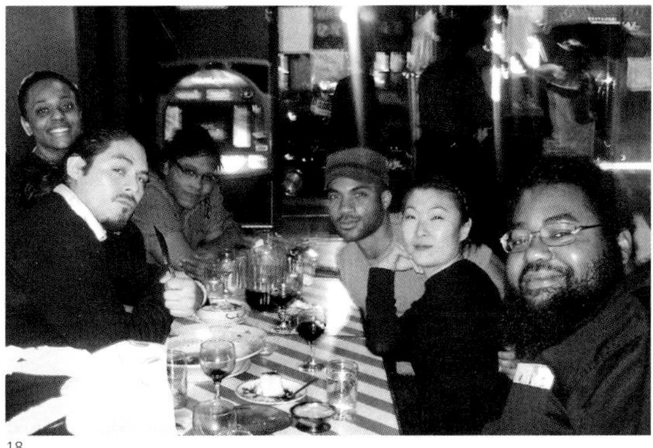
18

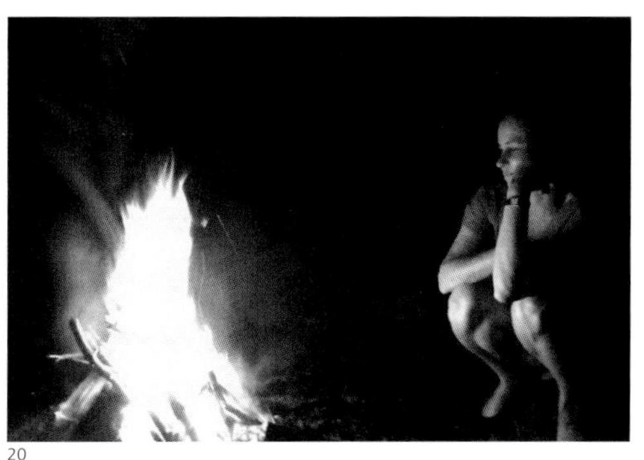
20

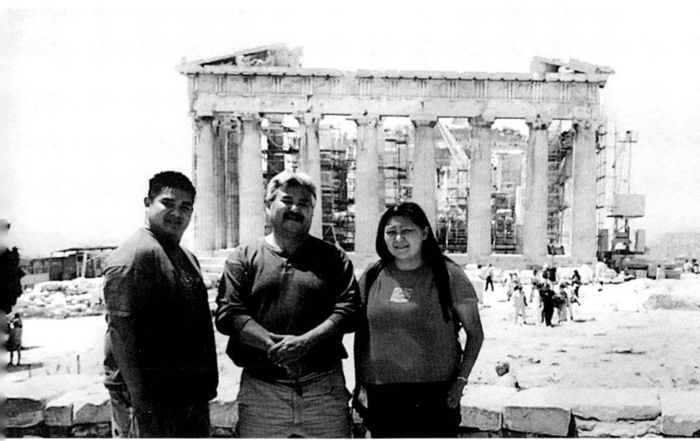

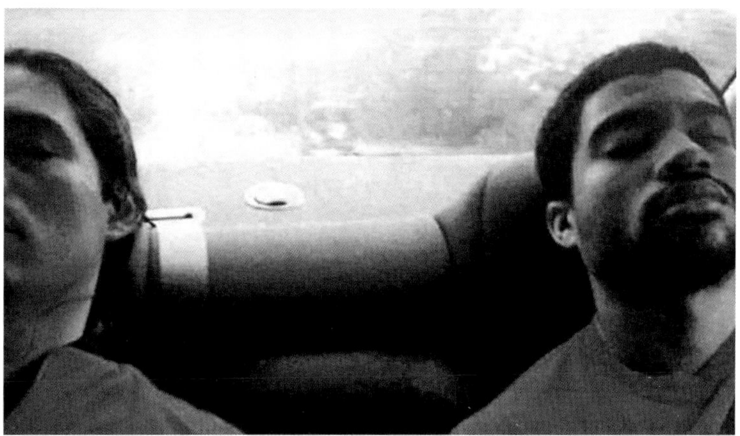
22

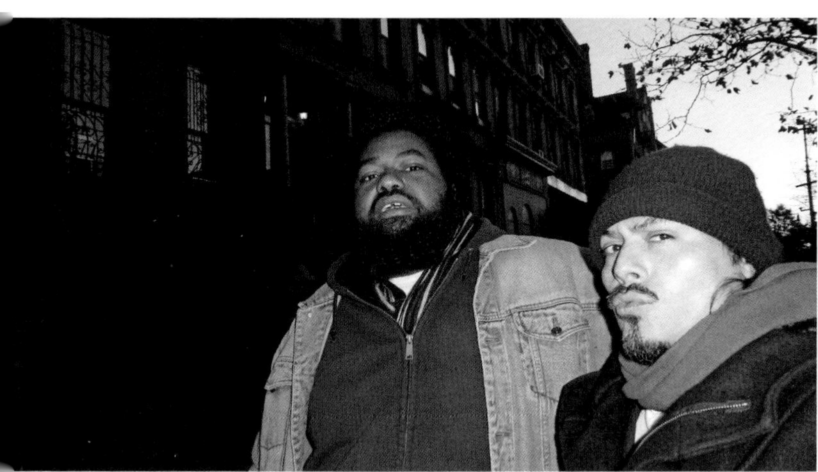

Roundtable discussion with Mike Cloud, william cordova, Shoshanna Weinberger, moderated by Bonnie Clearwater

(April 2, 2022, NSU Art Museum Fort Lauderdale)[1]

Bonnie Clearwater: What happened at Yale that made it such a significant period of time for the artists who studied there between 2000 and 2010?

william cordova: Every generation is influenced, informed, and changed by the steps of those who came before it. Our generation started to come of age in the late 1990s. Hip-hop had a great deal to do with the major influences on youth culture. But it was particularly influential on people of color in part because we were the main architects. We have to observe and understand how hip-hop as a phenomenon evolved on a global scale. It wasn't simply music or aesthetics. Its roots were complex and deep. It included a great mix of 1960s Black, Asian, Latino, national ideologies in the arts, music, culture, religion, cinema, politics, literature, and so forth. This mix of racial, ethnic, cultural, and national influences shaped what was to become hip-hop after the 1970s… Artist Sol Sax (Yale MFA1995) saw this coming in the mid 1990s and understood there had to be a *coup d'état* in the institutions of higher learning. I see him as an early alliance because he broke many windows by articulating the coming of the next wave and breaching into the White castle. This is a generalization of most institutions of higher learning at the time because they tended to only validate the Western canon and dismiss everything else. Jane Balin, Howardena Pindell, Barkley Hendricks, Angela Bassett, David Alan Grier, Dawoud Bey, Sol Sax, MiYoung Sohn, and SunTek Chung all started to change the shape of things prior to the 1960s and well into the 2000s. What we are talking about isn't exclusive to Yale University. I am only highlighting to contextualize how the first ten years of the new millennium began. It was formed by many generations of practitioners who came before us. Without their sense of working collectively, grassroots philosophies, and principles we would not have been able to arrive at our theories and practice. We collectively knew we had arrived but the institutions didn't realize this until they started to hire artist Coco Fusco and author Greg Tate, around 2005. Tate's own *Flyboy in the Buttermilk: Essays on Contemporary America* (1992) was our own Funk & Wagnalls but the institution took a while to catch up to it until we started to shake up the art world(s) in general. The other artists in the exhibition have their own reasons why we gravitated, why we network. My reason was it's just an extension of family. We had similar or common interests that were not necessarily common or studied in school. That could be different theories, different logics, music. But that's on the surface. A lot of the deeper things are implied in the conversation that we don't go into. Their conversation activates certain ideas, certain perspectives. And I would carry that back to my studio at home and work or share with Loren Holland, Ronny Quevedo, Leslie Hewitt, and other artists. After graduation, I would come back and do unofficial studio visits with new students of color. Everything was by word-of-mouth and never official because it was too slow and difficult through proper channels. My conclusion is that we shaped a fragile point in time (2000 to 2010) that prompted me to create a project to illuminate the importance of our collective presence and its contributions as a community.

Shoshanna Weinberger: I went to the School of the Art Institute of Chicago in '91 and graduated in '95. I took six years off between undergrad and graduate school. I thought it was really important to make my own work outside of undergrad and find my own voice. I was working at LaSalle Bank Photography Collection in Chicago. My application to Yale, in the winter of 2000, was encouraged by the curator of LaSalle bank, who said, "You should just apply. You've been getting those applications, the books from Yale for four years."

Getting into Yale, there was a big weight and a big relief. But I think when we got there—you're there for a reason. You have this dedication. I think getting there and finding a community that was slightly polarizing, and finding the old guard, and being amongst this history and being around privilege in a way that kind of manifested, I was able to negotiate many different avenues that I may not have had, because I had two parents that were artists, I was always thinking about, "Okay, how am I going to pay for all this when I'm done?" But I think that finding similar faces and finding that connectivity with people who didn't come from all of this privilege was why we gravitated to each other.

Mike Cloud: I never did well in art classes. So I changed my major to Art Education. Before I graduated I had to take one more art class, and I was like, "Oh my God. I'm going to fail this art class." I took painting and I really enjoyed it, so I stayed for another semester and took more painting classes. When I was younger, I painted murals in Chicago. I didn't think I was a very good painter, even though I loved it. Kerry Marshall suggested that I attend Yale, because they had separate programs, that that would be a place where I would learn to paint better than other programs where it was more interdisciplinary. A lot of my professors discouraged me from applying there because nobody, except a very few people, and no one from our program ever got accepted there. I was like, "Oh, maybe I shouldn't apply. They only accept five or six people." And Kerry Marshall said, "Well, you only need one space." And that was when I made the decision to apply.

BC: What is the application process? I know that it's different for each of the departments.

MC: Well, it was 20-some odd years ago, but you did have to actually go there and bring a painting. We're all sitting out in this hall, and everyone's got their silly painting. And you have to go in there and sit your painting down, and there's two professors, and I think they're trying to get under your skin. So generally you have kind of a bad interview. Everybody does.

SW: I photocopied the entire application, and then I put it up in my apartment, and I highlighted everything that they said.

wc: The application process was tedious. The slide carousel box had to be covered with butcher paper on top but not the sides. I actually prepared two packages. And then eventually after some feedback from grad students, I sent in one version but I was a nervous wreck after going through the process.

MC: william's strategy of making two is brilliant. Because even if they throw one out, they still would get one from him.

wc: [The interview process was] like the film *Blade Runner*. At the beginning [of the film], there's an interview process with the replicant….

MC: "Tell us about your mother."

wc: Yeah. "My mother? You want me to talk about my mother?"

SW: I had all my work shipped. I brought work up. And I was rigorous. It felt like a bad interview. I approached it like it was a job interview, and I remember just sending bullet questions off. Why do you want to be here? What is this about? What's this? Oh, are you doing this? He was like, "Okay." I knew what I was doing. It wasn't like I didn't know what I was doing.

BC: The committee though was all faculty. It didn't include students.

wc: No grad students participated in the interview or selection process for the Painting department, but they did in the Sculpture department.

BC: Let's hear from the Sculpture department [seated in the audience]. You had a different process. Right?

Anna Tsouhlarakis: So all of the second-year students that were in the sculpture program were on the admissions committee, in my time, with only one faculty member, the chair of the department. And so it was a much smaller group, but the students had the bulk of the decision of who was making up the next class, which I think is phenomenal to think about.

BC: And did you have a good interview or a bad interview?

AT: I thought I had a great interview, and we weren't required to bring work with us. I think I brought slides of new work, but we didn't even get to that in my interview. I thought it went well.

MC: Before I applied, I bought a book about applying to graduate school, and they said apply to seven schools. So I applied to seven schools. So [Yale] was one of many. It was less nerve-wracking in some way, even though it was different from all the other applications because the others weren't like, "You have to wrap the slide carousel in that particular way." And I didn't have to go there and bring work for the others.

WC: I had a wonderful interview experience. The [application committee] was really engaged in the way I was thinking, producing, and the direction I was coming from. I was talking Third Cinema, OSPAAAL graphic design ideologies, and literary folks from Peru and the Caribbean. They knew some of the visual artists I was referencing but not many. The interview lasted 30 minutes. I felt very happy. But of course, you never know. You could be happy and they're kind of thinking, "This guy doesn't know what he's talking about."

BC: Why did you chose to go to the school?

WC: I knew that I needed to go to grad school. I reached the point where I couldn't develop on my own critically. I thought I could just go to undergrad and that's it. But then my friends applied and went. Then, within a short amount of time, I saw a huge development in their work. But it took me a little while [until] a friend of mine, the late [artist] Michael Richards said, "You need to go to grad school. You need to go to these schools." I did want to study with filmmaker, D. A. Pennebaker, and art historian, Dr. Kellie Jones. And both of them were at Yale University. I made a promise to myself and Michael, after his passing, that I would apply and attend Yale and Studio Museum in Harlem, and that is exactly what I did. RIP Michael.

MC: I would just also say that william was doing work that is more interdisciplinary than they were used to. And more international than they were used to. Shoshanna was interested in work about identity that they were not used to, or maybe even interested in. And I was just an abstract painter, working in a language they understood. So they looked at us very differently.

SW: As a female student, it was quite an interesting kind of experience of being like, "Oh. Why are you giving that person a studio visit with so and so, and there's some people here that would like to get a studio visit." There was a little bit of favoritism.

MC: And with that gender issue too, and also racial, and also this idea of—lineage. I understood that, in our political system, to be in a lineage, not only do you have to be inspired by somebody, but you have to be able to inspire further people down the line. And so it was understood that you cannot be a part of a lineage unless other artists recognize your legitimacy.

WC: I had a particular way of speaking during crits at Miami Dade College and SAIC [School of the Art Institute of Chicago]. But I also realized that those environments were much more interdisciplinary, gender, and racially diverse. In grad school I felt that I constantly had to explain what every little thing was. Like a poet explaining their poem to the crowd, right after reading it to them. It was an uncomfortable feeling, not that critiques are supposed to be easy. Rather it was more like me teaching the students and faculty about my identity, race, culture, customs and then after all that I still couldn't get any critical feedback.

BC: And that's when you started reaching out to other students?

wc: We had to find alternatives, and found them in conversations with other artists of color in different departments. Students, Doreen Adengo in architecture, Irene Small, Courtney J. Martin, and Dr. Imo Nse Imeh in the Art History department. Also, Dr. Kellie Jones and the late D.A. Pennebaker in Film and Media Studies department.

BC: And the role of visiting artists and critics was also very important and filled in the gaps?

wc: There was a lot of visiting artists and scholars coming to the Art History department at the time, circa 2002–2004. But there must have been a disconnect with the Art History department and the Painting, Sculpture, Photography, Graphic Design, Architecture departments, because we would rarely find out when they had visiting lecturers. Our departments were much closer and disseminated information much better. I hope things have changed between Art History and the MFA departments.

SW: I was really spoiled at The Art Institute of Chicago. I had a lot of professors that were female and a real diverse set of faculty there,

so as an undergrad I had faculty that looked like me, who [I] could identify [with]. I was expecting that kind of engagement with [Yale] faculty. So I came into that with like, "Hey, I applied and I got in with the slides that I put in the carousels." [The faculty] would tell me "Adrian Piper was the only artist that did identity art. As she's done it you don't have to do that." I remember doing our own critiques—a lot of moments of sitting in the lounge or coming to the studio, and each of us critiquing each other's work and getting feedback. I had a few people in the Sculpture department that would come, and I would go to their studios. Having that community, and making my own interdisciplinary courses, I was like, "I'm just going to do this. I'm paying for this." So I think that's how we started to evolve and create on our own and to forget the faculty.

BC: Mike, you were in painting.

MC: And I was painting abstract paintings as the professors understood.

BC: So they understood your work? Did you make it so they would understand it, or this is what you wanted to make, and they understood it?

MC: I guess that's where my trick worked too well in the end. I'll say that that kind of trauma of the professors sitting there, and pulling out of you rather than giving you, that was so real that for many years afterwards, when I would be a Visiting Artist, I would go to the studio of

minority MFA students, and I would say, "Do not become a storyteller. I'm going to sit here and just give me a minute, and I'll look at the work, and then I'll talk to you." Because if you start talking about where you came from, why you're making the work, then the professor will just sit there and listen. And then, you won't get anything. The reason why I think we [Yale MFAs] started talking to each other is just that we were willing to give and not take anything. So william would come into my studio and start judging things and talking about them without asking me to do any work for him. This just became a thing we would do.

I would also say that with gender and with race in the art world as well, there was this idea that you could be famous but not significant. You couldn't be assigned within this symbolic language of history. I think that that idea that minority and women artists can be famous but not significant, maybe [the faculty] felt like our work operated in a post-critical space. We didn't even need to be critiqued because of the way our work was going to operate in the world. So if you were a Black artist painting Black bodies, then you were fine, and they didn't need to engage with your work critically. If you were a white guy painting geometric abstraction, you were fine. They didn't need to engage with you critically.

wc: Also, the legacy we spoke of in the year 2000 was not what it is today. Today, people are very familiar with Barkley Hendricks. Back then, the public in general was not very familiar with his work. When Kehinde [Wiley] started to get attention for his figurative paintings most people didn't reference Barkley, because they didn't know about Barkley even though he graduated from Yale. Out of sight out of mind. Howardena Pindell, who was an artist and a curator at MoMA from '68 to '78, was not even part of the conversation. But we were aware of them. I was aware of them in undergrad. Even reached out to Barkley when I was in grad school to propose a documentary. I have to admit, in general, I was trying to create a video archive back then because I felt that we *were* because of Barkley and Howardena's legacy, but it wasn't part of this mainstream legacy, it wasn't part of the conversation until [the curator] Trevor Schoonmaker illuminated Barkley Hendricks' career.[2]

We were far and few at Yale. Who's afraid of Black, Brown, Red, and Yellow? I used to say… slowly many students of color gravitated to one another. This is how I met Monique Walton and Andia Winslow (both BFA 2004), and participated in their documentary *Still, Black at Yale* (2004). Which is an account of student life at Yale. We all continued to work collectively in various projects or just studio visits and conversations for moral support. I know Michael [Cloud] didn't participate but at the same time he did more than he knows. He'd share a thought, a phrase but they resonated like a Big Daddy Kane lyric. I remember Mike once said, "People group (art) work in a way that diffuses the power of the most uncanny objects."

MC: I was not invited in.

WC: You were always invited. But by the time Michael graduated, he already had commercial gallery representation in New York. It was a very uncommon situation for a student to have so early in their career.

MC: That was that moment that my trick worked too well. Because I made this work that professors would understand, so that they could talk about it. And then they talked about it. But then when I went out to the art world, I did a show, and [Grace Glueck] of *The New York Times* [September 24, 2004] wrote a review of it. She was talking about me being a New York School painter like Ad Reinhardt and I was like, "Whoa, whoa, whoa, whoa." The language I had learnt at school worked fine—in our context of school we could talk—but out in the world I didn't want to be misidentified in that way. So I had to change what I was doing and learned other languages from the world.

BC: And language actually entered your work, but coded information as well, or symbolic information. How did you arrive at what you're doing now?

MC: Teaching helped a lot. One reason I liked teaching at Yale as a Visiting Critic, is because the issues that are going to be important are already important there. The students are wrestling with things that are going to be an issue in a few years in the world. One of the

issues that came up there early was empathy. You hear empathy a lot now in culture. Arthur Jafa did this video, *Love is the Message, The Message is Death* [2016]. After George Floyd's killing, a lot of cultural institutions all over the world showed the work simultaneously. Arthur Jafa was asked how he felt about it, and he would say how people would come up to him, and they would be crying and tell him how much they were moved by the work. But he was ambivalent because he wasn't sure how he felt about this kind of microwave empathy, [I think that's] what he called it. I had students who were asking the same kind of question. "I'm making this work about this group of people I feel passionate about. But how does the audience actually feel?" And I thought to myself, *well, you can do an experiment*. What you would do is, make work about another community and then see how you felt, and then that would logically be how the audience would feel when you make work about your community. So that wrestling with empathy [which is what] all of my students were doing is what led me out of my favored mode of painting, which is painting abstract spaces that have atmosphere, maybe some architecture, maybe some text, maybe some geometry, but I don't paint people. In order to engage with what the [students] were wrestling with, I had to start painting people somehow. That wrestling with how to paint people and objects is what led to the kind of [painting I'm doing now]. Also, empathy is a kind of filter so that I don't experience all of the pain of the world.

And messing with that filter let in so much kind of trauma that it really shattered my ability to make pictures. So that created the kind of struggle that my paintings try to embody, and it came a lot from teaching.

BC: william, what was interesting about the Miami artists was that you, Luis Gispert, and John Espinosa came from an environment in Miami, which in the 1990s, was already a growing international art scene. You came with a different perspective than other students that went to Yale. You also came from the South Florida community and an art world that was very diverse. Going to Yale is a very different experience. How did your work change being at Yale?

wc: I remember practitioners, Gean Moreno, Eugenia Vargas, and Jorge Pantoja creating platforms in the late 1990s where artists could critically address their concerns, challenge one another about their practices, politics, and community. This was due in part to the lack of diversity in the Miami art world. Miami's a big place so diversity may not have been equally represented in all of South Florida at the time. Some of us also studied undergrad outside of Florida. Leaving and coming back that first time around gave us the opportunity to reflect and realize how much had changed and how much still needed to change at home. We made mistakes, learned from our experiences in a short period of time. Eventually, we started to leave for grad school.

I have to give thanks to my friend Genaro Ambrosino and Lou Anne Colodny for supporting my practice before and after grad school.

[It] was around 2009 when I started reflecting on the fact that many of the artists I was closely working with were mostly from Yale. It's also hard to reflect or pace yourself when you're just starting your career but after the Whitney Biennial (2008) I began to pace myself differently. My practice also didn't evolve within the commercial art world. I had different agendas and the pressure to create or develop was not based on monetary examples. Still, I'd curated or organized many small exhibitions focused on artists of color from Yale; *Paradise City* (2002), *Skillz* (2004), *Supersonic* (2005), *Gimme Shelter* (2006), *Passin' it On* (2007) *Casa de Carton* (2008). So I wasn't oblivious of what we were slowly crafting together. Then I spoke to Coco Fusco, artist-curator-author, about this. I stated the fact that most of the students who came out of Yale that were either academically, critically or economically successful were artists of color who had graduated within the millennium. I added that some of us were similar in age, interests, background, and values but not all. Still we all shared a unique experience that brought us together.

MC: You reminded me of something Professor Mel Bochner said, where he said that the problem with being of the moment is that you have to wait for someone else to define the moment. And I think that maybe being not

accepted there forced that generation of artists of color to invent new modes of working.

BC: That is what interested me in this period of Yale graduate students, and why I wanted to develop it into an exhibition. I was interested in how collectively you made a change and contributed to the change not only in the art discourse but the broader general public discourse and brought a new perspective to the way art is being taught.

<hr>

[1] This text has been edited by the artists from the original video transcript. See QR code on p. 5 for the video of the Roundtable.

[2] Trevor Schoonmaker, *Barkley L. Hendricks: Birth of the Cool* (Durham, North Carolina: Duke University Press Books, 2018).

Oral Histories[1]

Hip Hop Culture: Sol Sax (Yale MFA 1995)

Hip-hop culture changed academic culture in a lot of ways, particularly in the artworld. When I was trying to get into art school in the '80s, all the art schools would reject you if you had any graffiti, or anything that looked like graffiti in your portfolio. The academy was very against the aesthetic of hip-hop and the cultural expression of people of color at that time. Nonetheless, so many gifted people from the culture made it into the schools and came through the academy withholding their culture. Young artists found that retaining hip-hop culture may not have been appreciated in the academy, but it was culturally popular to a growing audience of people that valued the conventional Eurocentric aesthetic of academic painting, sculpture, new media, and performance. Artists of color developed multi-cultural studio practices drenched in references to hip-hop that just didn't happen by most academically trained artists of color in the '60s and '70s. By the '90s and 2000s, a lot of artists of color were using street culture to reframe multiculturalism in the academy. If it weren't for racism, I often think about what would've happened, if we had a history of cultural subjectivity, cultural respect for one another. How different our society would be if there was more balance and cultural exchange. But our history of a completely Eurocentric Academy left street culture as the only voice of African retention, and it has been confronting the European Academy for a hundred years from the blues to hip-hop. Hip-hop is the modern African American academy. In my neighborhood, we had street psychologists, we had street lawyers, a whole culture kept underfoot. When I joined Robert Farris Thomas's lecture at Yale, he made an announcement to the class, "This is the first time that one of my informants has become one of my students." I think that's what our generation really was, we're some of the first people of color to be accepted into these elite schools in large numbers. Many took the opportunity to start writing our identity into the academy as practitioners of the cultures that had been separated and kept apart from the academic culture of this country. Our generation is using the aesthetic of hip-hop culture as a bridge to reclaim the many cultures and histories excluded from contributing to the Academy. We have to continue to focus and make our obsidian tower, our ebony tower, our mahogany tower, our maple tower of people of color telling our history and with our own academic voice.[2]

Anna Tsouhlarakis: What drives me to make work is the idea that culture must evolve to grow, and if we don't, it will be stagnant; it will die. When I began making work, I learned how to do traditional arts, like pottery and beadwork, and silversmithing. My dad makes traditional Native American jewelry and I learned from him. As a teen, I remember hearing a story of an elder and a young boy in a sweat lodge. In a sweat lodge you sing songs. The elder looked at the boy and said, "Okay, it's your turn. You need to make a song for us." And the boy responded, "Me? I can't make a song. I don't know those ways and how to do all that." And the elder said, "If you don't create new songs, our culture will die. You have to keep making songs and know that it's within you." That's the way I see my work, it's an evolution of Native art.

In the early 2000s I was one of a handful of Native women artists to create nonlinear video and performance art. Now, I'm probably one in a thousand and that is amazing. There's so much new work out there that we couldn't even imagine 20 years ago. And I'm proud of being at least one little step in that long journey. I think our communities are very flexible and adaptable. We've adapted to be here. My people were supposed to have been dead 400 years ago, but somehow, we're still here. And I know that we have the mindset and the growth to evolve and work in new ways. When I started making the work I do, I was nervous. But my father, who is a well-known artist, is my biggest supporter, and he'd say, "I have no idea what you're doing, but I will help you build this." I knew that if he could try to understand and learn to appreciate it, then I could make work like this.

In 2007, the Navajo Nation Museum in Arizona asked me to travel a solo exhibition I had in a New York gallery to the Navajo Nation Museum. It was the first time I know of that any of these new mediums had ever been shown on the reservation: installation, video, and performance work. All of a sudden, kids on the reservation were being exposed to work in their community and hearing, "Yes, this is art. This is Navajo art." But the best part about that particular exhibition was that the work was dealing with my Greek identity. It was showing them that we are complex, complicated people, and that's okay. We don't have to explain that to people. We can just be. To me, that's always been a big thing because culturally, in the Navajo way, it's maternal, matrilineal, and so I am fully Navajo. But Greek is patrilineal, so I'm fully Greek as well. I'm not half this or half that.

Shoshanna Weinberger: It all starts with my parents. My father and mother met at the School of Visual Arts in New York City in the mid-1960s. My mother was born and raised in Kingston, Jamaica. After attending school, my parents moved to Jamaica, and had me, then my sister. In the mid-1970s, we then moved to America, and I grew up in Montclair, New Jersey. During my childhood, my parents would take my sister and I back to Jamaica to visit family and stay connected to the culture.

A lot of my history is about being on the periphery as sort of a "Double Consciousness." I'm not Jamaican enough in Jamaica; I'm not American enough in America; and I am "Shoshanna Weinberger," and the irony is that I wasn't raised in either the Jewish faith nor was I raised as a Christian. However, both religions informed me growing up. My whole experience has been standing on the periphery. Referencing writer Nella Larsen, whose fictional stories about women, as "emotional nomads" navigating on impulse to shape-shift among society in order to survive or "pass" is easily identifiable to me. I can identify as a nomad that can go in and out of different private and public spaces, but also dealing with the macro-aggressions of, "You don't look Jamaican?" And to that, I say… "Well, what is a Jamaican supposed to look like…?" It seems at times I have to navigate my identity by proving my heritage.

I consider myself a visual anthropologist, cataloging these experiences through my work. Thinking about one's identity based on first impressions and society's assumed norms, I use this to reinvent, critique, and create specimens or "muses." My muses remain within frame. Thinking about how women are objectified throughout history. Thinking about female exposé and presentation, especially how Black and brown bodies have been portrayed or not included or if included within a certain stereotype in mainstream, growing up.

Two of the three works in the *Lux et Veritas* exhibition: *Potbelly Porn Star and the Rise of Bacon* and *Muffin Top Banana Bottom* are self-portraits. Thinking about how my body moves among and within space because of this surveilled history. For a lot of women, we think about, how our bodies appear in any given space and that is what these works evoke. These are excessive, unapologetic images of female bodies occupying space. I want viewers to see them as flipping back and forth from: human to animal; dominant to passive; and grotesque to beautiful.

Mamiko Otsubo: I was born in Japan. My family and I moved to New York when I was nine months old. Two years later we moved to Seattle. Two years after that we moved back to Tokyo. When I was eight, we moved to Los Angeles. I would say that I grew up both here (USA) and there (Japan) and have been shaped by the reality that I am considered foreign or otherwise "other" in both places. I wasn't always aware of this when I first started making art, but my artworks have always focused on how different parts meet. "Parts" is a general and perhaps inadequate word to use here. I use this word, both to refer to things that are visible to the eye in an artwork (i.e.: materials, different sculptural elements), as well as those things that are more visible to the mind (i.e.: histories, vernaculars, strategies). This preoccupation with how different parts meet is at its most basic core about trying to understand the clash—the experience of being Japanese and also American, by continually recreating it. Often you will see that the manner of this meeting is abrupt and comically obvious, sometimes clean and surgical, other times, with undertones of force and violence. For all its variations, it is, however, never seamless. The parts never blend into each other. They remain distinct. I am hesitant to refer to this preoccupation as the subject of the work. Instead, I would offer that now having been engaged with making my work for some time, I recognize this as a throughline in all my works. It is the point at which my work most obviously opens.

Abigail DeVille: I was born and raised, a native New Yorker. I'm from the Bronx. I went to the Fashion Institute of Technology, for undergrad, and it's a general fine arts program. There's no area of specificity, so I ended up doing all things at all times, which defines my practice. I'm more interested in what's the best medium for the message versus being indebted to a kind of specific technical practice or specific material practice.

Eric N. Mack: I experienced [Sam] Gilliam at a really important time when I was learning the rules of abstraction. I went to a show at the Corcoran [Art Gallery, Washington, D.C.] when I was in high school. This was really important because you could see these massive installations hanging from classical architecture. A few years later I saw a Morris Louis show in D.C., and that began to spur similar questions. In reading about both of them, but particularly Sam, there was a real critique about Sam's work in relation to Louis. Sam was disregarded as parody early on. That exclusion and resistance to him [had a lot do to with him] as a Black abstractionist and there were all these maneuvers to push artists out of the forefront. But he continued to have this kind of innovation. You can look at the work in relation to the [structural support of the painting] and Arte Povera. There are so many points of dexterity that have to do with his work: his relentless dedication to paint, the soaked canvas and his connection to [Helen] Frankenthaler; the way he can really attack the architecture and

impose his own kind of language is always fascinating.[3]

Art School

Luis Gispert: We felt like we came into [Yale] at a very interesting time, an in-between time. The class that was ahead of us, the second year [students], was an interesting, eclectic group of people. At the time, there was an organized effort between [the departments of] photography, sculpture, and painting, to have cross crits and cross dialogue, and hanging out, and having friends across departments. At the time, students that were more concept-based found themselves looking for discourse in photography. They were doing a lot of videos, because there was a lot of painters that were also filming the videos.

There's a network of Yalies and Non-Yalies that are still there. But it comes and it goes. william cordova, who graduated two classes later… maintained a network. The first decade after graduation there was definitely a vibrant network of graduates and of following classes. For example, I maintain a dialogue connection with Christian Curiel, who graduated from painting a couple of classes after me, who's also originally from Miami. Mickalene Thomas, Kehinde Wiley, [and I] were all in the same class… we were aware of each other. We kind of are in conversation.[4]

AT: A network definitely evolved from my time at Yale. I was much more connected than I was when I started out, with friends and classmates that I made in the Sculpture department. Even today, there are people that I stay in contact with and who are good friends. I was the only Native grad student at the School of Art during my time on campus. Before my time, there was another Native art grad student in the mid-'90s. I was alone in the program in that way. My people came from the School of Forestry and Yale Law School. While I had friends at the art school, my closest friends were in other areas. I took Federal Indian Law. I was told I was the first art graduate student to take that course at Yale Law School. In my law class there were two other Native grad students from the School of Forestry. It was a way for me to connect and survive. No matter where I am, I do better when I have other Natives around me for dialog and conversation. During the time I was at Yale, there were a lot of contemporary Native artists working, specifically in the '80s and '90s, but a lot of them had not yet reached new media, and there weren't many that were branching out yet to video and performance. I was interested in working in these new ways because they didn't have the baggage of expectation as a Native artist. I loved video. I loved performance. I loved installation. There was a freedom working in these ways.

Mike Cloud: The first time I lived away from home was when I went to graduate school at Yale. I didn't have that much experience in painting before then. When I was there, if you brought work that wasn't painting to critique, you were welcome to do that, but people wouldn't talk about it. In the Painting department they would only talk about painting. That was fine for me because it taught me how to be a better painter. It was a really good group of painters at the time. So I must have gotten five years better in the two years. I was there.[5]

SW: "Art School" started at home during my early childhood. My mother always had me doing something creative when we moved to America. She was my first art teacher. My father was a photographer and my second teacher, who taught me existentialism with questions at the age of 10: "How do you visualize the calendar year?" Every Saturday, from the age of 15 until I graduated high school, my mother took me into New York City, where she and I would spend eight hours doing figure-drawing classes at The Art Student's League. I understood from my parents that being an artist is a profession, and with that you have training and learn the formal rules in order to challenge them. Although I don't use traditional figure drawing or realism, I have learned how to give my muses a physical gesture, attitude or a specific posture. Growing up, I was raised in a world where I was taught to take experience and translate it into something artistic using what was available or through invention. After high school, I went to the School of the Art Institute of Chicago and graduated in '95. After undergrad, I secured a position, as a Curatorial Assistant for the LaSalle National Bank Photography Collection in Chicago, and after six years became the Collection Manager there. I learned a great deal about how to care for art, hang, and store it. I took six years off before applying to Yale because I wanted to make work that was not part of my undergrad canon and create from lived experience. When I got into Yale, I was excited to return to making work instead of caring for it. I never thought I would be part of Yale's history, but here I was. While attending, I had only a handful of professors that I could have a dialogue with, but the majority of the professors were kind of "old guard." I was feeling a little bit like I was on a lifeboat, finding myself rowing ashore, meeting and connecting more with my peers in painting and printmaking, but also finding connections in the Sculpture, Photography, Graphic Design, and even Architecture departments. The critiques were often steered by the old guard, and there were lots of favoritism that seemed to be part of the typical patriarchy and the same canon of art that we are all supposed to think about and read about and contemplate.[6]

william cordova: I often think of entering Yale as a moment when my generation departed the '90s with a completely new set of rules and logic. A generation collectively engendering alternative ideas and challenging the status quo by pausing and debunking institutionalized aesthetic standards. I was thinking of a fourth dimension that constantly oscillates and is defined by an alternate theory based on spirituality Black, Brown, Red, and Yellow consciousness, woven into a non-linear narrative.

In my work, I wanted to illuminate the synthesis of memory, ritual, and mythologies that have the capacity to disrupt, challenge, and reassess definitions of our collective landscape. I'm talking about hip-hop, Native American mathematics, sacred geometries. We were improvising on top of the rules and the rulers, and being conceptualists as a state of being. There was much confusion and pushback [from some of the faculty which is] why we found common bonds and built support groups. We networked throughout the 2000s and built a presence despite the lack of informed hip-hop scholarship at the time, despite the lack of academic interest in *our own side of the mountain*.

We all grew up with the same music and literature, we all grew up in the 1980s and '90s. We all graduated from the hip-hop before the genre was embraced by institutions of higher learning. There was no scholarship on hip-hop in the 1990s and early 2000s in major universities. It wasn't until Franklin Sirmans curated *One Planet Under the Groove* at the Bronx Museum (2001) that academics started to realize that *Flyboy in the Buttermilk* (1992) by Greg Tate (RIP) was hip-hop's thesis statement gone unnoticed for almost a decade.

Today, universities incorporate and teach *Bulletproof Diva* (1994) by Lisa Jones, *No Disrespect* (1996) by Sister Souljah, *Holler if You Hear Me* (2001) by Michael Eric Dyson, and *Can't Stop, Won't Stop* by Jeff Chang as part of their regular curriculums without pause, without reservation. I remember, UCLA teaching classes

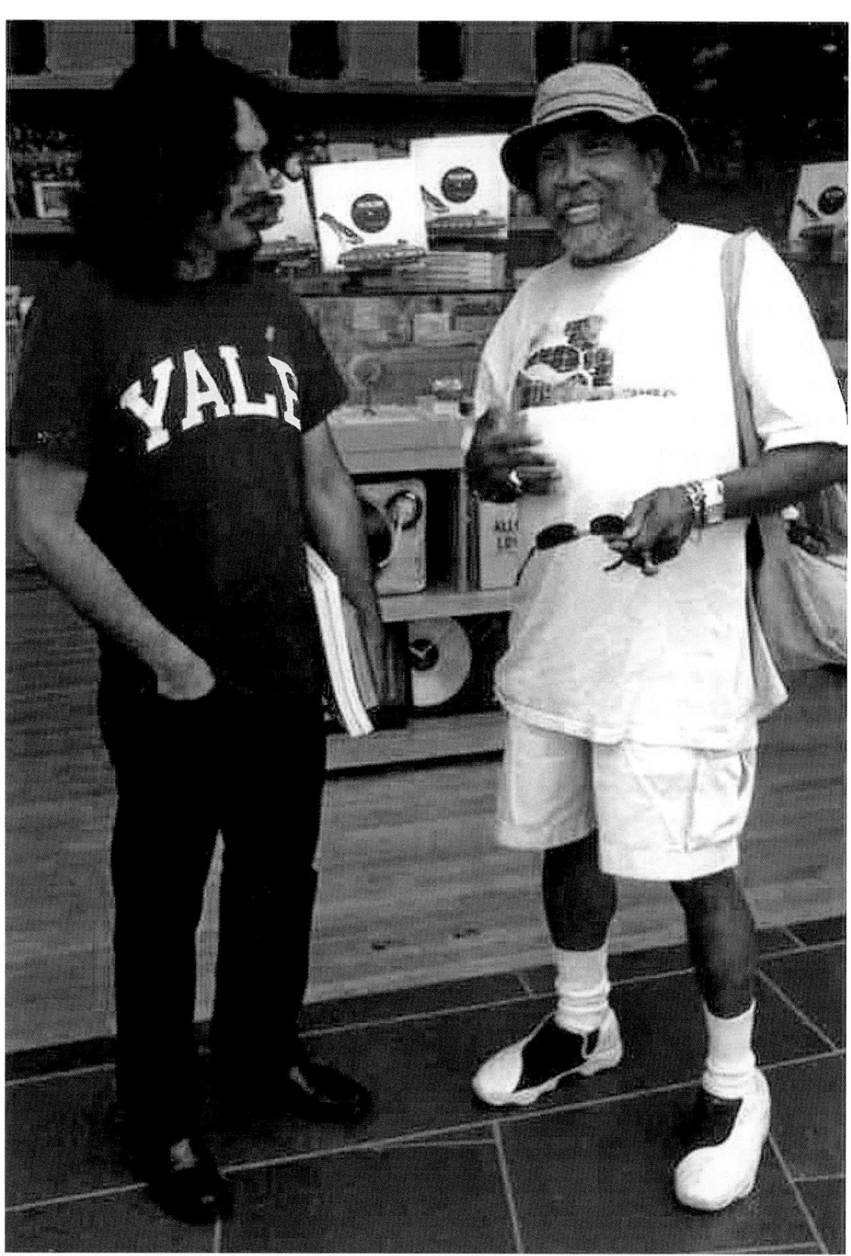

william cordova and Barkley Hendricks (Yale MFA 1971) at Nasher Museum, 2008. Barkley Hendricks was a huge influence on artist Kehinde Wiley and other figurative painters in the early 2000s. In the Fall of 2002, cordova reached out to Hendricks in hopes of making a documentary on the artists life while a student at Yale.
Photo by Trevor Schoonmaker

on Tupac Amaru Shakur in 2007. So the infrastructure we helped develop contributed in the articulation of a new veneer, *no wall paper*, just the alchemy of a generation whose theories were formed outside the institutions of higher learning: Mao Tse Tung, the Quran, Lisa Jones, Sonia Sanchez, Malcolm X, bell hooks, Kellie Jones, Pedro Pietri, Gil Scott-Heron, Toni Morrison, Piri Thomas, Natanya Ann Pulley, John Trudell, Felipe Luciano, NWA, Last Poets, Rammellzee, KRS-One.

While in grad school, I kept a video journal of my experience but also felt it important to document my peers' work, presence, and contributions. I always thought we'd use this material history in the future. We were in the trenches and knew we were building something different.[7]

Loren Holland: I initially went to Brown University as an engineering student because I love science and math. I was also pressured and encouraged by my family to do something that would make money, so that seemed like the right thing at the time. However, I have always made art. Ever since I was a child, I have always loved art and that is where my real passion was.

I chose Brown University because they had a cross-registration program with the Rhode Island School of Design, and I knew I would be able to take classes there and could explore different things. I came in as an engineering student, decided that that was boring and switched to Pre-Med. My undergraduate degrees are in Neuroscience and the Visual Arts. My

undergraduate experiences were extremely shaping and a big part of why I chose to become an artist. I had some amazing professors who believed in me, helped me get to where I needed to go and promoted my work. Through Brown, I attended a small program called the Yale-Norfolk Summer Program where I got a taste of working with contemporary artists and some of the professors that would be at Yale later. They were the first people to actually encourage it as a profession. While still a senior, I had just begun to hear about Wangechi Mutu's work, and my professors were all buzzing about her. I think she was at The Studio Museum in Harlem at the time, and I was intrigued. She was one of the first artists, in addition to Kara Walker, who addressed the subject of Black women and the "deviant" manner in which they are often viewed by society. She was creating creature-type bodies out of very sexualized images by collaging and rearranging them. I was simply in awe that art could actually incorporate these things. A lot of the art that I grew up on and loved came from the more traditional canons in art, such as Romare Bearden, Jacob Lawrence, Faith Ringgold; these are the artists typically associated with being successful Black artists. But the subject matter was extremely different from what I was seeing people closer to my age were making, and it really opened my eyes.

Jamerry Kim: At the School of Art, there were open interdisciplinary quick sessions, artist talks, and we were also functioning within the academic institution, which had its own history.

All of this became part of the experience of grad school. I think there was an instinctual attraction that happens, and you end up gravitating towards like-minded peers. The relationships that developed were influential and they became a support system for me that continued after grad school. Even to this day, whether it's through actual conversations or through the work as an artist, designer, educator, it's an embodied experience that is living and breathing. It connects us to a time period at Yale when we were there. But it also connects us further to the past before and, more importantly to the future ahead.[8]

Irene Small: In terms of thinking about contemporary art, one of the defining elements of my graduate experience was interacting with the MFA program. I had come to the Ph.D. program at Yale without any formal art history background but having worked in the contemporary art world. One of the things that really helped me in terms of bridging my interests in global contemporary art and the longer trajectories of modern and contemporary art outside of Western Europe and the United States was having dialogues with artists in the MFA program and going to crits. There was a really different discourse around art there than in my art history program, and it felt urgent. Going to those crits really helped me think about what it means to understand the work of art as an entity that is continually finding and making meaning. It also helped me recognize and articulate the

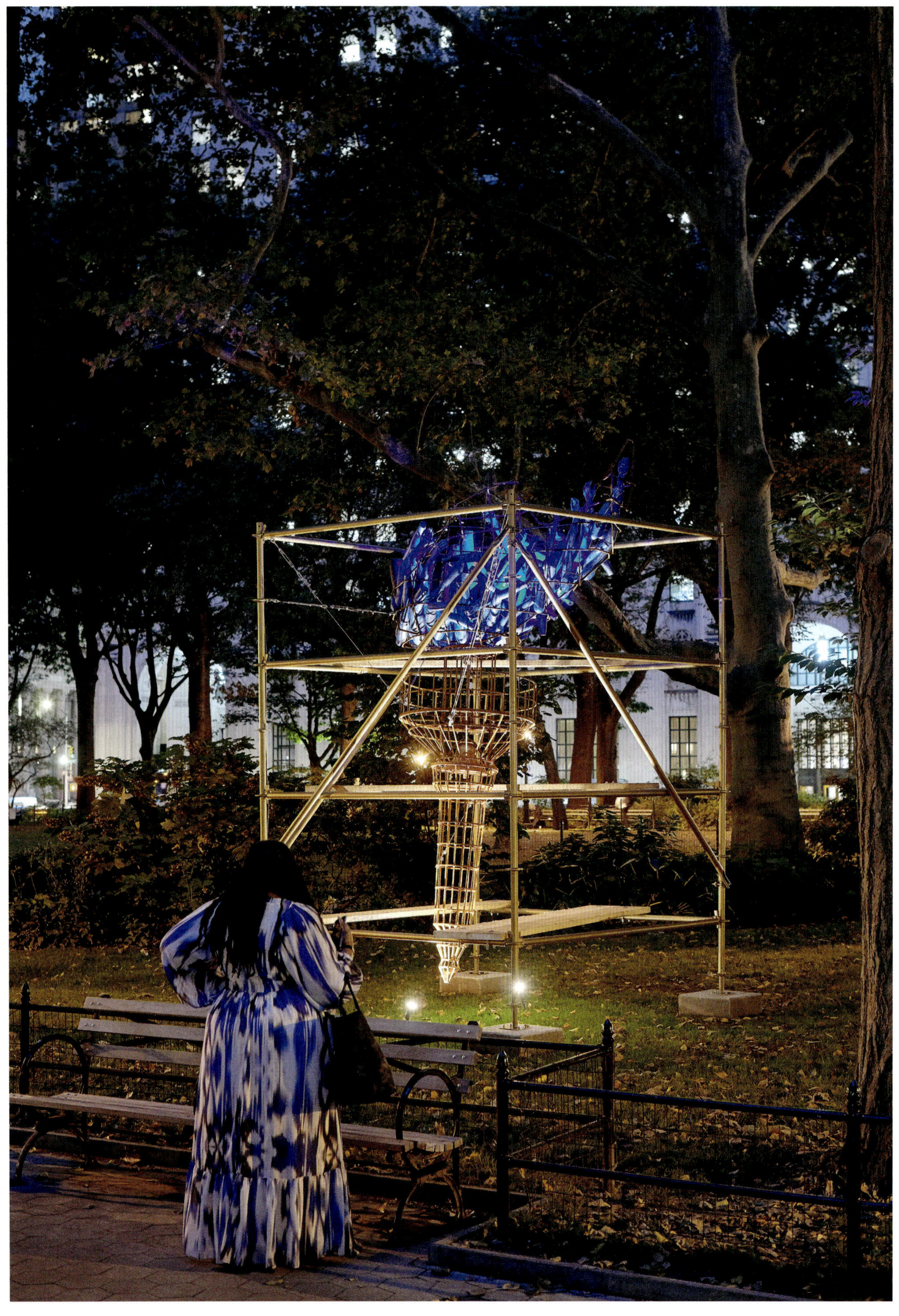

legacies of the past that really impacted practices in the present.[9]

AD: I was at Yale in the latter end of the decade. I feel like the [artists who attended at] the early part [of the decade] really impacted the influx of Black and brown students that applied to the school [towards the end of the decade]. I never heard of the Yale School of Art until Kehinde Wiley. I went to an exhibition of his work in 2005 at Deitch Projects [*Kehinde Wiley: Rumors of War*, November 11 to December 10, 2005]. That's when I saw his résumé. I saw that [he went to the Yale School of Art] and I was like, "What's that?" And then I just sent away for the brochure for the school to find out more about it. I ended up there four years later.

[When I attended Yale, of the] 40 people in painting at least 15 to 18 people were Black and brown, which is kind of insane. I made some of the best friends of my life in that moment. I still talk to Eric Mack and Troy Montes-Michie every single day 12 years out. I think that was a magical moment in terms of thinking about the kinds of ties that you were able to make cross outside of the School of Art. I went to a fashion school for undergrad [where] the liberal arts courses were limited. [It was while I attended Yale that] I was able to take an African art history course and an African American studies course. My first semester, I took a class with Elizabeth Alexander. She was very supportive of all of the artists at the School of Art. I know that she's had ongoing relationships with people from different moments during that program.

There were a lot of people at the university to speak to, even if you didn't find your people within the School of Art.

Art is a carrier of cultural belief of a particular moment in time, and it acts as a witness to that time and also like a time capsule of the things that were important in that moment. I have always used derelict materials or materials that could quickly speak to larger concerns because of the political and social implications of the specific material. I think there are lots of ways where Eric Mack and I overlap in terms of thinking about time and our place in time and the dematerializing of the body, and how to show the body without actually showing the body.

EM: I've always loved [Helen] Frankenthaler's paintings and there were epiphanies I had in undergrad. I went to Cooper Union [as an undergraduate] and was taught by a number of professors that either identified as abstract expressionists or 9th Street artists. I felt very connected to the culture of those images and the principles of making that developed out of so many veins of life but were synthesized as within principles of abstract expressionism.

Shinique Smith [Visiting Artist 2010] was one of my professors at Yale and Mickalene [Thomas] was in one of my final critiques at Yale. One of my first shows leaving Graduate school was curated by LaToya Ruby Frazier. Each affected my practice in different ways. Each worked in textiles and were thinking about the decorative and the ornate. Latoya's [photograph with her mother] particularly speaks within the intimacy of the ornate decorative language. Shinique is also from Maryland, and she's been an inspiration for me. I was happy to work with her when I was at Yale. There's a lot of shared commonalities. If there is any lineage with the Washington Colorfield school, she would be a part of that. In grad school she gave me all this fabric. There are swatches I use still to this day. Early on I felt the burdens of the work was the wooden support. There was so much that went into the process of stretching the canvas that people would go on autopilot. There was such a strict tradition that felt untouched especially in school. I did research and found moments in history in which there were artists challenging those constructs and getting into interesting places, even finding sculpture and installation.

[One of the first things I did after grad school was to eliminate the wooden stretcher]. The idea of carrying around stretcher bars seemed kind of silly as an unseen construct in a painting. I felt I had to invent something so I didn't have to carry around all this wood that no one would ever see. I started working with moving blankets [used for shipping objects and art]. The question was to see how they could be the surrogate for the painting object. How it could be a readymade. How the border could mimic the frame and how the chevron of the quilted material changed the material identity of the piece. I was really interested in the softness of it.

The most important thing to me within graduate school had to do with gesture and

how gesture could become a material object.
In one of my early pieces I just used bungee cord
rope and threaded it through the surface of the
canvas. [The question was] how do you make an
object become singular, how do make a material
become singular? And how to maintain
anonymity. I didn't want to give myself over too
quickly. I felt it was important that the gestures
and the ways I communicated through my own
touch, to have the viewer be able to unpack
that. A lot of those things are still with the work.
It's a very digested relationship to gesture itself.
Whenever I find those moments, it's always
exciting and revelatory. It's about a degree of
freedom for myself. It's all the degrees of
questions that maneuver and problem solve
with a kind of wit and resourcefulness that
eludes traditional means of value.[10]

[1] Unless otherwise noted, texts have been edited by the
artists from the original transcripts of the Artist Gallery Talks
on April 2, 2022. Use the QR Code on page 5 to view the
edited video.

[2] Sol Sax correspondence with the author. Published by
permission of the artist.

[3] Text edited from the transcription of video: Eric N. Mack
Gallery Discussion with Bonnie Clearwater, 2021.

[4] Text edited from the documentary video, *Penumbras: Lux et
Veritas*, 2022, by cordova, commissioned by NSU Art Museum
Fort Lauderdale. Use the QR Code on page 5 to view the
edited video.

[5] From *Penumbras*, cit.

[6] From *Penumbras*, cit.

[7] From *Penumbras*, cit.

[8] From *Penumbras*, cit.

[9] From *Penumbras*, cit.

[10] From Eric N. Mack Gallery Discussion with Bonnie Clearwater.

1

Wardell Milan, Yale Photo Studio, 2003. Courtesy of william cordova

2

Luis Gispert arriving at Yale for the first time, greeted by John Espinosa, 1999. Courtesy of william cordova

3

Shoshanna Weinberger and Torkwase Dyson, Yale graduation 2003. Courtesy of Shoshanna Weinberger

4

Loren Holland and Mikah Ganski at their Yale MFA Thesis reception, 2005. Holland is a Los Angeles-based painter and Ganski is a Hawaiian-born artist now living on the west coast. Photo by William cordova

5

Ken Lovell (left) and Lee Faulkner (right), Associate Directors of the Yale Digital Media Center for the Arts (1998–2016). Courtesy of william cordova. Photo by Ken Lovell

6

william cordova, Lourdes Correa Carlo (Yale MFA 2009), Eric N. Mack as part of the coffee cup collective at Denniston Hill Art Residency, NY. Photo by william cordova

7

Kehinde Wiley, Yale Sculpture Department, New Haven, CT, 2000. Yale art departments were in different buildings. Students often would reach out to one another for support as they shared common ideas and interests. Courtesy of william cordova. Photo by Luis Gispert

8

Torkwase Dyson at Halloween Party, Yale Sculpture Department. October 31, 2002. Photo by william cordova

9

Irene V. Small, 2009. Courtesy of Irene V. Small. Photo by Tumelo Mosaka

10

Artists Derrick Adams, Miguel Luciano (Yale faculty), william cordova, Michael Chuapoco, Wardell Milan, Leslie Hewitt and friend (rear) at Whitney Museum exhibition, *Pacha, Llaqta, Wasichay: Indigenous Space, Modern Architecture, New Art*, curated by Marcela Guerrero with Alana Hernandez, 2018. Exhibition included Yale MFA Alumni Ronny Quevedo and william cordova. Photo by william cordova

11

BASE collective members at PS1/MOMA, 2010: Leslie Hewitt, Rashida Bumbray, Ronny Quevedo and Jamerry Kim. Photo by william cordova

12

Filmmaker Monique Walton (Yale BFA 2004) and william cordova work on their collaborate film *spillage* in Saint Malo, Louisiana. 2013. *spillage* would later be used for cordova's installation in the Prospect Triennial, New Orleans, LA. Photo by Jerome Reyes

13

Rashawn Griffin, Wardell Milan, and Jamerry Kim; BASE collective dinner at Pio Pio Long Island, 2008. Courtesy of william cordova

14

william cordova, Mike Cloud, Wardell Milan, close friends and collaborators. Wardell Milan was one of the founders of the BASE collective. This photo was taken at Sikkema Jenkins during cordova's exhibition reception, 2017. Photo by william cordova

15

Rashawn Griffin and Rashayla Marie Brown, 2006. Courtesy of william cordova

16

Mamiko Otsubo. Photo courtesy of Leslie Hewitt

17

Rashawn Griffin, Ronny Quevedo, and Carol Pereira-Olson, 2008. Courtesy of william cordova

18

william cordova, Leslie Hewitt, Rashawn Griffin, Wardell Milan, Jamerry Kim, and Mike Cloud; BASE collective dinner at Pio Pio Long Island, 2008. Courtesy of william cordova

19

Yale visiting artist Terry Adkins (RIP), Leslie Hewitt, and william cordova, Whitney Biennial after-party, 2008. Photo by william cordova

20

Lourdes Correa Carlo (Yale MFA 2009), 2013. Courtesy of william cordova

21

Left to Right: George C. Tsouhlarakis, George E. Tsouhlarakis, Anna Tsouhlarakis; 2002. Photo courtesy of Anna Tsouhlarakis

22

william cordova and Wardell Milan sleeping in car, Skowhegan, 2003. Photo courtesy of Nyeema Morgan

23

Mike Cloud and william cordova, 2013. Courtesy of Nyeema Morgan

Checklist of works in the exhibition

Njideka Akunyili Crosby
(b. 1983, Enugu, Nigeria;
lives and works in Los Angeles, CA)

Nyado: The Thing Around Her Neck
2011
Acrylic, photographic transfers, colored
pencil, charcoal, and collage on paper
81 ½ × 81 ¾ in / 207 × 207.6 cm
Collection of the artist
Courtesy of David Zwirner and Victoria Miro
© Njideka Akunyili Crosby
(pp. 56, 133)

Mike Cloud
(b.1974, Chicago, IL;
lives and works in Chicago, IL)

Advice Getting Puppy
2020
Oil on canvas and mixed media
27 × 33 × 3 in / 68.6 × 83.8 × 7.6 cm
Courtesy of the Landing Gallery
© Mike Cloud, 2020
(pp. 43, 48, 93)

Bomb Bambuti Pigmy
2020
Oil on canvas and mixed media
109 × 59 × 3 ½ in /
276.9 × 149.9 × 8.9 cm
Courtesy of the Landing Gallery
© Mike Cloud, 2020
(pp. 46, 94)

*Business Idea Beyond Grub
and Weevil*
2020
Oil on canvas and mixed media
118 × 33 × 2 ½ in / 299.7 × 83.8 × 6.3 cm
Courtesy of the Landing Gallery
© Mike Cloud, 2020
(pp. 46–47, 95)

Hero Portrait Georgine Carrigan
2020
Oil on canvas and mixed media
30 × 70 × 1 ½ in / 76.2 × 177.8 × 3.8 cm
Courtesy of the Landing Gallery
© Mike Cloud, 2020
(pp. 43, 47, 48, 96)

*Mixed Marriage Dr. Strasser
and Balaji Pandian*
2020
Oil on canvas and mixed media
71 × 71 × 7 in / 180.3 × 180.3 × 17.8 cm
Courtesy of the Landing Gallery
© Mike Cloud, 2020
(pp. 43, 48, 97)

william cordova
(b. 1971, Lima, Peru; lives and works in
Miami, FL, New York, NY, and Lima, Peru)

*machu picchu after dark (pa' victoria santa
cruz, macario sakay y damion thurston)*
2003–2014
Reclaimed speakers, candy, pennies, vinyl
record jackets, and candles
Dimensions variable
Courtesy of 80m2 Livia Benavides
and the artist
© william cordova
(pp. 43, 44, 48,105)

quotidian palimpsest
2021
Mixed media collage, gold leaf on paper
44 ½ × 96 in / 113 × 243.8 cm
NSU Art Museum Fort Lauderdale;
purchased wiwth funds provided by
Michael and Dianne Bienes by exchange
Courtesy of the artist and Sikkema Jenkins
& Co., New York, NY
© william cordova
(pp. 40, 106–107)

Abigail Deville
(b. 1981, New York City, NY;
lives and works in New York City, NY)

Lady Liberty
2022
Mixed media
6 × 5 × 3 ft / 1.8 × 1.5 × 0.9 m
Courtesy of the artist
© Abigail DeVille
(pp. 34, 135)

Libertas (study in off white)
2022
Magazine stand, disarticulated skeleton,
glass bottle, mannequin parts, mirror tile,
wood base, and graphite
6 × 3 × 3 ft / 1.8 × 0.9 × 0.9 m
Courtesy of the artist
© Abigail DeVille
(pp. 35, 38, 135)

Pharaoh March
2022
Rope, bungee cords, plastic chain, metal
wire, mannequin hangers, and metal
hangers
6 × 3 3 ft / 1.8 × 0.9 × 0.9 m
Courtesy of the artist
© Abigail DeVille
(pp. 34–35, 135)

Torkwase Dyson
(b. 1973, Chicago, Illinois;
lives and works in Beacon, NY)

I BELONG TO THE DISTANCE (#2)
2022
Plywood, steel, and graphite
25 ft × 30 ft × 84 in / 7.6 × 9.1 × 2.1 cm
Courtesy of the artist and Pace Gallery
© Torkwase Dyson
(pp. 14–15, 99)

John Espinosa
(b. 1966, Bogotá, Colombia;
lives and works in Los Angeles, CA)

People with Eyes
2004
Found images on wood panel
17 ¾ × 22 ⅜ in / 45.1 × 56.8 cm
Collection of Paul Berg
© John Espinosa
(pp. 41, 76–77)

Rut and Reconstitution
2001
Mixed media on paper
20 × 25 ¾ in / 5.8 × 65.4 cm
Collection of the Museum of
Contemporary Art, North Miami
Gift of Fredric and Kathy Snitzer
© John Espinosa
(pp. 41, 75)

Luis Gispert
(b. 1972, Jersey City, NJ;
lives and works in Brooklyn, NY)

Luis Gispert; Jeffrey Reed
Stereomongrel
2005
Super 35mm film, color, sound, 12 mins,
transferred to video
Courtesy of Lundgren Gallery
© Luis Gispert and Jeffrey Reed
(pp. 35, 38–39, 79)

Bojangles
2016
Emulsified bitumen, gold chains
Framed: 61 ½ × 77 ½ in / 156.2 × 196.8 cm;
Object: 61 ¼ × 71 ¾ in / 155.6 × 182.2 cm
NSU Art Museum Fort Lauderdale
Gift of Dr. Robert B. Feldman
© Luis Gispert
(pp. 39, 80)

Secret Pilgrim
2015
Emulsified bitumen, gold chains
Framed: 77 ½ × 61 ½ in / 196.8 × 156.2 cm;
Object: 71 ¾ × 61 ¾ in / 182.2 × 155.6 cm
NSU Art Museum Fort Lauderdale
Gift of Dr. Robert B. Feldman
© Luis Gispert
(pp. 39, 81)

Rashawn Griffin
(b. 1980, Los Angeles, CA;
lives and works in New York City,
NY, and Kansas City, KS)

The Changing Room
2022
Pool top felt, fabric, glass, wood, mirrored
plexi glass, ceramics, acrylic, oil, gouache,
and mixed media
84 × 107 ½ × 87 ½ in /
213.3 × 273 × 222.2 cm
Courtesy of the artist
© Rashawn Griffin
(pp. 65, 121, 122–123)

Leslie Hewitt
(b. 1977, New York, NY;
lives and works in New York, NY)

Aura
2016
Digital chromogenic print
3/3 + AP
30 × 30 in / 76.2 × 76.2 cm
Courtesy of the artist and Perrotin
© Leslie Hewitt
(pp. 43, 44, 109)

Color Study_01
2016
Digital chromogenic print
3/3 + AP
15 × 15 in / 38.1 × 38.1 cm
Courtesy of the artist and Perrotin
© Leslie Hewitt
(pp. 43, 44, 48, 109)

Object
2016
Digital chromogenic print
1/3 + AP
30 × 30 in / 76.2 × 76.2 cm
Courtesy of the artist and Perrotin
© Leslie Hewitt
(pp. 43, 45, 109)

Screen
2016
Digital chromogenic print
1/3 + AP
30 × 30 in / 76.2 × 76.2 cm
Courtesy of the artist and Perrotin
© Leslie Hewitt
(pp. 43, 45, 109)

RAM
2017
Digital chromogenic print
1/3
30 × 40 in / 76.2 × 101.6 cm
Courtesy of the artist and Perrotin
© Leslie Hewitt
(pp. 50, 111)

Topologies (Fanon mildly out of focus)
2017
Traditional chromogenic print
2/3
30 × 30 in / 76.2 × 76.2 cm
Courtesy of the artist and Perrotin
© Leslie Hewitt
(pp. 43, 45, 110)

Topologies (folded memory object)
2017
Traditional chromogenic print
2/3
30 × 30 in / 76.2 × 76.2 cm
Courtesy of the artist and Perrotin
© Leslie Hewitt
(pp. 43, 45, 110)

Topologies (Veblen with camera shake)
2017
Traditional chromogenic print
3/3
30 × 30 in / 76.2 × 76.2 cm
Courtesy of the artist and Perrotin
© Leslie Hewitt
(pp. 43, 45, 110)

Untitled
2019
Sheet metal, powder coat
11 ½ × 72 × 29 in /
29.2 × 182.9 × 73.7 cm
Courtesy of the artist and Perrotin
© Leslie Hewitt
(pp. 45, 50)

Loren Holland
(b. Los Angeles, CA;
lives and works in Los Angeles, CA)

The Bathers
2018
Oil on canvas (3 panels)
Each: 35 × 14 in / 88.9 × 35.6 cm
Courtesy of the artist
© Loren Holland
(pp. 35, 36, 37, 127)

The Shadow Queen
2018
Oil on canvas
30 × 24 in / 76.2 × 61 cm
Courtesy of the artist
© Loren Holland
(pp. 35, 37, 128)

Bait and Switch
2019
Oil on canvas
30 × 24 in / 76.2 × 61 cm
Courtesy of the artist
© Loren Holland
(pp. 35, 37, 38, 129)

Titus Kaphar
(b. 1976, Kalamazoo, MI; lives and works
in New Haven, CT)

Untitled (Self-Portrait)
2007
Oil and tar on board
Framed: 19 × 14 in / 48.3 × 35.6 cm
Private collection
© Titus Kaphar
(p. 29)

Untitled 8
2009
Gouache on paper and collage
8 ¼ × 7 ½ in / 21 × 19 cm
Collection Pérez Art Museum Miami
Gift of Nigel Margesson and Idamar
Siverio
© Titus Kaphar
(p. 29)

Another Fight for Remembrance (Study)
2014
Oil and gold leaf on canvas
59 × 40 ⅔ in / 149.9 × 102.5 cm
Private collection
Courtesy of the artist and Gagosian
© Titus Kaphar
(pp. 29, 131)

Jamerry Kim
(b. 1975, Germany;
lives and works in New York, NY)

*To Translate is to Cross a Bridge: Flushing
Remonstrance, A Protest*
2019–2021
Video, 32 mins
Courtesy of the artist
© Jamerry Kim
(pp. 61, 124, 125)

Eric N. Mack
(b. 1987, Columbia, MD;
lives and works in New York, NY)

Tessuti Raponi (Ciao Milano)
2018
Fabric
193 × 322 ½ in × 87 in /
490.2 × 819.1 × 221 cm
NSU Art Museum Fort Lauderdale;
purchased with funds provided by
Michael and Dianne Bienes, by exchange
© Eric N. Mack
(pp. 67, 137)

Wardell Milan
(b. 1977, Knoxville, TN;
lives and works in New York, NY)

Battle Royale
2007
20 individual mixed media paper collages
Each: 8 ¾ × 10 in / 22.2 × 25.4 cm
Courtesy of the artist
and David Nolan Gallery
© Wardell Milan
(pp. 29, 30–31, 113)

*I'm trying to keep my faith. But,
I'm searching for more. Somewhere
I can be safe*
2017–2018
Digital C-print, mounted on Dibond
Edition 3 of 3, with 2 APs
Unframed: 44 × 98 in / 111.8 × 248.9 cm
Courtesy of the artist
and David Nolan Gallery
© Wardell Milan
(pp. 34, 114-115)

Wangechi Mutu
(b. 1972, Nairobi, Kenya;
lives and works in Nairobi,
Kenya and New York, NY)

The Original Nine Daughters
2012
Suite of nine etchings with aquatint,
linocut, and collage
4/30
Each: 18 ¾ × 10 in / 47.6 × 25.4 cm
NSU Art Museum Fort Lauderdale;
purchased with funds provided by Michael
and Dianne Bienes by exchange
(pp. 20–21, 23)

Mirror Faced I
2020
Red soil, paper pulp, wood glue, emulsion
paint, gourd, brass beads, mirror, teak
base, and wrought iron stand
Bust: 22 ⅞ × 11 ⅛ × 12 ⅛ in /
58.1 × 28.3 × 30.8 cm;
Object: 68 ½ × 14 ⅝ × 13 ⅜ in /
173.99 × 37.1 × 34 cm;
Pedestal: 46 ¼ × 14 ⅝ × 13 ⅜ in /
117.5 × 37.2 × 34 cm
Collection of Ecaterina Vlad
© Wangechi Mutu
(pp. 22, 25, 26)

Mirror Faced II
2020
Red soil, paper pulp, wood glue,
emulsion paint, desiccated baobab
fruit, brass beads, mirror, teak base,
and wrought iron stand
Bust: 19 ¾ × 9 ⅞ × 11 ⅛ in /
50.2 × 25 × 28.3 cm;
Object: 66 ⅛ × 12 ⅜ × 14 ⅛ in /
168 × 31.4 × 35.9 cm
Courtesy of the artist and Gladstone
Gallery
© Wangechi Mutu
(pp. 22, 25, 26)

Seeing Cowries
2020
Red soil, paper pulp, wood glue,
emulsion paint, charcoal, ink, wood,
shell, and mixed media
39 × 39 ⅜ × 23 ⅝ in / 99.1 × 100 × 60 cm
Courtesy of the artist and Gladstone
Gallery
© Wangechi Mutu
(pp. 19, 20,71)

My Cave Call
2021
Digital film (2K HD), anamorphic format
16:9, 1920 × 1080p, 12 mins 35 secs
Edition of 5 plus 2 artist's proofs
Courtesy of the artist and Gladstone
Gallery
© Wangechi Mutu
(pp. 18–19, 72)

Sentinel VI
2022
Red soil, paper pulp, wood glue, emulsion
paint, coral bean (Erythrina herbacea),
dead base rock, gourd, brass ornament,
plastic bead, tiger cowry (Cypraea tigris),
jawbone, chiffon, and brass bell
90 ¾ × 35 ⅛ × 36 ⅛ in /
230.5 × 89.2 × 91.8 cm
Courtesy of the artist and Gladstone
Gallery
© Wangechi Mutu
(pp. 18, 23, 73)

Mamiko Otsubo
(b. 1974, Nishinomiya City, Japan;
lives and works in Los Angeles, CA)

Time Traveler
2016
200-year-old Japanese Ash,
hand rubbed lacquer, and cast bronze
11 ¼ × 53 ½ × 9 ½ in /
28.6 × 135.9 × 24.1 cm
Courtesy of the artist
© Mamiko Otsubo
(pp. 51, 118)

Keeping Your Ear To the Ground
2016
Cast bronze, steel
Dimensions variable
Courtesy of the artist
© Mamiko Otsubo
(pp. 49, 51, 117)

On the Edge of the Western World
2022
Ceramic, urethane casting resin,
mirror polished stainless steel, aluminum,
and epoxy adhesive
20 × 16 × 2 ⅜ in / 50.8 × 40.6 × 6 cm
Courtesy of the artist
© Mamiko Otsubo
(pp. 49, 119)

Ronny Quevedo
(b. 1981, Guayaquil, Ecuador;
lives and works in the Bronx, New York, NY)

Critical Mass
2013
Video
Courtesy of the artist and Alexander Gray
Associates, New York
© Ronny Quevedo
(pp. 55, 138)

errantry (the benefit of being offsides)
2019
Gold leaf on linoleum tiles and cement
Dimensions variable
Courtesy of the artist and Alexander Gray
Associates, New York
© Ronny Quevedo
(pp. 64–65, 66)

migration lines
2019
Gold leaf on carbon paper
35 × 25 ½ in / 88.9 × 64.8 cm
Courtesy of the artist and Alexander Gray
Associates, New York
© Ronny Quevedo
(pp. 64, 139)

Mickalene Thomas
(b.1971, Camden, NJ;
lives and works in New York, NY)

October 1950
2021
Rhinestones, glitter, acrylic, and oil on
canvas mounted on wood panel with
mahogany frame
106 × 90 × 8 in / 269.2 × 228.6 × 20.3 cm
Courtesy of Mickalene Thomas
© Mickalene Thomas
(pp. 22, 25, 27, 87)

Anna Tsouhlarakis
(b. 1977, Lawrence, KS;
lives and works in Boulder, CO)

Rocketship 3/4
2002–2022
Wood, aluminum, steel fabric, turf,
paint, duct tape, foamboard, aluminum
tape, plexiglass, IKEA remnants, plastic
bucket, tarp, fleece, step ladder, and
nylon cord
Dimensions variable
Courtesy of the artist
© Anna Tsouhlarakis
(pp. 62, 63, 66, 89, 90, 91)

Shoshanna Weinberger
(b. 1973, Kingston, Jamaica;
lives and works in Newark, NJ)

Potbelly Porn Star and the Rise of Bacon
2012–2013
Gouache on paper
60 × 74 ¼ in / 152.4 × 188.6 cm
Courtesy of the artist
© Shoshanna Weinberger
(pp. 55, 57, 101)

Ménage à Trois
2013
Gouache on paper
60 × 72 ¼ in / 152.4 × 183.5 cm
Courtesy of the artist
© Shoshanna Weinberger
(pp. 54, 57, 102)

Muffin Top Banana Bottom
2014
Gouache on paper
60 × 74 ¼ in / 152.4 × 189 cm
Courtesy of Carol Jazzar
Contemporary, Miami
© Shoshanna Weinberger
(pp. 54, 57, 103)

Kehinde Wiley
(b.1977, Los Angeles, CA;
lives and works in Brooklyn, NY)

The Apostle Peter
2006
Oil on canvas
96 × 72 in / 243.8 × 182.9 cm
Courtesy of Laurie Karen Silverman, N.Y.C.
© Kehinde Wiley
(pp. 25, 26, 83)

Sir Richard Owen 1804–1892
2013
Oil on canvas
48 × 36 in / 121.9 × 91.4 cm
Courtesy of Laurie Karen Silverman, N.Y.C.
© Kehinde Wiley
(pp. 25, 26, 85)

Karl Spindler
2017
Oil on linen
72 × 60 in / 233.7 × 208.3 cm
Courtesy of S. Donald Sussman
© Kehinde Wiley
(pp. 2, 25, 27, 84)

Installation photographs
Steven Brooke

NSU Art Museum Fort Lauderdale Staff

NSU Art Museum Fort Lauderdale Board of Governors